Independent for Life

P9-DDF-701

Independent for Life

*Homes and Neighborhoods
for an Aging America*

Edited by
Henry Cisneros
Margaret Dyer-Chamberlain
Jane Hickie

University of Texas Press ⬥ Austin

Requests for permission to reproduce material from this work should be sent to:
Permissions
University of Texas Press
P.O. Box 7819
Austin, TX 78713-7819
www.utexas.edu/utpress/about/bpermission.html

♾ The paper used in this book meets the minimum requirements of ANSI/NISO Z39.48-1992 (R1997) (Permanence of Paper).

LIBRARY OF CONGRESS CATALOGING-IN-PUBLICATION DATA

Independent for Life : homes and neighborhoods for an aging America / edited by Henry Cisneros, Margaret Dyer-Chamberlain, Jane Hickie.
    p.   cm.
Includes bibliographical references and index.
    ISBN 978-0-292-73791-4 (cl. : alk. paper) — ISBN 978-0-292-73792-1 (pbk. : alk. paper) — ISBN 978-0-292-73793-8 (e-book)
    1. Older people—Housing—United States.   2. Older people—Services for—United States.
I. Cisneros, Henry.   II. Dyer-Chamberlain, Margaret.   III. Hickie, Jane.
    HD7287.92.U54L58   2012
    363.5′9460973—dc23   2011049654

This volume was prepared for publication and designed by Motto Publishing Services.

For our parents

Contents

Foreword

John W. Rowe

According to a recent report issued by the MacArthur Foundation Research Network on an Aging Society, an aging society is one in which people over sixty outnumber those under fifteen.[1] The MacArthur Foundation Research Network on an Aging Society, an interdisciplinary group of experts on longevity, conducts analyses and proposes public policies relevant to the challenges and opportunities of an aging society. The network has pointed out that inevitable demographic shifts mean that our country will become increasingly older in coming decades. We are woefully unprepared to deal with the myriad consequences of this impending reality, nor have we challenged ourselves to imagine the opportunities that an aging America will present.

The aging of our society is not merely a possibility, contingent on future increases in life expectancy. It is a certainty driven by well-defined factors, including the aging of the baby boom generation, dramatic increases in life expectancy that occurred in the twentieth century, and the more recent compression of morbidity.[2] Compression of morbidity means that many more of us will live disease- and illness-free right up until the end of our lives. These forces, despite sustained fertility rates and continued immigration, will result in an America populated by increasing numbers and percentages of older people.[3]

As we enter these uncharted waters, the greatest unknowns relate to the future behavior of the baby boom generation. How will they work, save, spend, study, help others, and vote? How and when will they retire? As they withdraw from paid

JOHN W. ROWE is a professor in the Department of Health Policy and Management at the Columbia University Mailman School of Public Health. Previously, he served as chairman and CEO of Aetna Inc. and was former president and CEO of Mount Sinai NYU Health. He was a professor of medicine and founding director of the Division on Aging at the Harvard Medical School, as well as chief of gerontology at Boston's Beth Israel Hospital. Currently, he leads the MacArthur Foundation's Research Network on an Aging Society and chairs the Institute of Medicine's Committee on the Future Health Care Workforce for Older Americans. He serves on the board of trustees of the Rockefeller Foundation. He chairs the board of trustees at the University of Connecticut and the Marine Biological Laboratory in Woods Hole, Massachusetts. He received an MD from the University of Rochester School of Medicine and Dentistry and a BS from Canisius College.

employment, how will they cope with their lack of engagement and control? Will the innovative and entrepreneurial spirit that has characterized this generation endure? What new ideas will they pursue? And, as investigated in detail in this volume, where and how will they live?

Considerable analysis and much political discussion have focused on the future of the US health care system, and the solvency and sustainability of the Social Security and Medicare trust funds. There has been much less focus on the realities of life in an aging America. We are entering a period of rapid change in many of our society's key institutions, including housing, retirement, labor markets, education, transportation, religious communities, neighborhoods, political parties, national defense, and the family itself. To cope with an aging population, these institutions must adapt to emerging structural and cultural changes. We also need to develop policies and strategies at the local, state, and national levels that will optimize opportunities for all age groups. Our whole society needs to think creatively about how to best support people to a very old age.

The future design, structure, and function of our housing, neighborhoods, and communities are central issues as we try to come to grips with an aging America. One important strategy will be to develop healthy communities that engage all residents and foster intergenerational experiences. Former secretary of the US Department of Housing and Urban Development, the Honorable Henry Cisneros, joined with the Stanford Center on Longevity to produce this volume, *Independent for Life: Homes and Neighborhoods for an Aging America*. The basic premise of this book is that Americans are aging in traditional homes, age-segregated neighborhoods, and communities that are designed for yesterday's demographic realities. Future demographic changes demand transformative efforts for successful aging in place. As Professor Andrew Scharlach says, "The ultimate goal of aging in place is about achieving true choice in housing—the ability to live wherever we want, regardless of age or ability."

This important and timely volume is an edited work from an interdisciplinary group of architects, urban planners, gerontologists, economists, civic leaders, elected officials, developers, and builders. It represents a very important contribution to the national discourse on strategies to assure the emergence of a productive and equitable aging America.

Independent for Life has been funded with generous grants from The Home Depot Foundation, MetLife, and Freddie Mac. Lead funding has been provided by the MacArthur Foundation Research Network on an Aging Society.

It is our hope that this book will stimulate thinking about how we can change the culture of our society to support successful aging in place. We are aware that the challenges are great and that the opportunities are real.

Notes

1. John W. Rowe, "Opportunities and Challenges of an Aging Society" (speech to the Institute for Survey Research, University of Michigan, Ann Arbor, September 2007), http://www.agingsocietynetwork .org/speech.

2. Sherwin B. Nuland, *The Art of Aging: A Doctor's Prescription for Well-Being* (New York: Random House, 2007).

3. Adele M. Hayutin, Miranda Dietz, and Lillian Mitchell, "New Realities of an Older America: Challenges, Changes, and Questions" (Stanford Center on Longevity, 2010), http://longevity.stanford .edu/article/new+realities+of+an+older+america.

Preface

In the past, old people either were expected to adapt to their existing homes and neighborhoods or expected to move into an institution. Rarely did older people insist that homes and neighborhoods be modified for them as they aged in place.

When only a small minority of the population was old, it was perhaps understandable that their housing and community needs could be ignored. Families managed on their own. But now that there are more people over sixty than people under fifteen in America, the challenges and opportunities of aging demand attention. These challenges do not affect only a few people, they affect many people, and the effects ripple throughout society.

The oldest old are the fastest-growing segment of the population. The disabilities that may result from the normal process of aging can create hardships in homes designed only for younger people. And the oldest old are among the most financially vulnerable. Although, in 2008, the poverty threshold for a person living alone was $10,400, estimates are that an older American in good health living alone would need about $16,300 to make ends meet if he or she owned a home free and clear. A higher amount would be required if he or she were renting or paying off an outstanding mortgage.[1] The challenges are particularly pressing for the "oldest old"—those who can no longer work, whose savings are being depleted, who are in poor health, and who need services that are unavailable in their homes or communities.

The issues are personal and they are big. The baby boomers are affected, and they are beginning to realize the importance of aging in their own lives. Solutions have to be:

Cost effective
Multigenerational
Practical
Enduring

Measurable and well managed
Creative and imaginative

We do not have enough affordable, appropriate housing and services to meet the needs of the projected population of older Americans. Federal and state budget deficits will constrain entitlement spending just as there are unprecedented numbers of older people. Growing minority populations, unless able to achieve higher educational levels, will be unable to find good jobs and maintain Social Security, Medicare, and Medicaid programs over time.

In addition, most Americans will have fewer personal resources in the future. The intersection of demographic, financial, and political realities will result in difficult choices and new opportunities. The issues to be resolved are vast, complex, and unavoidable.

Each of us must not only develop our own plan for a long life, but as a society we must also find solutions that reflect the needs of older people and the limitations of public funding. Solutions need to be offered by private and public sector leaders. We must challenge ourselves to consider new ideas that test the usual assumptions about lifestyle. We believe that people will need to:

- Anticipate aging in their current homes, knowing that needs for accessibility and services will change over time.
- Remodel and/or develop new living arrangements such as cohousing, accessory dwelling units, and shared housing.
- Insist that communities be well managed and supportive of older people.
- Work full- or part-time to older ages, perhaps becoming entrepreneurs in new ways.
- Volunteer for their own kids and for poor kids who are at risk for poverty. Help young people get an education and find and hold better jobs.
- Stay healthy and avoid medical costs. Eat nutritiously. Walk.
- Save and share resources; expect to give and receive care from friends and family.
- Use technology to stay connected and make all aspects of life more efficient.
- Engage fully in community in order to find joy in a world of scarce resources.

It is critical to raise awareness of longevity today, as the oldest of the baby boomers turn sixty-five and while there is still time to act to change policies and to reallocate resources on a national scale. The transformational change that is urgently needed can only come from bringing together academics, policy makers, and practitioners. Transformational change also requires a new and better vision of aging, one that responds to the overwhelming desire of older people to age in the homes and communities they have chosen. As a nation, we need to find ways to support aging in place for those unprecedented numbers of Americans seeking to live healthy lives in their own homes. These changes will enable older Americans to make even greater contributions to their communities, thereby strengthening our society as a whole. This book is intended to describe that new vision of aging in place and the encouraging progress already under way to make that vision a reality.

Notes

1. Virginia P. Reno and Benjamin Veghte, "Economic Status of the Elderly in the United States" (working paper, National Academy of Social Insurance, Washington, DC, 2010); based on the chapter "Economic Status of the Aged," in *The Handbook of Aging and the Social Sciences,* 7th ed., ed. R. H. Binstock and L. George (New York: Elsevier, 2011).

Acknowledgments

Our heartfelt thanks go to the chapter authors, who have written with both depth of expertise and new thinking intended to transform an aging America. If the book makes such a contribution, these experts are due the credit. The chapter authors were willing to exchange ideas creatively, work collaboratively, and establish new parameters within which the topic of aging in place will be explored more fully. They are exceptional authorities, colleagues, and friends.

Essential to the life of this project is the MacArthur Foundation Research Network on an Aging Society, headed by Jack Rowe, which is a project of the John D. and Catherine T. MacArthur Foundation. The network's funding was joined by important support from The Home Depot Foundation, MetLife, and Freddie Mac. We hope that this book is a credit in the continuing work of these generous institutions in improving the lives of older Americans.

We are grateful to the University of Texas Press, especially to our editor, Jim Burr, who guided us through the publishing process. We also thank Joanna Hitchcock and Dave Hamrick, the former and current director of the press, respectively, who made quick decisions to acquire and produce the book so well.

We thank the staff of CityView and of the Stanford Center on Longevity. This book could not have been completed without them. Among those who worked with such willing good humor, we are particularly grateful to the late Sharon Vazquez.

Finally, we thank our families, especially Mary Alice, Page, and Michele for their patience, companionship, and support. They have been key to the fruition of this project, embracing its importance to us and sharing our joy in its conclusion.

The Editors

Independent for Life

INTRODUCTION
Independent/Successful Longevity

In order to remodel and rebuild communities to support aging in place, we need to understand the history of longevity and the physical and cognitive realities of normal aging. The evidence is abundant from studies of history and science that Americans can live for many more years without the painful, costly, dispiriting effects of debilitating diseases.

Older Americans can continue to contribute and can remain self-reliant for longer, able to articulate their own priorities. We can find solutions to the problems that old people identify only if we fully appreciate the importance of their concerns.

"Aging in place," as we discuss it in this book, refers to a range of housing and services, a continuum of options, that together support older people as they age and change. Older people can age in place well in assisted living or age poorly in a single-family home in a traditional neighborhood. The goal is to find the balance of housing and care that offers the right environmental, emotional, and economic fit.

A central purpose of our society should be to change our culture to support both old and young people so that very long lives are lived well.

Chapter 1

New Visions for Aging in Place

Henry Cisneros

My Family Experience

My mother, Elvira Cisneros, is over eighty-five years old and lives independently. She lives in the home in the West Side neighborhood of San Antonio, Texas, that she and my father, George, bought as newlyweds in 1945, across the alley from the home of her mother and father, my grandparents, where she grew up. Most rooms of my mother's home, a 1920s bungalow, are exactly as I remember them my entire life, down to the placement of the furniture in the rooms and the figurines on the shelves. I am the oldest of five siblings and will always remember a home that was a nurturing place full of encouragement, ambition, and pride in our Latino heritage. The neighborhood around us was supportive and active; every house on the block belonged to a hard-working, lower-middle-class Latino family with multiple children. I have often described it as a block that could well have been lifted from a Norman Rockwell painting, except that all of the faces would have been brown.

Over the years, some exterior modifications were made to the home to accommodate the realities of debilitation and aging. My father suffered a stroke at age fifty-nine in 1976 while on Army Reserve duty and lost full use of his left arm and left leg. Though some doctors advised that the stroke would accelerate the aging process and that he would likely live only another few years, owing to his disciplined commitment to therapy and exercise and to my mother's care in their home, my dad lived thirty years after his stroke. He died at age eighty-nine in 2006.

HENRY CISNEROS, former secretary of the US Department of Housing and Urban Development and four-term mayor of San Antonio, Texas, is also executive chairman of CityView, a company that specializes in urban real estate, in-city housing, and metropolitan infrastructure. He is a member of the advisory boards of the Bill and Melinda Gates Foundation and the Broad Foundation. He has served as president of the National League of Cities. He is the author of several books, including *Interwoven Destinies: Cities and the Nation* and *Our Communities, Our Homes: Pathways to Housing and Homeownership in America's Cities and States*. He holds a master's degree from Harvard University and a doctoral degree from George Washington University.

Elvira Cisneros and her neighbor, Stella Tenorio, on the ramp built adjacent to Mrs. Cisneros's home in San Antonio, Texas. Photo by Charlie Elizalde.

To help him remain as active as his disabilities allowed—which included founding the San Antonio Stroke Club and creating a one-arm golf tournament—the house was modified to include a ramp along one side, a deck connected to the ramp to eliminate steep back-door steps, and a metal handrail leading up to the front porch. Inside, bathroom modifications, including lowered fixtures and a roll-in shower, made possible my dad's use of a wheelchair in his later years.

Only in the last two years has my mom begun to visibly slow down and show some frailty herself. She hurt her knee rushing into the passenger seat of a car on a rainy day in 2009, and from the knee trauma came foot, ankle, and hip pain that lasted months. Pushed by her strong character, she worked hard to remain mobile and the earlier home modifications helped. She loves being in her home full of memories and has never for an instant considered moving to senior housing. She recognizes that she is slower and that organizing complex family events in her traditional manner is beyond her, so she now accepts that Christmas dinner can be at my home instead of stubbornly insisting that her home must be the holiday gathering place for my brothers and sisters and their families. I noticed recently that she wrote instructions to herself for operating the kitchen oven in large letters on masking tape and affixed them to the handles of a new stove. She accepted the installation of a security alarm system one Christmas and a Life Alert personal communications device the next year. By making these concessions, she contends that she can live in her beloved home for years to come.

Her attitude is mirrored by other seniors in this neighborhood that has itself aged, both in the longevity of the residents and in the physical attributes of the housing stock. Stella Tenorio, the ninety-four-year-old next-door neighbor who never married, keeps an immaculate house and mows her own yard with a manual reel mower. About ten years ago, she repelled a violent intruder by sliding under her bed and biting him when he reached for her. Rebecca Gonzalez, the neighbor on the other side, lived in her home until her nineties, and Lydia Mass across the street was at home until she died at age ninety-seven.

Many other older people in the innermost circle of my life have demonstrated similar attachments to their homes over the years. My wife's father, Porfirio Perez, lived at home and worked with his wife, Annie, in the store they owned adjacent to their home until 2000, when he went to the hospital and passed away a few weeks later at age ninety-two. And Mrs. Perez died in her bed at home six years later at age ninety. My maternal grandfather, Romulo Munguia, worked in the print shop he founded and operated with a son until the day before he died at age ninety-three. He and my grandmother lived independently in the home that my wife and I later remodeled in that central city neighborhood and in which we raised our family.

It may seem from these examples that the older people in my life are all unusually long-lived and have particularly strong attachments to their homes. I do believe that Latinos develop intense love for their homes as places that evoke the memories of large extended families and years of lively social gatherings. But Latinos are by no means unique in their desire to be as independent as possible and to live in familiar surroundings for as long as they can. I cite the experiences of my family and neighbors only because they are personally vivid examples of the following themes that are becoming more important in our country:

- The reality that large numbers of Americans will be living into their eighties and beyond
- The desire of many older Americans to live in their homes for as long as they can
- The fact that existing neighborhoods all across the nation will increasingly comprise aging residents
- The awareness that homes and communities and services will have to be adapted, or new ones built, to accommodate older Americans who want to function actively, even though they may slow down a step in their pace, lose some acuity of vision, or function with slightly less upper body strength

The aging attributes of the Latino neighborhood I have described in San Antonio could just as easily be a Polish American parish in Chicago, Illinois; an African American community of row houses in Washington, DC; a Chinese American neighborhood in San Francisco, California; or a small town of German American heritage in Nebraska. The same ripples are spreading out across the nation: the growth of the aged population, the desire or need of older people to stay at home, and the imperative to engage family and community resources to create living settings that will enable people to live with dignity and to manage the process of aging supported by the comforting familiarity of the homes and communities in which they live.

The Focus of This Book

As former secretary of the US Department of Housing and Urban Development (HUD) and mayor of San Antonio and in my current role as a home-building executive, I have long been interested in housing and communities. With the sweeping demographic changes that are facing our nation, the ways our communities function must change. We, as a nation, must examine ways to support aging in place for the unprecedented numbers of older Americans seeking to live healthy and contributing lives in communities that serve all ages. Americans are aging in traditional homes, neighborhoods, and communities that were designed for yesterday's demographic realities, not those of today or the future. The sheer size of the baby boom generation guarantees that, as the health and mobility of so many begins to deteriorate, communities could be saddled with an enormous burden. What can be done quickly and affordably to support successful aging in communities throughout the United States? What will be our plan for supporting the oldest of the old among us?

Fast-arriving changes in age, race, and ethnic composition of the population will have significant consequences for the creation of what have been called livable communities. Large segments of the population are at risk for health, social, and economic hardship. Suburbs, where most of the growth in the senior population will occur, create dependency on the automobile, with many homes being distant from jobs, services, and amenities.[1] Rural communities struggle with transportation and service delivery issues. We can change our communities so that people living very long lives can live well. These changes must be made soon.

As we age, our needs and interests evolve and change, so our choices of housing should be wide ranging, as should be the spectrum of activities and services. There are a number of proven, affordable models that enhance independent living. Homes can be retrofitted, new age-appropriate homes built, existing neighborhoods reconnected, and new communities planned.

The enormity and complexity of such change is daunting. Financial strategies must adapt to new needs and opportunities. Public opinion must be better aligned with the values of accessibility, affordability, connectivity, and diversity. All levels of government must address these challenges with bold solutions.

During the years that I served as the mayor of San Antonio and spent many evenings listening to residents in neighborhood meetings across the city, I noticed repeated development patterns related to aging. In the same neighborhoods in which the population was aging, the housing stock was deteriorating and social needs were intensifying. As I listened to the older residents of those neighborhoods, I did not know then that those patterns were the local manifestations of what we now know to be the national forces of aging demographics, of physical isolation experienced by many older people, of unaffordable housing, and of diminishing social services funding. Over all these years, the frightened faces and plaintive voices of those older residents have stayed with me and spurred this search for public and private answers.

For this book, we have brought together experts in aging, architecture, construction, health, finance, and politics. We have asked experts on home renovation, urban design, community services, and finance to apply their professional knowledge to the needs of older Americans. Although diverse in expertise, they share a sense of urgency and determination to describe a new vision for aging in place and for living well at all ages.

Demographics

The number of Americans who will make up the population over age sixty-five is growing rapidly. When the first baby boomers, one of the largest cohorts of people in American history, reach sixty-five in 2011, the older population will explode. The US Census Bureau projects that the over-sixty-five population in the United States will grow from thirty-five million in 2000 to seventy-two million in 2030 to eighty-nine million in 2050. The number of people eighty-five and over will grow from 4.2 million in 2000 to 9 million in 2030 to 19 million in 2050.[2] Dr. Sherwin Nuland tells us in his book, *The Art of Aging*, that today 64 percent of Americans can expect to live to seventy-five and 35 percent should plan to reach eighty-five.[3]

The rate of growth in the numbers of older Americans has implications for numerous dimensions of American life, from consumer products to finances to living arrangements. The relative percentage of older Americans in the population is also larger,[4] so there will be changes in the ratios of workers to retirees and of schoolchildren to elderly people. The US Census Bureau projects that the ratio of working-age people (those aged fifteen to sixty-four) to retirement-age people (those aged sixty-five plus) will drop from 5.2 in 2010 to 3.0 in 2050. This change will occur not because we will have fewer workers or children but because we will have so many more retirees.[5] These retirees may not be able to rely on Social Security to the same degree that their parents could, but will instead need to work longer and draw upon other personal resources to fund their retirement.

The evidence is abundant that many Americans can live for many more years without the painful, costly, dispiriting effects of debilitating diseases. Others may not be so fortunate. Many older Americans can continue to contribute and can remain self-reliant for longer, pushing serious debilitation until the very end of life. One of the central purposes of our society should be to change our culture to support both old and young people so that very long lives are lived well.

Compression of Morbidity and the Longevity Dividend

Dr. James Fries of Stanford University articulated the idea of "compression of morbidity" in 1980.[6] In *The Art of Aging*, Dr. Sherwin Nuland provides a clear description of the concept:

Fries hypothesized that measures could be taken to change the long, gradually drooping arc [of aging decline] with a pattern that more resembled a relatively horizontal line ending in a rapid drop-off shortly before death. If this was accomplished, he pointed out, "then lifetime disability could be compressed into a shorter average period and cumulative lifetime disability could be reduced." In other words, instead of a long period of worsening frailty and illness, our bodies would stay relatively intact and then give out much closer to the time of eventual demise.[7]

When I visit my mother in her home and see her neighbors—like Stella Tenorio next door trimming her roses at age ninety-four—I am struck by evidence of how important compression of morbidity is as I see its benefits in the people I love. It is a walking, talking, living reality that goes far beyond an interesting concept and has everything to do with dignity in people's older years. It is my strong conviction that the physical environment in which older people live—with the security, stability, comfort, and psychological nurturing it offers—has a lot to do with staying healthy and independent longer.

A metric has been devised to bring solidity to the concept. It is referred to as ALE, or active life expectancy, and it quantifies the number of years that people can expect to live without disability. It is indicative of our hopeful standards of quality of life that we, as a society, are now measuring, not simply years of longevity but also the number of those years in which longer life can be of high quality: healthy, active, and free of impairment.[8]

The benefits to individuals of being alert and involved in activities with colleagues, friends, and family are clear. There are also benefits for caregivers, for younger family members, for networks of friends, for employers, and for the recipients of volunteer time. Preventive measures, such as establishing activity centers and supporting wellness programs, are valuable investments. Everyone benefits by reducing expenditures for costly medical interventions and emergency responses due to diabetes, stroke, and heart attack. The costs of Medicare and Medicaid might be reduced if individuals used the most expensive long-term institutional and end-of-life care less.

The late Dr. Robert Butler, former president and CEO of the International Longevity Center in New York City, explicitly extended the idea of compression of morbidity for individuals to a benefit, or "longevity dividend," for society at large.[9] If compression of morbidity for individuals and a longevity dividend for society are worthy goals, then it is important to consider ways in which they can be achieved. Among the elements of a strategy to reach those goals are continued progress in medical research and care, increased accessibility to health care, governmental attention to solvency of the key health insurance and finance systems, wellness education, nutritional improvements, and disincentives to use cigarettes, alcohol, and other harmful products. Increasingly, health and aging experts are adding another set of societal actions to the compression of morbidity agenda—that is, the redesign of physical environments to facilitate wellness, healthy activity, social engagement, and self-reliance. A place to live that is physically manageable and emotionally uplifting is connected with independence, peace of mind, and self-improvement. Services designed particularly for the needs of seniors are essential. Support systems can be added to existing homes or can be built into new homes to help people remain safe, mobile, self-reliant, fit, and strong.

The central assertion of this book is that we, as a nation, need to find ways to modify or build homes and communities to support aging in place for those unprecedented numbers of Americans seeking to live healthy lives in their own homes. These changes will enable older Americans to make even greater contributions to their communities, thereby strengthening our society as a whole.

Transforming Existing Homes into "Lifelong" Homes

Why should we pay attention to housing with respect to aging? It is estimated that 70 percent of Americans aged sixty-five and older live in single-family detached homes, and at least 89 percent intend to remain permanently in their homes.[10] The normal process of aging imposes infirmities that can create hardships in homes if these environments are designed only for younger people. Some of the hardships are easy to address. Declining eyesight, for example, can be aided by simple interventions based on knowledge about aging, such as brighter lightbulbs, better locations for light sources, accessible controls, guide lights for nighttime, and contrasting colors on the edges of furniture or steps.[11]

But many homes need more significant modifications to support healthy living, and older Americans may ignore necessary changes until there is a crisis. Renovations and necessary maintenance can be expensive, there may be a fear of becoming victimized by predatory elements of the home-remodeling industries, and there may be challenges in managing major repair projects.

For years, city officials and remodeling contractors have organized and certified packages of home renovations for energy efficiency and savings in order to weatherize homes. I was a city councilman in the 1970s and a mayor in the 1980s when the concept of weatherization of homes was first advanced on a large scale. The concept went from general awareness of the energy losses from poorly insulated homes and from recognition of the financial burdens of utility costs to action on pilot projects and then widespread national action. It is now time to follow that path from awareness to action concerning the modification of existing homes to meet the needs of aging Americans. The need for an affordable and effective package of modifications and regular maintenance to make existing homes more suitable for older people should be organized as a renovation package to create homes that could be used for a lifetime. A certified renovation package for aging in place could include roll-under kitchen and bathroom sinks, grab bars, curbless showers, lever faucets and door handles, a zero-step entrance, and wider doors and hallways. In multifamily homes, adding elevators may be the key for aging in place.

New Homes for Aging in Place

A 2002 report published by the National Association of Home Builders indicates that 31 percent of homebuyers aged fifty-five and older would seriously consider buying townhomes, duplexes, and multifamily condo units, but only 15 percent of homeowners aged fifty-five and older live in such housing.[12] As a society, we need to be producing more housing that is of smaller scale, affordably priced, suitable for multifamily use, located in walkable communities, and close to amenities, commercial districts, health facilities, and public transit. The goal should be to support communities in which older people can choose from a variety of types of homes: single-family and multifamily units, rentals and owner-occupied homes.

New forms of supportive housing are being developed that enable older residents to live independently with assistive services. Cohousing is a residential model that locates individual dwelling units around common spaces, often including dining facilities and a great room, and incorporates accessible design.[13] Accessory dwelling units (ADUs) located on the same lot as a primary home may be ideal for multigenerational families.[14] Because of their physical proximity, they provide the added advantage of enabling the younger generation to look in on older residents. Some cities promote the building of ADUs on single-family lots to expand the supply of affordable housing on more dense, transit-accessible infill sites. Other cities are revising zoning policies to encourage more compact and affordable housing types in areas where the population is aging.

Another housing innovation for older people who wish to continue working in a small, self-employed setting is the live/work flex house, a dwelling that includes a workspace. It might be a row house in which the living space is typically above the business use, or a loft/studio in which the office or shop is on the same level as the living area. These "mixed uses" create settings where older people can comfortably pursue careers. Some of these configurations evolve naturally in existing homes and neighborhoods; in newly constructed communities, their inclusion can create a diversity of uses that is ideal for all ages.

Henry Cisneros and his wife, city councilwoman Mary Alice Cisneros, at a town hall meeting organized to discuss the housing concerns of older San Antonians. Photo by Charlie Elizalde.

Adapting Existing Communities for Aging Populations

In addition to individual homes that support aging in place, we need thoughtfully created communities—both existing and new neighborhoods—that feature safe streets, usable sidewalks, stores offering groceries and pharmaceuticals, public parks, churches, and services. All across America, neighborhoods such as the one where my mother lives are aging. Planners have given them a name: naturally occurring retirement communities (NORCs). As a councilman and mayor, I advanced ideas on a piecemeal basis when I saw the pattern of older residents left behind in increasingly concentrated pockets. I suggested, with some success, to our police department, for example, that we use crime data to identify those concentrations of aging citizens victimized by local thugs in order to patrol those neighborhoods in different ways, such as on foot or in teams capable of doing spot checks by knocking on seniors' doors. I have visited more than two hundred American cities as secretary of HUD and in my private community-building work, and I have come to believe that we should go beyond piecemeal ideas and create more comprehensive municipal responses to aging that can include the following elements:

- Supporting certified home renovation programs
- Establishing accessible senior nutrition and fitness programs
- Providing utility assistance
- Arranging health consultations and interventions
- Offering special programs at branch libraries and literacy centers
- Extending appropriate transportation programs
- Training and deploying aging specialists
- Developing the capabilities among those specialists to help seniors with daily activities such as preparing meals, cleaning, and bathing
- Tailoring community policing to special needs
- Designing local senior services based on statistical evidence and on advice from community-based organizations about elderly population needs

In this way, an existing neighborhood can overcome the seemingly immutable physical features that otherwise render it socially disconnected, geographically isolated, underprotected, and underserved. Such seemingly unchangeable barriers as the street layout, distance from necessary stores and services, and even criminal incidence can be overcome with an intentionally designed overlay of community services that pull together a cohesive NORC. Also, organizations such as the Village to Village Network offer new ways to weave together a fabric of unifying services to overcome the barriers that isolate residents in an existing NORC.[15]

Planning New Communities to Age in Place

Admittedly, it can be difficult to place new communities of significant scale, including homes for older people, in already dense, built-up urban environments, although the recycling of obsolete urban areas through clearance and restoration is an attractive option in many cities. But there are abundant opportunities for newly designed communities in the less dense first-ring suburbs and in the green-grass exurbs. In such places, there is physical space to build entirely new concepts of communities, as well as homes of various sizes, price points, and configurations, designed for young singles, families, and people seeking to age in place. This mix of ages and homes can be consciously woven together as communities of cohesion and mutual support. The suburbs are where the fastest growth of the older populations will occur. The Brookings Institution draws the following conclusion about the "graying of suburbia":

> In 2008, 71 percent of pre-seniors lived in suburbs, and their numbers (as well as those of seniors) grew faster in suburbs than in cities during the 2000s. This reflects boomers' status as America's

"first suburban generation," and signals their likelihood to remain in these communities as they grow older.[16]

The work of the New Urbanists has advanced smart growth principles, which are highly applicable to the creation of communities suitable for Americans of all ages. New Urbanist principles provide a guide for community building that stair-steps through levels of urban geography: from the regional level to the neighborhood to the specific street to the individual building or dwelling unit.[17] These principles can be applied when a failed retail center in an inner suburb is cleared and a new neighborhood is put in its place or when an open tract of land adjacent to an edge city farther out from the urban core is linked to mass transportation and planned as an urban village. These concepts and models are useful in examining and assessing the characteristics of existing as well as new communities. The challenge is to finance and otherwise enable this type of change to occur across the country.

Listening to Older People

Listening carefully to the concerns of older people about their present living arrangements is an important way to identify what should be done to make their lives better. At an AARP-sponsored town hall meeting,[18] at which I presented aging-in-place ideas, older residents described their concerns and fears, the things that made life difficult for them in their present homes. Among the concerns they listed were the following:

- Frustration at being immobile and being dependent on others to run errands and drive them to appointments
- Deterioration of their homes
- High utility costs, particularly for heating and cooling
- Fear of crime, including assaults on the street or burglaries of their homes
- Debilitating effects of major impairments and serious frailties
- Loneliness as a result of isolation from friends and family
- Fear of falling, getting hurt, becoming ill, and not being able to communicate
- Pain or feelings of inadequacy in managing the activities of daily living
- Lack of money for home improvements or maintenance
- Fear of high volumes of fast-moving traffic on neighborhood streets
- Danger of misusing appliances such as a stove or oven

Clearly, not all of these concerns can be addressed by reshaping the physical environment, but a number of features in homes and communities can help. Services to support people in their communities and homes are essential and need to be well coordinated. Table 1.1 sets forth responses for addressing specific

Concerns of older residents about aging at home	Features of a home (remodeled or new)	Existing communities	New communities
Frustration of immobility; dependent on being driven for errands	Use technology to create links to delivery services, such as grocery valet services	Provide van transport programs Zoning changes—overlay amenities and retrofitting big-box stores	Design walkable neighborhoods with manageable distances to amenities
Deterioration of the home	Undertake age-appropriate modifications on existing homes Repair and maintenance programs	Offer a package of certified "lifelong" improvements at a reasonable cost	Build sustainable homes with green technologies and build healthy homes with safe materials
High utility costs for heating and cooling	Include weatherization modifications in a "lifelong" package for existing homes	Design certified energy efficiency programs targeted to the homes of older residents	Be attentive to the orientation of new homes to the sun's seasonal path and to prevailing breezes Build sustainable homes
Fear of crime: burglaries of homes and assaults	Use technology to increase in-home security (e.g., alarm systems)	Community policing in NORCs focused on older residents	Design of the streetscape to increase "eyes on the street"
Overall effects of impairments and frailties	Install a "lifelong" package: bathroom and kitchen modifications, proper lighting, etc. Apply new communications technologies	Maintain walkable sidewalks, curb cuts, ramps, street lighting, pocket parks, etc.	Construct street and sidewalk systems for safety; properly equip neighborhood parks
Isolation from friends and family	Reorient spaces in existing homes as welcoming settings for visitors In new homes, design ample social spaces in floor plans	Provide transportation to community social settings, such as senior fitness centers and nutrition centers, religious institutions	Design neighborhoods within easy walking distance of public spaces and amenities Zone communities for compact mixed-use development
Fear of falling or getting sick without being able to communicate	Build in communications technologies, such as visual aids, to offer links to emergency services	Create a community outreach capacity to check on seniors, especially those who are more frail Offer aging-in-place specialists	A core public service of a new community should include aging-in-place specialists to regularly assist older residents
Pain or inadequacy in managing daily activities in the home	"Lifelong" package should at least meet visibility standards and strive for universal design	Offer community-based home care appropriate to the level of disability	Match community-based home care with community care facilities as part of the community design
Lack of money to undertake home improvement projects	Access federal/state programs for "lifelong" packages Improve social security system Maintain public programs supporting housing and services for vulnerable populations	Focus on neighborhood-wide modifications in a NORC Offer public financial supports adequate for aging based on community economic levels	Incorporate age-related modifications from the earliest design and constructions to reduce costs Plan for infrastructure efficiencies in capital and operating costs Housing community affordability

(continued)

Table 1.1 Responses to the fears and concerns of older Americans about aging in place. Source: Henry Cisneros.

Concerns of older residents about aging at home	Features of a home (remodeled or new)	Existing communities	New communities
Fear of high volumes of fast-moving traffic on neighborhood streets		Be attentive to traffic flow issues Mitigate with speed bumps, targeted enforcement, traffic signage and stop lights, communications devices for personalized service	Design neighborhood streets to be narrower, with shorter straightaways to reduce and slow traffic
Danger of misusing appliances such as a stove or oven	When replacing appliances in existing homes, install with age-appropriate controls and handles In new homes, install specially designed appliances with large readouts and easy-to-use controls	Conduct community briefings that include reminders of safety precautions Train professional and informal caregivers in safety measures	Include instruction in safety precautions in community orientations

Table 1.1 (*continued*)

concerns. Table 1.2 provides helpful information from the MetLife Mature Market Institute report titled *Aging in Place 2.0: Rethinking Solutions to the Home Care Challenge* about categories and expenses related to homes and services.

Paying for Aging in Place

No consideration of preparing our homes and communities for the surge of older Americans who wish to age in place can be complete without exploration of the economic resources needed for home maintenance, retrofitting, new construction, and the integrated delivery of services. To list useful renovations and products without regard to how individuals or society are going to pay for them is not likely to result in progress.

There are resources that can be prioritized, including personal savings, retirement earnings, and state and local tax relief measures, that would be helpful for wealthier families. Social services and federal housing and income security programs are important for those with fewer resources. It is important to remember that modest expenditures to extend the years of aging in place can save money for individuals, for families, and for society. The interplay of personal savings and retirement earnings with governmental grants, loans, tax relief, and incentives is complex. It is important for leaders to create age-appropriate homes available within the price ranges of people who need them. Table 1.3 offers ways in which economic resources can be matched to our goals for aging in place. It is particularly important to consider the ways in which scarce resources can be brought to bear in assisting the frail elderly who are poor. Table 1.4 summarizes income eligibility for various programs and resources.

The Challenge

As our country recognizes the growth in the number of older people, it is important that we mobilize our resources to enhance the quality of life for our aging population. We can support the vitality of older people, enhancing their independence, supporting their mobility, and sustaining their dignity. By doing this, we will reap the benefits of the wisdom and experience of seniors at a time when our society needs every citizen to be productive. We can help transform individual lives from dependence and decline to lives of purpose and involvement by being attentive to the ways that we build homes and communities.

To date, these concepts have been applied principally to senior facilities of a

Home*	**Modifications**			**Capital investment**
		Assessment, design, etc.	$300–$10,000	
		Ramp, landscape, lifts	$2,500–$20,000	
		Grab bars	$250/2 installed	
		Bathroom	$3,500–$35,000	
		Door widening	$800–$1,200	
		Elevator	$20,000–$35,000	
		Stair glide	$3,000–$12,000	
		Master addition	$35,000–$100,000	
	Maintenance			
	Regular	Furnace	$100 x 2/year	
		Gutter cleaning	$70–$350	
	Seasonal	Snow, grass, leaves, mulch, weeds	$10–$25/week	
	Long term	Roof, paint	$1,000–$5,000	
Services**	**Ceiling lift**		$5,000–$12,000	**Regular and variable expenses**
	Personal emergency response (PERS)		$50 install, $15–$35/month monitor	
	Pill dispenser monitor		$160; $15–$35/month or w/PERS	
	Multiple element monitoring	Purchase/install/monitor	$2,400–$3,400, $49/month	
	Paid assistance	Homemaker, personal assistance	$19/hour	
		Home health aide	$21/hour	
		Nurse	$38/hour	
	Money management, bill paying, etc.		$50–$75/hour, $2,400–$6,000/year	
	Transportation	Public		
		Family, cabs, volunteers	$45/hour accompanied	
	Prescription deliveries and other errands			
	Food	Meals delivery	$6–$10/day	
		Grocery delivery	$8–$10/week	
	Lifestyle	Adult day care	$67/day	
		Senior/social center	$0–$75/year	
	Brain fitness	Internet-based programs	$400–$1,250	
	Care management	Community social worker	$0–$100/hour	
		Private geriatric care manager	$90–$150/hour, $2,500–$5,000/year	
		Nurse case manager	$0–$55/hour	

*Prices depend on existing design and conditions.
**Costs depend on family and personal resources, health status.

Table 1.2 Potential costs of aging in place. Source: MetLife Mature Market Institute, *Aging in Place 2.0: Rethinking Solutions to the Home Care Challenge*, http://www.metlife.com/mmi/research/aging-in-place.html#insights.

specialized character, affordable to people with substantial retirement resources in resort-like settings. But the population of older people in our country is now becoming so large that strategies of improving existing homes, of incorporating universally useful features in new homes, of building thoughtful new communities, and of retooling existing neighborhoods must be broadly integrated into our community-building strategies at the local level across the United States. This initiative is not a matter of creating homes for seniors as acts of obligation, although, as a nation, we certainly owe a debt of gratitude that would make obligation reason enough. Rather, it is in the interest of our nation that we all benefit from the longevity dividend, that we secure the best quality of life for all our

Aging-in-Place economic goals	Personal/private funds	State and local funds	Federal funds
Personal economic security: living-related personal finances	Personal savings Family and friends Retirement earnings Health, disability, and long-term care insurance Reverse mortgages HELOCs	Senior homestead exemption from property taxes "Circuit breakers" for senior renters	Social Security Medicare/Medicaid Expanded health care coverage
Funds to modify existing homes	Personal savings Family and friends Loans Reverse mortgages HELOCs Foundations/NGOs—Habitat for Humanity	Tax credit or deferred loan programs Housing trust funds Acquisition capital for developers to preserve affordable housing	Weatherization Assistance Program to include "lifelong" elements CDBG/home funds HUD programs for preservation of the affordable housing stock Upgrade and expand existing Section 202 properties Section 504 programs VA programs
Funds for age-appropriate new home construction	Sale of present home to move to smaller housing Personal savings for home upgrades with new technologies Foundations/NGOs—Habitat for Humanity	Senior homestead exemption from property taxes Housing trust funds Predevelopment loans to builders State housing finance agency mortgage products Deferred loans and incentives for universal design features	Section 202 Supportive Housing for the Elderly Low-income-housing tax credits HOME program FHA mortgage products Financial support for universal design and visitability standards Section 504 programs VA programs
Funds for "lifelong" naturally occurring retirement communities SSPs	Personal membership and senior tax relief contributions (such as "village-to-village" network services)	State supplemental transportation programs: to improve accessibility Flexible zoning Housing affordability State funds for home- and community-based services	NORC SSP grants DOT public transit funding Medicaid funding for home- and community-based services/PACE OAA community Service coordinator programs Veterans Directed Home and Community Based Services Program
Funds to incorporate age-appropriate features in new communities	Reduce home expenditures in planned communities with common amenities	Senior property tax relief programs Expedited zoning, permitting, and fees to reduce new construction costs	Federal transit programs for multifamily housing at transit stops Supportive housing funds for continuing care retirement

Table 1.3 Categories of resources for aging in place. Source: Henry Cisneros.

Income level	Extremely low 30% of median and below	Very low 31%–50% of median	Low 51%–80% of median	Moderate 81%+ of median
Programs currently financing new construction or rental assistance vouchers	Section 202 Housing choice vouchers HOME Section 515 Public housing/ HOPE VI	Section 202 Housing choice vouchers LIHTC HOME Section 515 Public housing/ HOPE VI 501(c)(3) Bonds (partial)	LIHTC (up to 60%) HOME (up to 65%) 501(c)(3) Bonds GSEs	HUD mortgage insurance GSEs 501(c)(3) Bonds (partial)

Table 1.4 Summary of income eligibility for programs of housing assistance. Source: *A Quiet Crisis in America* **(Report to Congress by the Commission on Affordable Housing and Health Facility Needs for Seniors in the 21st Century, June 30, 2002).**

citizens, and that we live up to the ideal that every single person can contribute to the nation's well-being over the span of an entire lifetime.

I have seen with my own eyes how a safe, decent, and financially secure place to live can add vitality to a person's older years. I know that my mother's ability to live in the cherished home she shared with my father and in the rooms where she raised her children is a big part of the life force that enables her to stay active, involved, upbeat, and determined to make the most of each day. She knows her way around the house and knows every creak and crack after sixty-five years there. She is deeply rooted in the neighborhood and follows the goings-on among the younger generations. She gains energy from the warm sun and the breeze as she tends her potted plants and fruit trees. In short, she loves her home—it is part of her, intellectually and spiritually.

She and we, her family, are living proof of the wisdom of Winston Churchill's observation: "We shape our buildings; thereafter they shape us." In the case of the Cisneros family, it is fitting to take license with the great statesman's idea: We spend sixty-five years lovingly shaping a home and all the while it is shaping us. After all, that home is the place where my brothers, sisters, and I learned about family loyalty, about social justice, about patriotism, about faith, about responsibility, about diversity, and about striving against adversity.

Not everyone can live in a home with as much tenure or memory as my mother's. But I have a deep conviction that a safe and decent home is a great boon in every person's life. We need to make sure that every American—especially those whose older age makes the quest for stability and peace of mind more urgent—has a safe and decent place to call home.

Notes

1. William H. Frey, "Age," in *State of Metropolitan America: On the Front Lines of Demographic Transformation* (Washington, DC: Brookings Institution, 2010), 77.

2. *2008 National Population Projections* (Washington, DC: US Census Bureau, 2008).

3. Sherwin B. Nuland, *The Art of Aging: A Doctor's Prescription for Well-Being* (New York: Random House, 2007), 242–43.

4. Paul R. Cullinan, "Social Security Spending and Revenue Options" (presentation, Bipartisan Policy Center's Debt Reduction Task Force, Washington, DC, April 15, 2010).

5. *2008 National Population Projections*.

6. Nuland, *Art of Aging*, 230.

7. Ibid.

8. Ibid., 244.

9. S. Jay Olshansky et al., "In Pursuit of the Longevity Dividend," *The Scientist* (March 2006): 28–36.

10. Keith Wardrip, "Strategies to Meet the Housing Needs of Older Adults," *Insight on the Issues*, no. 38 (March 2010): 2.

11. Esther Greenhouse, "Physiological Changes in Typical Aging in Relation to the Built Environment" (unpublished manuscript, 2010).

12. Margaret Wylde, *Boomers on the Horizon: Housing Preferences of the 55+ Market* (Washington, DC: BuilderBooks, National Association of Home Builders, 2002).

13. Wardrip, "Strategies to Meet the Housing Needs of Older Adults," 9.

14. Andres Duany, Jeff Speck, and Mike Lydon, *The Smart Growth Manual* (New York: McGraw Hill, 2010), 12.10.

15. Judy Caldwell-Midero, "Market Expert Predicts the Future of Senior Living," *Housing for Seniors Report*, no. 10-03 (2010): 8.

16. Frey, "Age," 77.

17. Duany et al., *Smart Growth Manual*, appendix.

18. AARP, "Political Empowerment through Neighborhood Revitalization: One Square Mile at a Time" (conference, San Antonio, TX, May 16, 2009).

Chapter 2

A Hopeful Future

Laura L. Carstensen

The Birth of Aging Societies

Americans aged sixty to seventy-five are the best educated and healthiest older people yet known. Throughout most of history, human life expectancy was about twenty years—barely long enough to ensure survival of the species. In fits and starts, life expectancy steadily crept up. But all prior increases pale in comparison to those made in the twentieth century, when life expectancy at birth nearly doubled in developed regions around the globe. In 1900, life expectancy in the United States was forty-seven; by 2000, it was seventy-seven. Even more dramatic increases occurred in Japan and parts of Western Europe. Demographer James Vaupel predicts that the majority of children born in the developed world since 2000 will live to be one hundred.[1]

Humans did not suddenly become more robust. Rather, improvements in living conditions raised the average life expectancy in entire populations. Scientific and technological discoveries, along with related cultural advances, paved the way for biological hardiness to profit from human ingenuity.

In other words, breathtaking gains in life expectancy were the product of culture: shared attitudes, values, goals, and practices. Our predecessors made the world safer for people of all ages, but the youngest in the population, whose early years had been highly precarious, benefited especially. We even created a new phase of life—adolescence—which focused on education, identity building, and a more gradual entry into adulthood. The fact that most people born in the Western

LAURA L. CARSTENSEN, founding director of the Stanford Center on Longevity, is professor of psychology at Stanford University, where she is the Fairleigh S. Dickinson Jr. Professor in Public Policy. She is a member of the MacArthur Foundation Research Network on an Aging Society and has chaired two studies for the National Academy of Sciences, resulting in *The Aging Mind* and *When I'm 64*. She received her bachelor of science from the University of Rochester and her doctorate in clinical psychology from West Virginia University. She is the author of *A Long Bright Future: Happiness, Health and Financial Security in an Age of Increased Longevity*.

world today have the opportunity to live out their full lives is nothing short of extraordinary.

The Challenge

Now we find ourselves at a peculiar point in human history. The advent of old age happened so fast that societies are unprepared to support the needs of older populations, or to make use of their expertise. Our lives are guided by outdated norms. Enduring life scripts that tell us when to get an education, have babies, work, and retire are the same as those that guided lives half as long. We live in homes and communities built to accommodate young parents and their children, when the typical household in the United States today consists of one or two adults.

We must imagine how lives doubled in length might benefit individuals of all ages. We need to rethink the design of our homes and communities. We must reinvent the social services and cultural norms that shape our collective life.

What Aging Is and Is Not

It is imperative that we gain a basic understanding of aging[2]—what is inevitable and what is avoidable—so we can build home and community environments that compensate for the weaknesses and facilitate the strengths of long-lived populations. We need to get rid of myths about aging so that we have a clear-eyed view of the possibilities that aging societies present.[3] We need to build solutions into communities in ways that benefit all.

At this point in our history, we need to help people plan for exceptionally long time horizons, to optimize learning throughout life, and to motivate older people to remain engaged in communities and workforces. We need to build social and physical environments to help individuals maintain their physical fitness, create new norms for cross-generational relations, and create financial opportunities that enable people to afford long lives.

We need to be realistic. There is no cream, potion, or pill that will stop the aging process, but there are a number of factors that can improve the likelihood of a happy and healthy old age. There are general trends that we should understand, associated with normal aging as it affects our emotional, social, physical, and mental processing. If we can appreciate these trends, we will be able to put in place the kinds of homes, communities, and services that best fit an aging society.

BIOLOGICAL AGING

Our body functions peak in the early twenties and decline with age. Lung capacity steadily decreases with age, bones gradually become thinner and more brittle, and muscles lose their elasticity. It takes longer for the body to respond to changes in ambient temperature—making extreme hot and cold temperatures hazardous. Thirty-year-olds notice that they can't pull all-nighters the way they did in their twenties, and runners at fifty know firsthand that they are at greater risk for injuries than they were at thirty. But there are substantial individual differences.

As anyone who watches the Senior Olympics can tell you, many people in their seventies, eighties, and beyond can be awe-inspiring athletes. Fifty-year-olds who exercise have better lung capacity than thirty-year-old couch potatoes.

The healthiness of older Americans is a remarkable achievement. That said, in an era of increased longevity, the oldest segment of the population (those eighty-five and older) will see an increase in the proportion of citizens who have chronic illnesses, many of whom will have associated functional disabilities.[4] Given that the majority of Americans prefer to live independently, homes and communities need to gear up to meet their needs.[5]

COGNITIVE AGING

Like other organs, the brain suffers with age. Memory loss is the most widely experienced cognitive change associated with normal aging. Just as physical decline starts early and declines steadily, memory and speed of information processing peak in the early twenties and decline thereafter.[6] Working memory, the ability to store pieces of information and manipulate them, like adding a series of numbers, takes a particularly strong hit with age. Similar changes occur in recollection, attention, and language, especially in retrieving the names of people.[7] Although these changes are noticeable and unwanted, they do not *prevent* learning or problem solving. Some aspects of memory, like how to ride a bike or type on a keyboard, change barely, if at all, as we age. Stores of knowledge, such as vocabulary and cultural acumen, continue to grow with age.[8]

Of course, not everyone follows the expected path of aging. Although many people reach old age without dementia, diseases such as Alzheimer's and other dementias are strongly correlated with age, and are climbing rapidly to the top of the list of public health crises. Older people suffering from cognitive decline may struggle to care for themselves in their homes. Community services are not always adequate, and family caregiving networks can be strained. Difficulties include everyday challenges such as taking medications correctly, dressing, preparing meals, shopping, getting to doctor and other appointments, and managing finances. Cognitive decline also affects the ability to take care of one's home and feel confident about living alone.

EMOTIONAL AND SOCIAL AGING

Emotionally speaking, life improves with age. Older adults suffer less from depression, anxiety, and substance abuse than younger people, and they report fewer negative emotions.[9] It's not the intensity of emotions that diminish with age. In experiments studying responses to negative memories, images, or text, older people report just as much distress as younger people, but negative emotions do not linger as long as they do in younger adults. Plus, as people begin to sense their own mortality, they tend to focus on what's most important.[10] With vast and nebulous futures, younger people tend to worry about everyone and everything. Older people seem less troubled by such matters. Older people instead concentrate on enjoying the present and are less concerned about the future.

Some improvement in emotional well-being is linked to improved social relationships. Social circles narrow with age, as people concentrate on deep, often decades-long relationships. Researchers now agree—after decades of failed interventions aimed at getting older people to play bingo or go to socials—that superficial social contacts confer few, if any, health benefits. Of course, social networks can narrow too much. Having fewer than three people you consider

THE POSITIVITY EFFECT

What if instead of conceiving of age as the years elapsed since birth, we considered time left before death? My colleagues and I have found that younger and older people have markedly different priorities, not because of chronological age but because of their estimations about the time they have left.

Socioemotional selectivity theory proposes that people's subjective understanding of the time left in their lives motivates their goals, preferences, and desires. There are two broad categories of goals: those that aim to gather experience and knowledge and those that focus on emotionally rewarding activities. When time horizons are expansive, people lean toward gathering new experiences, because the future is long and nebulous, and just about anything could prove useful in the years ahead. When time horizons are short, people choose to spend time on pursuits that matter most to them, which tends to make them happy.[a]

Goals affect attention and memory. Older adults show preferences for positive over negative or neutral information. Researchers call this the positivity effect. Because older people remember positive events and associations better than they do those that are negative, they tend to be less influenced by negative experiences, and this benefits mental health. However, in situations where negative information is important, a tendency to focus on the positive can put people at risk. For example, older adults may buy into financial scams because they are selectively focused on the positive information—friendly telephone calls and the anticipation of financial rewards—rather than the negative—manipulative sales techniques and unlikely promises.

So, if you had expected to live for twenty more years, but just now learned that you only have six months left, you might be inclined to close this book and call your best friend to meet for lunch.

[a]Laura L. Carstensen, "The Influence of a Sense of Time on Human Development," *Science* 312, no. 5782 (2006): 1913.

very close is a risk factor for mental and physical health problems. Feeling socially isolated is as great a risk to health as cigarette smoking.[11]

As people age, they also become more deeply concerned about younger family members, the environment, and social justice. There is little evidence of so-called intergenerational warfare. Older people care about future generations and their legacy, and younger people care about older people. Younger voters tend to support government programs for the elderly, just as older people support programs that benefit youth.[12]

However, we live in a highly age-segregated society, and eliminating age segregation should be one of the pressing goals of this century. Constructing communities in ways that intentionally integrate housing designed for young families and elders can help, as can careful modification of existing housing stock. Public facilities, such as libraries, can bring together generational interests and provide needed social supports.

Exercise and Diet

The news that exercise and diet are important for longevity is neither new nor surprising. But most people underestimate their effects. Exercise helps to maintain strong bones and muscles, benefits emotional well-being, and plays a role in staving off cognitive decline, too. Psychologist K. Warner Schaie describes an exchange he had with a friend who wanted to know how many Sudoku puzzles he should do each day to keep his mind sharp. Schaie's response: "It depends on how many you can do on your thirty-minute walk."

Despite exhortations to exercise and eat properly, a significant majority of Americans do not exercise and remain overweight. Willpower may work for some, but a community's infrastructure has a far better chance of integrating activity into daily life. If a community has inviting walkable areas, and if amenities and services are located within a walkable radius of housing, residents will stand a greater chance of continuing to be mobile and independent as they age.

Aging and Where We Live

Research shows that humans are highly attuned to their environments and that where we live affects our overall well-being. We must begin to design homes, workplaces, schools, and communities that address the realities of normal aging. The built environment can support healthy nutrition, exercise, and social engagement to help people live well from the beginning of life. We know that if fast-food restaurants pepper your neighborhood, you will weigh more than if you live near a farmers' market. If there are accessible paths on which to walk from your home to the corner store, you're likely to be a walker.[13] Proximity even predicts our good friends.[14,15] Lessons learned about the power of environments can help us to live lives that are emotionally rich, engaged, and satisfying.

One important step is to create physical and social environments that optimize the daily lives of frail elders to allow them to stay in the homes they have chosen. Basic building requirements should make modifications, like ramps or grab bars, easy to add and aesthetically pleasing. Homes of the future will likely be filled with technologies that make them safer and healthier for older people. And making homes safer for older people will make them safer for younger people as well.

The emotional connection to home cannot be overestimated. The author Mihaly Csikszentmihalyi has written insightfully about this question. He gathered data from a sample across age groups, and his findings about the elder generation (what he calls grandparents) reaffirm the importance of aging in place.

> Those who were able to remain in their old places stress the importance of the continuity of memories and experiences the home represents:
>
>> It's home to us because we raised our children here. . . .
>> I lived in it for 34 years; it's like an old bathrobe: when you put it on, it feels so good.
>> It's just a nice place to go to. It's got so many memories. With never—I'm very lucky—never a bad time.[16]

Csikszentmihalyi's insights, after completing this study, include the following:

> The importance of the home derives from the fact that it provides a space of action and interaction in which one can develop, maintain and change one's identity. . . . The home is a shelter for those persons and objects that define the self; thus it becomes, for most people, an indispensable symbolic environment.[17]

How we modify and design homes and neighborhoods will make a difference. A group of researchers in Australia examined how the modification of homes for older residents can strengthen the personal and social meaning of the home, as well as its safety and comfort.[18] Research also has found a link between housing quality and psychological well-being among the elderly.[19] Other researchers believe there is evidence to suggest that housing dissatisfaction and neighborhood deprivation can lead to declines in cognitive function in older populations.[20]

Education, Work, and Retirement

Factors related to the stages of our lives—education, work, and retirement—are integrally related to how we live, age, and interact in the community.

EDUCATION

When people can effectively solve the problems they face, they fare better. Low levels of education are associated with increasing disabilities that begin early in adulthood and continue to old age.[21] Indeed, education is a better predictor of mortality than age.[22] Americans with the highest levels of income also enjoy the greatest wealth, but education appears even more influential than income in old-age outcomes. People with high levels of education are less likely to get sick, and when they do, they manage their illnesses more effectively than people with less education.[23] Education early in life even appears to bolster memory performance in old age.[24] The steady increase in high school graduation rates in the second half of the twentieth century is believed to have played an important role in recent declines in disability among the elderly.[25]

However, the quality of public education is declining. Although half of Americans have some college education, far fewer (closer to a quarter) obtain a college degree. Differences in educational attainment by race and social class threaten to solidify castelike divisions. In California, for example, the statewide high school dropout rate in 2008 varied widely—amounting to 8 percent for Asian students, 12 percent for white students, 33 percent for black students, and 24 percent for both Native American and Hispanic students.[26]

WORK AND RETIREMENT

For some people, the end of grueling or tiresome work couldn't come too soon, but many Americans between sixty and seventy-five find a mismatch between their abilities and their working lives. Healthy and educated retirees often describe themselves as underutilized. Many in this age group might like to continue working, perhaps on a part-time basis or in a different job.

Disability has been pushed farther into advanced ages, too, so much so that if age is calculated by mortality risk rather than chronological age, a sixty-five-year-old man today is the same age as a fifty-nine-year-old in 1970.[27] But across the same years that life expectancy increased, retirement age declined.

There are two principal problems with retirements that last decades. First, most people find it impossible to save enough in forty years to finance a retirement that lasts twenty or thirty years, particularly if the cost of living in retirement isn't substantially reduced from its cost during working life. Half of Americans older than fifty have no retirement savings.[28] Monthly Social Security checks alone will not allow recipients to live the lifestyles they enjoyed while working.

Second, there is no reason to think that extended retirements are desirable psychologically or emotionally. Most Americans like their work. Leisure is important throughout life, but a life of leisure is a different matter. Not only does work provide people with income, but research findings also suggest that work offers stimulation that helps to maintain cognitive performance[29] and self-esteem.[30] For those who would like to change their work as they reach retirement age, or for those who cannot continue in taxing physical jobs, there need to be new options and creative thinking about work.

Vision for the Future

It is imperative that we envision futures that are very different from those our ancestors considered. When most people think about buying a home, getting married, having children, or completing an education, they look to the past, referencing the ages of their parents or grandparents when they achieved these same milestones. But generations alive today can think differently. If we are living longer, child-bearing years do not have to co-occur with the peaks of careers,

THE SWAMPSCOTT EXPERIENCE

Consider an example from Swampscott, Massachusetts, a small town fifteen miles north of Boston. As the town prepared to build a new high school, space constraints led town leaders to propose that a senior center be included in the same building. For the senior center, it meant moving out of an old, cramped building with limited handicap accessibility into a brand-new space that would have been infeasible as a stand-alone project. It took some convincing, but in 2007 a beautiful new high school was built with a senior center. The seniors were able to take advantage of many school facilities when not in use by students, including the gym, lecture halls, performance spaces, and music, dance, and art studios. The students provided popular tutorials for seniors on computer skills, and social studies classes included World War II and Korean War veterans from the center, along with Veterans Day remembrances.[a]

But perhaps the best benefit of the colocation came as economic times grew tougher. Facing budget cuts, the high school announced that the school library was in jeopardy. When the members of the senior center heard about the cutbacks, they volunteered to manage the library.[b] If the senior center had remained on the other side of town, it is unlikely these older adults would have known about the problem, let alone been able to solve it. This is just one example of how generations can support one another.

[a]Philip J. Poinelli, "Mixing Generations: New High School Enriches Senior/Student Life," *Educational Facility Planner* 43, no. 1 (2008): 21–23.
[b]Donna Butts and Lindsay Moore, "Generations Unite: Mix Wisdom with Energy" (Aging Services of California), http://www.aging.org/i4a/pages/index.cfm?pageid=2182.

Senior Corps reading program. Courtesy of the Corporation for National and Community Service.

education can be extended, and work and leisure can be integrated throughout life. We can envision our homes and communities differently as well.

We are fortunate to be learning a great deal about the factors that influence not only how long we will live but, more important, the quality of life in old age. Aging outcomes vary enormously, and although luck and chance play a role, lifestyle, habits, and life choices exert more influence. Where you live makes a difference. The formula for a long, bright future is relatively straightforward: Exercise, make sure that you are deeply embedded in a strong social network, save money and invest it wisely, dedicate your time and effort to something that matters, get a good education early, and continue to challenge yourself to learn new things throughout your life. Try not to worry too much.

For many older adults, their later years are the best years in life, the time to savor decades-long relationships, engage in gratifying work, and invest selectively in close friends and family. Their gains in emotional stability and experience allow them to serve key roles in families and communities. Industries will need to find ways to harness the experience of people who have been in the workforce for thirty or forty years.[31] Incentives that encourage seasoned entrepreneurs to start businesses and create jobs that can employ younger workers will improve the workforce. Second careers can become the norm. Careers can be revised so that work becomes more satisfying over the years instead of more of a grind. Disincentives to work, like those built into Social Security and Medicare, must be changed. We need to revise many of our current policies so that they are adapted to long life.

Conclusion

With shared attitudes, values, goals, and practices focused on improving an aging society, people of all ages will thrive. There is no better place to start thinking than in the places we call home—from the houses and apartments we inhabit to the neighborhoods in which we work and shop. Community-level changes like integrating generations and individual changes like increasing exercise are all reflected in the places we choose to live. The next time you see children playing in a park or schoolyard, understand that you are observing the first centenarians of the twenty-second century. Ask yourself what sort of a world we need to create so that they arrive at old age physically fit, mentally sharp, and financially secure.

Notes

1. James W. Vaupel, "Biodemography of Human Ageing," *Nature* 464 (2010): 536–42.

2. John W. Rowe and Robert L. Kahn, "Successful Aging," *The Gerontologist* 37, no. 4 (1996): 433–40.

3. MacArthur Foundation Research Network on an Aging Society, "Facts and Fictions about an Aging Society," *Contexts* 8 (2009): 16–21.

4. E. M. Crimmins and H. Beltrán-Sánchez, "Mortality and Morbidity Trends: Is There Compression of Morbidity?" *Journals of Gerontology: Series B* 66 (2011): 75–86.

5. Stanley K. Smith, Stefan Rayer, and Eleanor A. Summer Smith, "Aging and Disability: Implications for the Housing Industry and Housing Policy in the United States," *Journal of the American Planning Association* 74, no. 3 (2008): 289–306.

6. Timothy A. Salthouse, "When Does Age-Related Cognitive Decline Begin?" *Neurobiological Aging* 30, no. 4 (2009): 507–14.

7. Denise C. Park, Gary Lautenschlager, Trey Hedden, Natalie S. Davidson, Anderson D. Smith, and Pamela K. Smith, "Models of Visuospatial and Verbal Memory across the Adult Life Span," *Psychology and Aging* 17, no. 2 (2002): 299–320.

8. K. Warner Schaie, "The Course of Adult Intellectual Development," *American Psychologist* 49 (1994): 304–13.

9. S. Charles and L. L. Carstensen, "Social and Emotional Aging," *Annual Review of Psychology* 61 (2010): 383–409.

10. Laura L. Carstensen, "The Influence of a Sense of Time on Human Development," *Science* 312, no. 5782 (2006): 1913–15.

11. Lisa F. Berkman and S. Leonard Syme, "Social Networks, Host Resistance, and Mortality: A Nine-Year Follow-Up Study of Alameda County Residents," *American Journal of Epidemiology* 109, no. 2 (1979): 186–204.

12. AARP Press Center, "Intergenerational Conflict? Think Again!" www.aarp.org.

13. Neville Owen, Nancy Humpel, Eva Leslie, Adrian Bauman, and James F. Sallis, "Understanding Environmental Influences on Walking: Review and Research Agenda," *American Journal of Preventive Medicine* 27, no. 1 (2004): 67–76.

14. Lucille Nahemow and M. Powell Lawton, "Similarity and Propinquity in Friendship Formation," *Journal of Personality and Social Psychology* 32 (1975): 205–13.

15. Bibb Latané, James H. Liu, Andrzej Nowak, Michael Bonevento, and Long Zheng, "Distance Matters: Physical Space and Social Impact," *Personality and Social Psychology Bulletin* 21 (1995): 795–805.

16. Mihaly Csikszentmihalyi, *The Meaning of Things: Domestic Symbols and the Self* (Cambridge: Cambridge University Press, 1981), 133–34.

17. Ibid., 144.

18. Bronwyn Tanner, Cheryl Tilse, and Desleigh de Jonge, "Restoring and Sustaining Home: The Impact of Home Modifications on the Meaning of Home

for Older People," *Journal of Housing for the Elderly* 22, no. 3 (2008): 195–215.

19. Gary Evans, Elyse Kantrowitz, and Paul Eshelman, "Housing Quality and Psychological Well-Being among the Elderly Population," *Journals of Gerontology: Series B* 57, no. 4 (2002): 381–83.

20. Iain Lang, David Llewellyn, Kenneth Langa, Robert Wallace, Felicia Huppert, and David Melzer, "Neighborhood Deprivation, Individual Socioeconomic Status, and Cognitive Function in Older People: Analyses from the English Longitudinal Study of Ageing," *Journal of the American Geriatrics Society* 56 (2008): 191–98; Richard Wight, Carol Aneshensel, Dana Miller-Martinez, Amanda Botticello, Janet Cummings, Arun Karlamangla, and Teresa Seeman, "Urban Neighborhood Context, Educational Attainment, and Cognitive Function among Older Adults," *American Journal of Epidemiology* 163, no. 12 (2006): 1071–78.

21. James S. House, Paula M. Lant, and Pamela Herd, "Continuity and Change in the Social Stratification of Aging and Health over the Life Course: Evidence from a Nationally Representative Longitudinal Study from 1986 to 2001/2002 (Americans' Changing Lives Study)," *Journals of Gerontology: Series B* 60, no. 2 (2005): 15–26.

22. S. Jay Olshansky, Dana P. Goldman, Yuhui Zheng, and John W. Rowe, "Aging in America in the Twenty-First Century: Demographic Forecasts from the MacArthur Foundation Research Network on an Aging Society," *Milbank Quarterly* 87, no. 4 (2009): 842–62.

23. Dana P. Goldman and James P. Smith, "Can Patient Self-Management Help Explain the SES Health Gradient?" *Proceedings of the National Academy of Sciences* 99, no. 16 (2002): 10929–34.

24. Maria M. Glymour, Ichiro Kawachi, Christopher S. Jencks, and Lisa F. Berkman, "Does Childhood Schooling Affect Old Age Memory or Mental Status? Using State Schooling Laws as Natural Experiments," *Journal of Epidemiology and Community Health* 62 (2008): 532–37.

25. Kenneth G. Manton and XiLiang Gu, "Changes in the Prevalence of Chronic Disability in the United States Black and Nonblack Population above Age 65 from 1982 to 1999," *Proceedings of the National Academy of Sciences* 98 (2001): 6354–59.

26. www.kidsdate.org (education and childcare statistics), doi:mckinsey.com/app_media/images/page_images/offices/socialsector/pdf/achievement_gap_report.pdf.

27. John B. Shoven, "New Age Thinking: Alternative Ways of Measuring Age, Their Relationship to Labor Force Participation, Government Policies and GDP" (working paper, National Bureau of Economic Research, Cambridge, MA, 2007), doi:www.nber.org/papers/w13476.

28. Colette Thayer, "Preparation for Retirement: The Haves and Have-Nots" (Washington, DC: AARP Knowledge Management, 2007), doi:assets.aarp.org/rgcenter/econ/retirement_prep.pdf.

29. Susann Rohwedder and Robert J. Willis, "Mental Retirement," *RAND Working Paper Series*, no. WR-711 (2009).

30. Richard W. Robins and Kali H. Trzesniewkski, "Self-Esteem Development across the Lifespan," *Current Directions in Psychological Science* 14, no. 3 (2005): 158–62.

31. Marc Freedman, *The Big Shift* (New York: Perseus Books, 2011).

DEMOGRAPHICS AND CHALLENGES

The demographic shifts facing the United States are known, predictable, and quantifiable. There will be many more old people in the very near future and many younger Hispanics and Asians. Financial problems face people of all ages, and living arrangements are changing. Demographic realities demand new solutions to meet the needs of an aging white and younger minority population.

There will be serious consequences if issues of aging in homes and communities are ignored and the nation stays on its current path. Without change, entitlements will require both unacceptably higher taxes and cuts to popular and needed programs for other segments of the population. A poorly educated workforce will have an even greater struggle to pay taxes, care for their family members, and provide for their own needs as older adults.

Chapter 3

Changing Demographic Realities

Adele M. Hayutin

Introduction

Demographic shifts under way in the United States will drive housing choices and living arrangements. Only by understanding those changes will policy makers, business leaders, and families be able to develop policies and practices that meet the needs of an aging society. Because key demographic changes are gaining momentum, it is urgent that we understand their impact and relevance.

The Demographics of an Older America

The unprecedented number of people reaching old age is a major part of the transformation that is reshaping our society. This increased longevity is occurring in the context of growing ethnic and racial diversity of the US population and reduced number of births per woman, even as the total population grows. All of these changes affect where and how Americans live and how communities and neighborhoods are changing.

THE NUMBER OF OLD PEOPLE WILL DOUBLE OVER THE NEXT THIRTY YEARS

Owing largely to the aging of the baby boomers (the cohort born between 1946 and 1964), the number of people aged sixty-five and over in the United States will double over the next thirty years, growing from forty million to eighty million people.[1] See Figure 3.1. The population aged sixty-five and older has been growing steadily since 1950, but as the boomers turn sixty-five over the next few decades, growth will accelerate. The first of the baby boomers turned sixty-five in 2011,

ADELE HAYUTIN is senior research scholar at the Stanford Center on Longevity and director of its Global Aging Program. Previously, she was chief economist of the Fremont Group (formerly Bechtel Investments), senior real estate analyst at Salomon Brothers in New York, and director of research at RREEF in San Francisco. She received a BA from Wellesley College and a master's degree in public policy and a PhD in economics from the University of California at Berkeley.

Population aged sixty-five and older

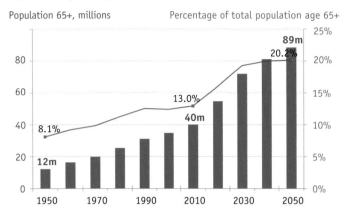

Figure 3.1 The population aged sixty-five and older will double over the next thirty years and increase from 13 to 20 percent of the total population as the baby boomers turn sixty-five. Source: Stanford Center on Longevity, using data from the US Census Bureau.

marking the beginning of a steep increase in the number of old people. After the last boomers turn sixty-five in 2029, growth will slow but will continue. By the middle of the century, the population aged sixty-five and older will total eighty-nine million, or 20 percent of the total population.

LIFE EXPECTANCY WILL INCREASE

In addition to the boomers turning sixty-five, increased life expectancy will contribute to the unprecedented number of old people. Not only are more people reaching old age, but once they reach old age they are living longer. According to the US Census Bureau, a baby born in 1950 in the early years of the baby boom could be expected to live to sixty-eight years. Since then, life expectancy for a baby has increased to seventy-eight years.[2]

Even more critical is the increased life expectancy for those reaching sixty-five. In 1950, a person who reached sixty-five could be expected to live another twelve to fifteen years. By 2010, a person reaching sixty-five could be expected to live another seventeen to nineteen years.[3] More people are reaching ever-higher age brackets. The population aged eighty-five and older, though small, is the fastest-growing age group in the United States.

Projections that life-expectancy gains will continue are controversial. Some researchers suggest that the dramatic increase in obesity rates could result in life expectancy remaining flat or even starting to decline over the next fifty years.[4]

Others assert that if current trends in increasing life expectancy continue, most babies born today in developed countries will reach one hundred.[5]

AGE MIX WILL SHIFT TO OLDER AGES

As the boomers reach sixty-five, then seventy-five, then eighty-five, the population in each age bracket will swell, and the age mix of the older population will shift upward. See Figure 3.2. The first boomers will turn eighty-five in 2031; by 2050, the number of people aged eighty-five

Age mix shifts upward

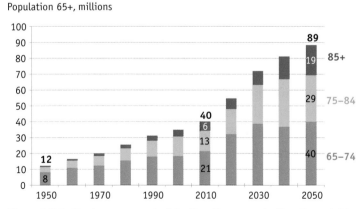

Figure 3.2 As the boomers reach sixty-five, then seventy-five, then eighty-five, the population in each age bracket will swell, and the age mix of the older population will shift upward. Source: Stanford Center on Longevity, using data from the US Census Bureau.

PROJECTIONS FROM THE MACARTHUR FOUNDATION RESEARCH NETWORK ON AN AGING SOCIETY

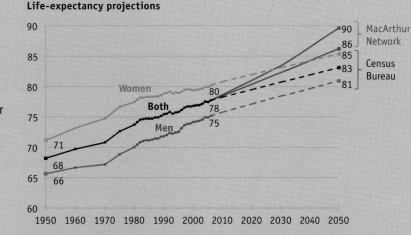

Life-expectancy projections

Figure A Longevity gains are projected to continue, but estimates vary. Source: MacArthur Foundation Research Network on an Aging Society and US Census Bureau.

A 2009 forecast by the MacArthur Foundation Research Network on an Aging Society suggests that the US government may be underestimating life-expectancy gains by three to eight years and that, by 2050, life expectancy at birth will be between eighty-six and ninety years. The Research Network forecasts an acceleration in life-expectancy improvements due to a combination of behavioral changes and new technologies. As shown in Figure A, the network forecasts that the population aged sixty-five and older could reach 99 million to 108 million by 2050, or 12 to 22 percent higher than the 89 million projected by the Census Bureau.[a]

The fiscal consequences of these projections are enormous. The Research Network on an Aging Society estimates that the cumulative outlays for Medicare and Social Security could be $3.2 to $8.3 trillion higher than the current government forecasts. Some of the economic, social, and health consequences could be offset if the extension of life is converted into healthy, productive years.

[a]S. Jay Olshansky, Dana P. Goldman, Yuhui Zheng, and John W. Rowe, "Aging in America in the Twenty-First Century: Demographic Forecasts from the MacArthur Foundation Research Network on an Aging Society," *Milbank Quarterly* 87, no. 4 (2009): 842–62.

and older will have more than tripled to nineteen million, or 22 percent of all old people. By then, more than one in five old people will be age eighty-five and older. It will be increasingly important as the age mix shifts upward to recognize that the health care, housing, and social needs of the oldest old group differ dramatically from those aged sixty-five to seventy-five. Differences in physical capabilities, cognitive skills, and financial resources will have important implications for their housing choices. Similarly, consideration of gender differences will be increasingly important. Because women live longer than men, by 2050 women will make up 61 percent of the nineteen million people aged eighty-five and older.

PHYSICAL LIMITATIONS AND COGNITIVE DECLINES WILL AFFECT HOUSING CHOICES OF OLDER PEOPLE

Physical Limitations with Aging

In 2005, 85 percent of Medicare beneficiaries with activity limitations lived in traditional housing. Improvements in the physical environment of homes will allow

Medicare beneficiaries aged sixty-five and older with functional limitations, by residential setting

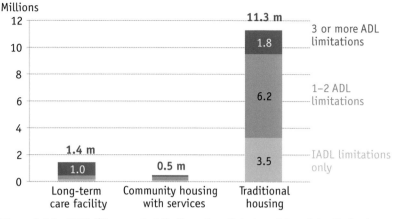

Millions

- 3 or more ADL limitations
- 1–2 ADL limitations
- IADL limitations only

Long-term care facility: 1.4 m (1.0)
Community housing with services: 0.5 m
Traditional housing: 11.3 m (1.8 / 6.2 / 3.5)

Figure 3.3 In 2005, 85 percent of Medicare beneficiaries with activity limitations lived in traditional housing. Note: ADL = activities of daily living related to personal care (e.g., bathing, eating, and getting out of bed); IADL = instrumental activities of daily living related to living independently (e.g., preparing meals, doing laundry, and taking medications). Source: Stanford Center on Longevity, using data from the Federal Interagency Forum on Aging-Related Statistics.

Activity limitations

Personal Care Activities of Daily Living (ADLs)	**Independent Living** Instrumental Activities of Daily Living (IADLs)
• Getting out of bed/chair • Bathing or showering • Dressing • Eating • Walking • Using the toilet	• Shopping for groceries • Preparing meals • Doing laundry/housework • Using a telephone • Managing money • Taking medications

Figure 3.4 Disability and limitation are often measured by asking whether a person needs help with personal care or independent living. Source: Centers for Disease Control and Prevention.

even more people with activity limitations to live independently. Because the vast majority of older people facing daily living challenges live in traditional homes and neighborhoods, new ways must be found to affordably and efficiently adapt existing spaces and deliver services. See Figures 3.3 and 3.4.

Disability and Activity Limitations

The Administration on Aging report, *A Profile of Older Americans: 2010*, states that "some type of disability (i.e., difficulty in hearing, vision, cognition, ambulation, self-care, or independent living) was reported by 37% of older persons in 2009. Some of these disabilities may be relatively minor but others cause people to require assistance to meet important personal needs."

People increasingly report disabilities at older ages. "56% of persons over 80 reported a severe disability and 29% of the over 80 population reported that they needed assistance."

Limitations due to chronic disease increase with age as well. The report notes that the rates of activity limitations in persons aged eighty-five and older are much higher than those for persons aged sixty-five to seventy-four and those aged seventy-five to eighty-four.

Chronic Disease

While death and disability rates are falling, particularly for heart disease and stroke, the prevalence of chronic disease is high in the older population. See

Figure 3.5. Although high blood pressure and arthritis occur in half of the older population, these chronic diseases do not prevent most people from aging in place, as advances in medical technologies, including drugs and assistive devices, have made independent living easier.

Cognitive Impairments

Cognitive impairments can dramatically affect the viability of housing choices and arrangements. The number of people with dementia is projected to more than double in the coming years (see Figure 3.6), causing challenges not only for friends and families but also for health care workers and other service providers.

ETHNICITY OF THE OLDER POPULATION

The older population will remain majority white non-Hispanic through 2050, even though minorities will account for nearly 60 percent of the

Reported prevalence of select chronic diseases in population aged sixty-five and older

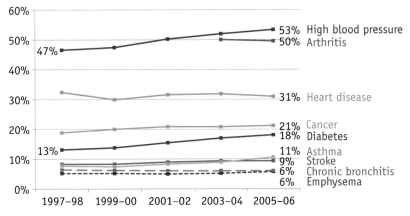

Figure 3.5 Chronic diseases with increasing prevalence in the older population include high blood pressure and diabetes. Source: Stanford Center on Longevity, using data from the Federal Interagency Forum on Aging-Related Statistics.

Projected dementia cases in the United States

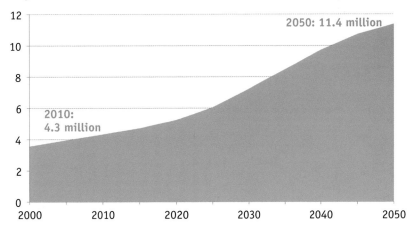

Figure 3.6 As the population ages, the number of dementia cases is projected to more than double, exceeding eleven million by 2050. Source: Stanford Center on Longevity.

growth among those aged sixty-five and older. See Figure 3.7. The white non-Hispanic share of the older population will decrease from 80 percent in 2010 to 58 percent by 2050. The Hispanic older population will increase sixfold over the next forty years, growing from three million in 2010 to eighteen million in 2050. By 2050, Hispanics will account for 20 percent of the older population and will be the largest minority group among those aged sixty-five and over. The number of black non-Hispanic people aged sixty-five and older will increase by roughly seven million in the next forty years, while the Asian non-Hispanic population aged sixty-five and older will grow by six million.

The older population will remain majority white, while the younger population

Population aged sixty-five and older by race and ethnicity

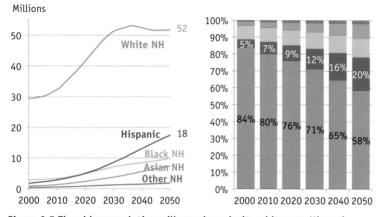

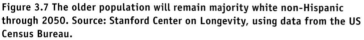

Figure 3.7 The older population will remain majority white non-Hispanic through 2050. Source: Stanford Center on Longevity, using data from the US Census Bureau.

Population age mix

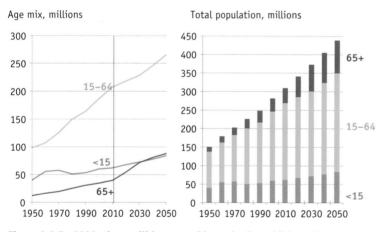

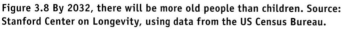

Figure 3.8 By 2032, there will be more old people than children. Source: Stanford Center on Longevity, using data from the US Census Bureau.

is becoming increasingly diverse. By 2042, the total US population will be "majority minority," which means that more than half of the population will be nonwhite or Hispanic.

THE PERCENTAGE OF OLD PEOPLE WILL INCREASE

At the same time that more people are reaching older ages, people are having fewer children. As a result, not only is the number of older people increasing, but the overall percentage, or share, of older people is increasing. By 2032, there will be more old people than children (see Figure 3.8); specifically, there will be more people aged sixty-five and older than there are children under the age of fifteen. By the middle of the century, there will be about four million more old people than young people.

This demographic pattern means that there will be fewer and fewer potential workers per retiree, which will occur just as the financial and social costs of an aging population are increasing.

Changes in Elderly Living Arrangements

Older people are more likely to live alone than younger people and that likelihood increases with age. In 2008, 41 percent of the population aged eighty-five and older lived alone, compared with 34 percent of those aged seventy-five to eighty-four and 22 percent of those aged sixty-five to seventy-four. Older men were more likely to live with a spouse, while older women were more likely to live alone or with other relatives. In 2007, 39 percent of women aged sixty-five and older lived alone compared with just 19 percent of older men.[6] There are significant differences in living arrangements by race and ethnicity; older Hispanic and Asian women, for example, are much less likely to live alone and are more likely to live with relatives. See Figure 3.9.

The availability of family members living nearby and able and willing to perform caregiving fundamentally affects these trends. Today's older population, the parents of the baby boomers, may have three or four adult children to share the caregiving responsibilities and costs. But the next generation of older Americans, the baby boomers, have fewer children and therefore fewer family resources to rely on for financial help and caregiving.

Even though the total population aged sixty-five and over increased, the number of nursing home residents remained stable at around 1.3 million between 1985 and 2004.[7] See Figure 3.10. In 2004, the number living in nursing homes declined to just 3.6 percent of the older population, down from 4.5 percent in the mid-1970s. The decline in nursing home residency was especially steep for those aged eighty-five and older, declining from nearly 26 percent in the mid-1970s to 14 percent in 2004. For seventy-five- to eighty-four-year-olds, the nursing home residency rate declined from 5.8 percent in the mid-1970s to just 3.6 percent in 2004. The decline for all ages may be attributable to better health status and to the wider range of options between a skilled nursing facility and other living arrangements.

Average household and family sizes have declined throughout the United States, and the number of single-person households has increased. These are trends that could reduce the numbers of caregivers available to older people. Some recent evidence suggests that these trends could be changing, and that the presence of potential caregivers could be increasing. A 2010 Pew Research Center report

Living arrangements of people aged sixty-five and older, 2007

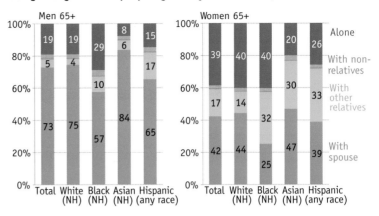

Figure 3.9 Older men are more likely to live with a spouse; older women are more likely to live alone or with other relatives. Note: NH = non-Hispanic; not shown but included in "Total" are non-Hispanic of two or more races: non-Hispanic American Indian and Alaska Native and non-Hispanic Native Hawaiian and Pacific Islander. Source: Stanford Center on Longevity, using data from the Federal Interagency Forum on Aging-Related Statistics.

Nursing home residents aged sixty-five and older

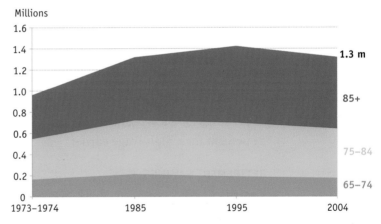

Figure 3.10 The nursing home population has remained relatively stable at around 1.3 million since 1985. Source: Stanford Center on Longevity, using data from the Centers for Disease Control and Prevention.

suggests that the multigenerational household is "staging a comeback," after steadily declining in popularity following World War II. According to the Pew report, older adults were historically the most likely of any age group to live in multigenerational households, but during the twentieth century, older adults became healthier, more prosperous, and more able and desirous of living independently. The multigenerational household could be staging a comeback due to an increase in age at first marriage, increased immigration, and the 2007–2009 recession.

Economic Drivers of Housing Decisions

Economic challenges facing the older population are increasingly important for housing choices, especially as longevity continues to increase.

INCOME AND FINANCIAL SECURITY

The older population has enjoyed increased income and a decline in the rate of poverty, but many households face a substantial risk of being unable to maintain their standard of living during their retirement years. Median household income for those aged sixty-five or older increased to $31,157 in 2008, which is 62 percent of the median income for all ages ($50,303). For the oldest households, those aged eighty and older, median income was $22,684. The highest income groups received the majority of their income from earnings and assets, while the lowest income groups relied on Social Security. In 2008, Social Security accounted for more than 90 percent of the income for 41 percent of elderly individual recipients. Social Security payments are less than preretirement income, replacing 55 percent of earnings for a low-wage earner, 41 percent for an average-wage earner, and 27 percent for a high-wage earner.[8]

RETIREMENT SAVINGS

There is significant debate about how well prepared the older population is for retirement. Median family net worth for older households exceeded $200,000 in 2007, but most likely declined substantially due to the sharp decline in housing prices and homeowner equity between 2007 and 2009.[9] The Center for Retirement Research at Boston College reports that 51 percent of households are at risk of being unable to maintain their standard of living in retirement. These calculations assume that people tend to need less income in retirement and assume that households work to age sixty-five and annuitize all their financial assets.[10] Other studies of retirement preparedness are more optimistic. One study found that, among households aged fifty-one to sixty-one in 1992, fewer than 20 percent had saved too little for retirement.[11] Another study found that about 20 percent of couples and about 50 percent of singles in their late sixties in 2004 were inadequately prepared for their retirement.[12]

POVERTY

Poverty among older adults declined dramatically from 35 percent in 1959 to around 15 percent in 1975, largely due to increases in Social Security benefits, and has since continued to decline. In 2008, the federal poverty level for people aged sixty-five and older was an annual income of $10,326 for an individual and $13,014 for a couple in which at least one member was aged sixty-five or older. The poverty rate in 2008 for older adults was 9.7 percent overall, but varied by gender, marital status, race and ethnicity, age, and education. Among older people, women had higher rates of poverty than men, and unmarried people had higher rates of poverty than married individuals. Hispanics and blacks had poverty rates more than double the rate for whites. The lower the educational level, the higher was the poverty rate. Also, the higher the age bracket, the higher was the poverty rate.[13]

HOUSING EXPENSE

Regardless of age and income level, housing is the largest household expense, as shown in Figure 3.11. On average, 34 percent of all household expenditures are devoted to housing. Spending patterns are similar across all age groups with the exception of spending on health care, which increases with age, and spending on personal insurance and pensions, which decreases with age. The actual dollar amount

Housing and health care spending

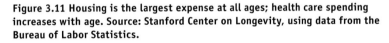

Figure 3.11 Housing is the largest expense at all ages; health care spending increases with age. Source: Stanford Center on Longevity, using data from the Bureau of Labor Statistics.

spent on housing declines with age, but increases as a share of total expenditures. For example, households with a household head aged seventy-five and older spent an average of 38 percent of household expenditures on housing compared with 32 percent for those aged fifty-five to sixty-four. The share is even higher for lower-income households, registering 40 percent or higher for those households with income less than $20,000.[14]

Conclusion

Disparate demographic shifts are under way and gaining momentum in the United States. As we look to the future and particularly as older people strive to age in place, we need to consider carefully how increased life expectancy, physical and cognitive challenges, caregiving patterns, family living arrangements, and financial realities affect older people's choices. Understanding the nature and scale of our changing demographic portrait is just a starting point; a far greater challenge is understanding how these changes will affect the realities of living for the older population.

Notes

1. Unless otherwise noted, projections cited in this chapter were taken from or calculated using data from the US Census Bureau *National Population Projections* released in August 2008 and cited as US Census Bureau, "Table 12: Projections of the Population by Age and Sex for the United States: 2010 to 2050 (NP2008-T12)," *2008 National Population Projections*, http://www.census.gov/population/www/projections /files/nation/summary/np2008-t12.xls. Unless otherwise noted, the historical data cited in this chapter were taken from or calculated using data from Frank Hobbs and Nicole Stoops, *Demographic Trends in the 20th Century (CENSR-4)* (Washington, DC: US Census Bureau, November 2002), http://www.census.gov /prod/2002pubs/censr-4.pdf.

2. *Health, United States, 2008, with Special Feature on the Health of Young Adults* (Washington, DC: US Department of Health and Human Services, Centers for Disease Control and Prevention, National Center for Health Statistics), http://www.cdc.gov /nchs/hus.htm (updated tables available here: http://www.cdc.gov/nchs/hus/updatedtables.htm); US Census Bureau, "Table 10: Projected Life Expectancy at Birth by Sex, Race, and Hispanic Origin for the United States: 2010 to 2050," *2008 National Population Projections*, http://www.census.gov /population/www/projections/files/nation/summary /np2008-t10.xls.

3. Felicitie C. Bell and Michael L. Miller, "Table 6: Period Life Tables for the Social Security Area by Calendar Year," *Life Tables for the United States Social Security Area 1900–2100* (Actuarial Study 120, US Social Security Administration), http://www.ssa.gov/OACT /NOTES/as120/LifeTables_Tbl_6.html.

4. S. Jay Olshansky, Douglas J. Passaro, Ronald C. Hershow, Jennifer Layden, Bruce A. Carnes, Jacob Brody, Leonard Hayflick, Robert N. Butler, David B. Allison, and David S. Ludwig, "A Potential Decline in Life Expectancy in the United States in the 21st Century," *New England Journal of Medicine* 352, no. 11 (2005): 1138–45.

5. Kaare Christensen, Gabriele Doblhammer, Roland Rau, and James W. Vaupel, "Ageing Populations: The Challenges Ahead," *The Lancet* 374, no. 9696 (2009): 1196–1208.

6. Federal Interagency Forum on Aging-Related Statistics, *Older Americans 2008: Key Indicators of Well-Being* (Washington, DC: US Government Printing Office, 2008), http://www.agingstats.gov.

7. *Health, United States, 2008*.

8. Patrick Purcell, "Income and Poverty among Older Americans in 2008" (RL32697, Congressional Research Service, October 2009), http://benefitslink .com/articles/guests/RL32697_Oct_2009.pdf.

9. "Changes in US Family Finances from 2004 to 2007: Evidence from the Survey of Consumer Finances," *Federal Reserve Bulletin*, February 2009, http://www.federalreserve.gov/pubs/bulletin/2009 /pdf/scf09.pdf.

10. Alicia H. Munnell, Anthony Webb, and Francesca Golub-Sass, "The National Retirement Risk Index: After the Crash" (Report 9-22, Center for Retirement Research, October 2009), http://crr.bc.edu /briefs/the_national_retirement_risk_index_after _the_crash.html.

11. John Karl Scholz, Ananth Seshadri, and Surachai Khitatrakun, "Are Americans Saving 'Optimally' for Retirement?" *Journal of Political Economy* 111, no. 4 (2006): 607–43.

12. Michael D. Hurd and Susann Rohwedder, "Alternative Measures of Replacement Rates" (Prepared for the Eighth Annual Joint Conference of the Retirement Research Consortium, "Pathways to a Secure Retirement," August 10–11, 2006).

13. Carmen DeNavas-Walt, Bernadette D. Proctor, and Jessica Smith. *Income, Poverty, and Health Insurance Coverage in the United States: 2008 (P60-236 RV)* (Washington, DC: US Census Bureau, September 2009), http://www.census.gov/prod/2009pubs /p60-236.pdf.

14. Bureau of Labor Statistics, "Table 3: Age of Reference Person: Average Annual Expenditures and Characteristics," *Consumer Expenditure Survey 2008*, http://www.bls.gov/cex/2008/Standard/age.pdf.

Chapter 4

Future Social and Economic Changes

Anthony Downs

Introduction

The worldwide financial crisis of 2007–2009 has radically changed conditions in all types of markets, especially real estate markets. I have written about the causes of this crisis, actions to combat it already adopted by the US government, further actions that might be undertaken, and future impacts of the crisis. This crisis has increased the impact and magnitude of the demographic shifts that the nation will experience in the next decades.

There are five major issues on which we must focus our attention:

- Federal spending on entitlement programs
- The education of the future American workforce
- Home sales and the real estate market
- The challenges of changing suburban lifestyles and patterns
- The need for many older people to work longer

It is critical that these realities and constraints be recognized as we plan for an aging society. If we fail to acknowledge the depth and significance of the financial and social realities facing our country, we will fail to develop the right solutions. The consequences of inaction are significant.

Since 1977, **ANTHONY DOWNS** has been a Senior Fellow at the Brookings Institution in Washington, DC. Before 1977, he was a member and then chair of Real Estate Research Corporation, consulting nationwide on real estate investment, housing policies, and urban affairs. His books include *An Economic Theory of Democracy*, *Inside Bureaucracy*, *Still Stuck in Traffic*, and *Real Estate and the Financial Crisis*. He received his MA and PhD in economics from Stanford University.

The Challenges

FEDERAL SPENDING ON ENTITLEMENT PROGRAMS:
SPENDING ON THE ELDERLY WILL SQUEEZE THE REST OF THE FEDERAL BUDGET

As the number of people aged sixty-five and over increases, federal entitlement spending programs serving the elderly will absorb ever-larger shares of future federal budgets. The most important such programs are Social Security, Medicare, and Medicaid. The Congressional Budget Office (CBO) projects that such spending will rise from slightly over $300 billion in 2000 to $1 trillion in 2015, tripling in fifteen years.[1] Figure 4.1 illustrates federal spending patterns on Medicare and Medicaid.

From 2009 to at least 2020, the CBO also projects that federal receipts from taxes and all other sources will remain below federal expenditures. Annual deficits will add $12.8 trillion to the total federal debt by 2020, more than tripling the Treasury's annual interest payments from $207 billion in 2010 to $723 billion in 2020.[2] Figure 4.2 graphically explains CBO projections of the president's budget from 2009 to 2020.

The portion of the federal budget tied up in Social Security, Medicare, Medicaid, and interest payments on the federal debt will rise from 44.4 percent in 2010 to 61.8 percent in 2020. Computed as shares of total future federal spending, all other activities supported by such spending will have to decline by 15.4 percentage points, or almost 40 percent of their relative level in 2010.[3] The result will be an acute shortage of federal funding available for many other programs beneficial to society. Examples are improvement

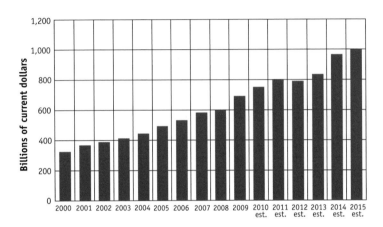

Figure 4.1 Projected federal spending on Medicare and Medicaid, 2000–2015. Source: Anthony Downs, based on Congressional Budget Office data.

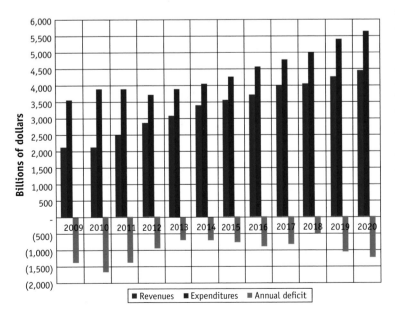

Figure 4.2 CBO projections of president's budget, 2009–2020. Source: Congressional Budget Office.

of education nationwide, highway construction, disaster relief, maintenance of national parks, food and drug safety, and foreign aid.

If we continue this pattern of "robbing the young to pay the old" we will increase political tension between elderly and younger age groups in America. Nonelderly workers will be paying ever-higher fractions of their paychecks to fund Social Security, Medicare, and Medicaid. Workers will be more and more opposed to continuing aid to the elderly while federal programs that might benefit younger people are severely reduced. Because working-age people are not likely to accept such deductions without major political protests, these high percentages may not actually be attained. And if they are not, elderly citizens will have to accept significant reductions in programs currently aiding them. Program reductions can be made by increasing the age of retirement eligibility, lowering benefits, and raising taxes on such benefits. In many communities, reductions will come at the same time that there is increasing demand for local facilities usable by retirees, such as parks, libraries, hospitals, and recreation centers. A stark political cleavage between younger and older citizens could weaken the social solidarity of the nation, adding to the already high level of political polarization.

THE EDUCATION OF THE FUTURE AMERICAN WORKFORCE: EDUCATION OF MINORITIES IS A PRESSING ISSUE

A second factor affecting the future strength of the American economy is the education received by our future workforce. As the percentage of Hispanic and African American children in school-age groups rises toward a majority, it will be increasingly important to improve their academic performance so as to maintain a well-educated and skilled national workforce. Because of large-scale immigration of Hispanics into the United States and higher birth rates among both Hispanics and African Americans, the share of those two minority groups among Americans of working ages (those aged twenty-five to sixty-four) grew to 27 percent in 2010; it will increase to 37 percent in 2040 and will top 39 percent in 2050. These groups will comprise 45 percent of all young people under the age of twenty-five by 2050.[4] Table 4.1 shows these demographic realities.

Unfortunately, the educational achievement of students in these two minority groups trails that of the Anglo and Asian American populations. The dropout rate from big-city high schools is 18 percent higher than that from suburban high schools.[5] Figure 4.3 shows these realities.

Year	All ages	0–24	25–64	65 and up
2000	25.32	32.56	23.31	9.37
2010	28.55	35.91	26.99	10.40
2020	31.30	38.62	30.83	12.15
2030	33.97	40.83	34.51	14.79
2040	36.60	42.94	37.04	17.25
2050	39.04	44.92	39.20	19.51

Table 4.1 Percentages of age groups comprising Hispanics and African Americans, 2000–2050. Source: Anthony Downs, based on US Census data.

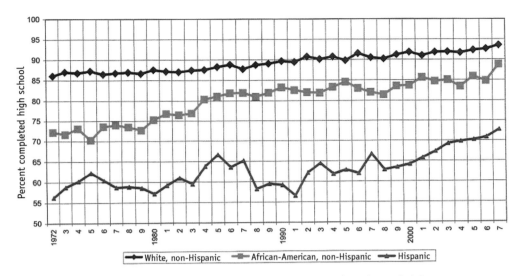

Figure 4.3 High school completion rates by ethnic group, 1972–2010 (people aged eighteen to twenty-four not enrolled in high school). Source: Anthony Downs, based on Department of Commerce data.v

Except for Asian Americans, experience shows that minority students attending schools dominated by other members of their own group or other minorities do not have test scores or graduation rates as high as those attending schools where a significant fraction of students are white or Asian American. A major cause of the lower educational performance of many Hispanic and African American students results from living in neighborhoods dominated by both poverty and a concentration of public school students from their own and other minority groups.

Unless we succeed in helping many more young members of those two minority groups stay in school longer, and improve their test scores, our future workforce is likely to be notably less well educated than our current workforce. Over the next four to five decades, the training and skills of the American labor force will deteriorate compared to their present levels. That fact could further weaken America's ability to compete in an increasingly interconnected world, a result that will be perilous for young and old alike.

HOME SALES AND THE REAL ESTATE MARKET:
HOMES SALES DECLINES WILL ADD TO FINANCIAL AND POLITICAL PRESSURES

Although a majority of retired elderly people in the United States want to remain living in their present homes until they die, there will be those who want or need to sell those homes and move into smaller homes, retirement communities, or assisted living facilities. Millions of elderly households will attempt to sell their homes so that they can harvest the equity in those homes for their living expenses or for unforeseen health crises.

Because immigration will remain the single largest source of future American population growth, immigrant households will comprise about 25 percent of net gains in homeowner households from 2005 to 2025, but will then rise to 38 percent by about 2037.[6] But many of those immigrant buyers may have notably low incomes, which either means that there will be fewer home sales or that sellers will have to settle for prices well below their expectations. If past events in American housing markets provide lessons for the future, in the next few decades there will probably be several more periods of home price increases followed by declines. These declines will increase the uncertainty of future home prices that elderly home sellers can expect to achieve. The situation will be affected by the quality of the American public school system. The better the education, the more young people will be able to earn and be able to afford as homebuyers.

THE CHALLENGES OF CHANGING SUBURBAN LIFESTYLES AND PATTERNS: SUBURBAN HOMEOWNERS OFTEN RESIST CHANGE

In suburban settings, there are challenges facing older people who strive to age in place. Many suburban homeowners oppose allowing new housing for their communities that is smaller or lower in value than existing single-family homes. They often oppose multifamily apartment units or assisted living developments in communities where single-family homes are predominant. They reject the concept of accessory apartments attached to, or within, larger homes owned by elderly people. Since such homeowners outnumber other local residents, they have been able to pressure local officials to adopt exclusionary zoning and other rules that make the construction of such housing in their communities very difficult. This restricts the ability of senior citizen households to adjust their living styles to better suit their changing needs.

In addition, many people aged sixty-five and over are unable to drive cars safely themselves, and many suburban communities were originally designed primarily for auto-using households. Lack of public transit can lead to older people becoming isolated from needed services and from other people.

THE NEED FOR MANY OLDER PEOPLE TO WORK LONGER

Many people over age sixty-five will need or want to continue working full-time or at least part-time to supplement their pensions and retirement funds. This is especially likely after the heavy financial losses suffered by millions of Americans from 2007 to 2009. On the other hand, millions of highly skilled workers in a wide variety of economic activities will retire. This retirement wave will cause some serious shortages of equally skilled workers to replace them. Workplace rules and expectations must be flexible to accommodate such diversity in the workforce. Employers will need to think ahead to be ready for these coming workforce changes.

Conclusion

The United States faces a diminished future unless we address these complex challenges, however daunting. We need new solutions, new ideas, a flourishing of creativity in social policies, and strategies for action. We must have a sense of urgency. And our first task is to understand the consequences of inaction, with an awareness that we can expect to live long enough to actually experience the world we are leaving for future generations.

Among these challenges will be the following:

- Reduced federal benefits for people who are old and people who are poor
- Increasing payroll taxes and taxes on benefits
- Homeowners unable to access needed home equity through home sales
- Old people seeking work, unable to retire
- Increasing demands for local services and amenities for old people
- Reduced federal support for many needed programs, including national defense
- Continued racial and ethnic segregation, particularly in public schools in large cities
- A poorly trained younger workforce
- Young people unable to afford homeownership
- Increased political polarization
- Diminished national economy
- Diminished global leadership for the United States

Overcoming these difficulties presents a major challenge to all Americans, young and old.

Notes

1. Congressional Budget Office, "The Budget and Economic Outlook: An Update," http://www.cbo.gov/ftpdocs/105xx/doc10521/08-25-BudgetUpdate.

2. Anthony Downs, based on Congressional Budget Office data.

3. Congressional Budget Office, "A Preliminary Analysis of the President's Budget and an Update of CBO's Budget and Economic Outlook," http://www.cbo.gov/ftpdocs/100xx/doc10014/03-20-PresidentBudget.

4. US Census Bureau, "Table 1: Projections of the Population and Components of Change for the United States: 2010 to 2050 (NP2008-T1)," *2008 National Population Projections*, http://www.census.gov/population/www/projections/files/nation/summary/np2008-t1.xls.

5. Editorial Projects in Education, "Cities in Crisis 2009: Closing the Graduation Gap," http://www.americaspromise.org/How-to-Help/Young-Leaders/My-Idea-Grants/~/media/3EF3A6C71DE3458787D979071E744EEA.

6. Dowell Myers and SungHo Ryu, "Aging Baby Boomers and the Generational Housing Bubble," *Journal of the American Planning Association* 13 (January 2008): 1–17.

HOUSING AND SERVICES

We need to understand the range of housing choices that exist today, from traditional housing to skilled nursing facilities. Ninety percent of older people say that they prefer to stay in their current homes and communities as they age, but there are other options for housing along a continuum of care services.

Even though older people want to age at home, the delivery of health and social services in home-based settings can be a challenge personally and financially, and may not be appropriate for everyone. Public funding has been biased toward institutional care, although innovative new programs are reversing this outdated pattern.

Chapter 5

From Home to Hospice

The Range of Housing Alternatives

Elinor Ginzler

Introduction

Aging in place" is a term that refers to aging independently while living in one's current residence for as long as possible. The ability to age in place is greatly determined by the physical design and accessibility of a home, as well as community features like the availability of nearby services and amenities, affordable housing, and transportation options.[1] When asked, most people report that they like where they live and they want to stay there for as long as possible.[2] AARP regularly polls the fifty-plus population on this topic, and the results are consistent. An AARP analysis of US Census Bureau data confirms that less than 10 percent of the sixty-plus population have moved in the five years preceding the Census.[3] Over two-thirds of older adults are living in owner-occupied units, of which almost 5 percent are manufactured homes. Over 11 percent of older people are in unsubsidized rental units, with half as many in government-subsidized rentals.[4] Table 5.1 shows the major types of housing occupied by older people in the United States.

Few of us are really surprised to learn that older people are determined to age in place. It makes perfect sense. Our homes and communities are where we have invested time, money, and energy. It is where we feel connected and where we have put down roots. Home and community care services are available to older individuals to enable them to remain in their current homes, including Meals on Wheels, friendly visiting, and shopper services, as well as adult day care.[5]

When those kinds of services are not enough, a variety of housing types with

ELINOR GINZLER was vice president for health portfolio in the Office of Integrated Value and Strategy at AARP from 1998 to 2011. She is now director of the Cahnmann Center for Supportive Services at the Jewish Council for the Aging in Rockville, Maryland. A leader in independent living/long-term care efforts, she has served on the Eldercare Locator Advisory Committee, the Board of Directors of the National Citizens' Coalition for Nursing Home Reform, and the Board of the National Hospice and Palliative Care Organization. She coauthored *Caring for Your Parents: The Complete AARP Guide*. She holds a BA from the University of Pennsylvania and completed her graduate studies at the University of Maryland.

Type of housing	Number of units[a]	Percentage distribution	Number of persons	Percentage distribution
Conventional housing units: senior householders[b,c]	**21,423,000**	**81.5**	**29,138,000**	**84.5**
Total owner-occupied units	17,196,000	65.4	24,216,000	70.2
1 unit, attached or detached	14,846,000	56.5		
2–49 units	836,000	3.2		
50+ units	259,000	1.0		
Manufactured homes	1,255,00	4.8		
Unsubsidized rental units	3,011,000	11.5	3,584,000	10.4
Government-subsidized rental units	1,216,000	4.6	1,338,000	3.9
Conventional housing units: younger householders (under age 65) occupied by at least one older (age 65 and older) person[c]	**2,166,000**	**8.2**	**2,336,000**	**6.8**
Owner-occupied dwellings	1,789,000	6.8	1,931,000	5.6
Renter-occupied dwellings	377,000	1.4	405,000	1.2
Supportive seniors housing units	**2,691,266**	**10.2**	**3,002,377**	**8.7**
Congregate care and CCRC[d] independent living	644,852	2.5	818,962	2.4
Assisted living[e]	507,414	1.9	644,415	1.9
Skilled nursing[f]	1,539,000	5.9	1,539,000	4.5
Total units/persons occupied by seniors[g]	**26,280,266**	**100.0**	**34,476,377**	**100.0**
All older householders	24,114,266		32,140,377	
All younger householders with senior occupants	2,166,000		2,336,000	

[a]Numbers all refer to units except for skilled nursing, which are reported in terms of beds and treated as one-person households.

[b]The householder is the first household member listed on the questionnaire who is an owner or renter of the housing unit.

[c]An unknown, but probably small, percentage of the units in this category are probably counted twice, because the US census erroneously treats them as households rather than "group housing" and they are also being counted in the "supportive seniors housing units" category. As this percentage increase in size, it artificially increases the relative shares of dwelling units considered as "conventional housing units."

[d]CCRC: continuing care retirement community.

[e]Includes board and care facilities.

[f]Includes hospital-based facilities, private-pay facilities, and facilities managed by the Department of Veterans Affairs.

[g]Including both "conventional housing units" and "supportive seniors housing units."

Table 5.1 Major types of housing occupied by senior householders and persons (aged sixty-five and older) in the United States, 1999. Source: *A Quiet Crisis in America* (Report to Congress by the Commission on Affordable Housing and Healthy Facility Needs for Seniors in the 21st Century, Washington, DC, June 30, 2002).

service options are available. However, older people often are not aware of these housing options. The economic downturn of 2007–2009 has affected those seniors who would like to move into housing with more services but cannot sell their current homes in order to do so. The clogged market helps explain why vacancies in senior living facilities are on the rise—most dramatically in areas where the market is most distressed. In Tampa, Florida, for instance, 12 percent of senior housing units are unoccupied, up from 4 percent in 2010.[6]

The homes that older people have long occupied may also be hard to sell. Outdated wallpaper, old appliances, and poor maintenance often deter buyers. According to a 2008 survey from the American Seniors Housing Association, nearly a quarter of seniors haven't made a home improvement in ten years, and 41 percent say they won't spend money to attract a buyer.[7] Many seniors live in manufactured housing, a housing form that often has resale and maintenance issues.

For those who have the financial means and desire to move, this chapter outlines the options currently available, ranging from independent living to skilled nursing facilities. The number of people living in alternatives to traditional housing is very small.[8] We need an increased awareness of the available options, and well-managed, affordable choices. Awareness of options is important because an extensive body of research literature "finds a relationship between the well-being of elderly people and their ability to exercise choice in living arrangements."[9] Organizations such as Caring.com provide a useful perspective on how to help older adults make decisions about their living arrangements. See Figure 5.1.

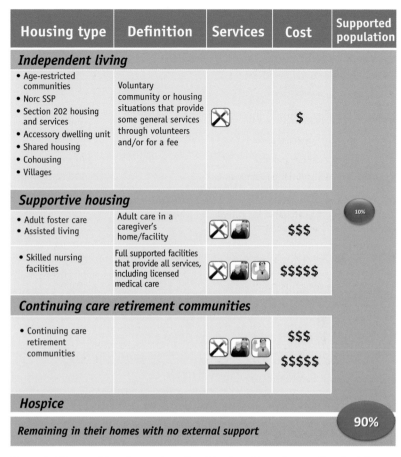

Figure 5.1 Range of housing options for older Americans. Source: Stanford Center on Longevity.

Options for Independent Living

The majority of Americans live independently as they age. Because aging in place is a preference for many of us, we will need to think more and more often about alternatives that enable independent living as the need for services increases. Several of these alternatives are outlined below.

AGE-RESTRICTED COMMUNITIES (SOMETIMES CALLED SENIOR RETIREMENT COMMUNITIES OR ACTIVE ADULT COMMUNITIES)

For some, the image of housing for older adults is synonymous with the name Del Webb and the place Sun City, Arizona. It was on January 1, 1960, that the first

MANUFACTURED HOMES AND OLDER RESIDENTS[a]

MANY OLDER, SINGLE RESIDENTS

Of the 3.3 million fifty-plus households living in a manufactured home in 2005, nearly 765,000 had a household head between sixty-five and seventy-four years of age, and around 695,000 were headed by a person age seventy-five or older.

About 45 percent of fifty-plus households living in manufactured homes were married-couple households, and 39 percent were single-person households.

HIGH PROPORTION HAVE LOW INCOME

The median income for fifty-plus households in manufactured housing was around $22,000 in 2005 compared with around $44,000 for fifty-plus residents of conventional single-family housing.

Limited financial resources make residents of manufactured housing particularly vulnerable to increases in park rents and unexpected home repair costs.

MANUFACTURED HOMES TYPICALLY SMALLER AND LESS EXPENSIVE

Manufactured homes are less expensive than conventional single-family homes. The median sales price for a new manufactured home in 2005 was $62,600 compared with $297,000 for a single-family detached home.

The median size of new manufactured homes in 2005 was 1,595 square feet compared with 2,414 square feet for new single-family homes.

[a]Jean Accius, "Issues in Manufactured Housing" (AARP Public Policy Institute, Washington, DC, October 2007).

planned active adult retirement community began selling homes. No one knew if anyone would even be interested. According to Del Webb records, over one hundred thousand visitors came to see the model homes in the first three days. Retirement communities had been born.[10]

Since that time, retirement communities have continued to grow. And while most people prefer to stay in their homes in mixed-age neighborhoods, some prefer the lifestyle choice of senior living or an active adult community that restricts the age of the residents, often to those aged fifty-five and older. Active adult communities are most appropriate for older people who are healthy, independent, and interested in the social benefits of living among their peers. They are rarely able to serve the poor. There is usually a mix of housing types—single-family homes, townhomes, and apartments—often connected by sidewalks or paths. Many communities have well-equipped clubhouses and other amenities, such as tennis courts and golf courses.

Active adult communities are not designed to include affordable housing, and they are not necessarily located near needed services. This housing alternative is not a setting designed to serve frail elderly. Should health conditions change, residents may be required to move to another setting where services are available.

NATURALLY OCCURRING RETIREMENT COMMUNITY SUPPORTIVE SERVICES PROGRAMS

In the mid-1980s, the Federation of Jewish Philanthropies of New York began targeting health and social services to older adults who were living in market-rate apartment buildings in New York City. These buildings became known as naturally occurring retirement communities (NORCs). Since then, the term "NORC" has been used to describe a community that was not intentionally built as housing for older adults, but has evolved to the point that it is comprised mostly of older residents.[11]

It is not surprising that the number of NORCs is increasing. Essentially, people have moved into a neighborhood and aged in place. New residents who move in are predominantly older adults, and younger people move away. There are various age and percentage thresholds used to define a NORC. For example, in New York, legislation passed in 1995 required that, for an area to be described as a NORC, more than half of the residents must be aged fifty or older.[12]

Today, NORCs exist in many settings: in an apartment complex that is either a rental or a condominium, which is referred to as a housing-based NORC or "vertical" NORC; or in a single-family neighborhood where a significant proportion of the residents are older adults, which is called a "horizontal" or an "open" NORC. NORCs are found in urban areas, in suburbs, and even in rural towns. When a significant proportion of older adults are housed in close proximity in a NORC, services can be provided effectively and efficiently to those in need.

Although AARP estimates that about five thousand NORCs exist across the country, it has also reported them to be "the most dormant and overlooked form of senior housing."[13] AARP, the National Academy on Aging, and the National Council on Aging believe that the vast aging in place of large concentrations of older adults living in NORCs can facilitate supportive communities.[14]

On-site services in NORCs are often public-private efforts, called NORC supportive services programs (NORC SSPs). Core program components of NORC SSPs include the following:

- Case management, assistance, and social work services
- Health care management, assistance, and prevention programs
- Education, socialization, and recreational activities
- Volunteer opportunities for program participants

Since 2001, the Administration on Aging (an agency of the US Department of Health and Human Services) has administered funding to support the development of NORCs in twenty-five states. In New York alone, there are over fifty thousand older adults benefiting from living in over fifty NORCs across the state.[15]

HOW TO KNOW IF IT'S TIME TO MOVE AN OLDER RELATIVE OUT OF THE FAMILY HOME[a]

The decision to move aging adults out of the family home is a complex one—both emotionally and practically. It requires a delicate balancing act between their safety and their emotional stake in staying put. Each of these is important, and helping them make the right decision (while remembering that as long as they are of sound mind, it's ultimately *their* decision) requires care and planning.

THE BASIC QUESTIONS TO ASK IN CONSIDERING A CHANGE IN HOUSING

Everyone is different, and the decision to move is an intensely personal one. But asking yourself, and those in your care, the following questions can help all of you navigate this difficult terrain.

- *Have there been any accidents recently—or close calls?* Who responded, and how long did it take?
- *Are activities of daily living getting harder?* If the answer is yes, are you able to get in-home help with chores like shopping, cooking, and laundry?
- *Are they becoming socially isolated?* Lack of companionship can leave older adults more vulnerable to heart problems and other health conditions. If they no longer see friends or visit with neighbors, moving to a place where they would be around other people could actually be a lifesaver.
- *Is the house clean and well cared for, and are basic home-maintenance tasks getting taken care of?* If not, are they open to getting more in-home help, can they afford it, and do you know how to help them find it?

- *Can someone check in on them on a regular basis?* If a family member, friend, or neighbor isn't nearby and available to do this, are they willing to consider a home-safety alarm system or daily calling service?
- *What's the plan for a worst-case scenario?* If there's a fire, earthquake, flood, or other disaster, is someone nearby prepared to assist them?
- *Are they clean and well-groomed?* If, say, an older man has always been known for his crisply ironed shirts but starts looking disheveled, that may be a clue it's time for another level of support.
- *What's in the refrigerator?* Is the freezer full of TV dinners and the vegetable drawer empty? Has the milk gone sour? A quick look can tell you whether they're eating well or whether they'll do better someplace where trained staff could make sure they're getting balanced meals.
- *How are the pets doing?* What about the plants? Their ability to take care of other living things may offer clues to their ability to manage their own care.
- *How did those you're caring for weather their most recent illness (for example, a flu or bad cold)?* Are they able and willing to seek medical care when needed, or did last winter's cold develop into untreated bronchitis?
- *What does the doctor think?* With appropriate permission, talk to their doctor. The doctor may share your concerns about their safety at home but may also be able to alleviate them. Sometimes your closeness to the issue can exaggerate your worries, and a little professional distance (and expertise) is just what's needed to clarify the picture.

- *How often do they get out—especially in the winter?* Are they spending days without leaving the house because they can no longer drive or are afraid to take the bus alone? While many older adults fear being "locked away" in a retirement home, many such facilities offer regular outings that may actually keep them more mobile and active, not less.

- *How are they doing compared with this time last year?* The holidays, when families get together after long periods apart, can be a good time to reflect on the previous year and take note of any significant changes. A marked decline from one year to the next may mean it's time to start looking—and planning—for a more supportive environment.

- *How are you doing?* While this decision is not primarily about you—the caregiver—your own exhaustion can be a good gauge of a decline in older adults' ability to care for themselves. If their need for care is just plain wearing you out, that may be a sign that it's time to start looking at other options.

- *How old are they?* Many continuing care facilities have age ceilings after which they won't admit older adults, no matter how healthy they are, so if you have your eye on a particular place, find out what its age cutoff is and plan accordingly.

- *Are the older adults you're caring for happy?* Safety is crucial, of course, but so is emotional well-being. If they're riddled with anxieties or increasingly lonely, then that may tip the scales toward a move that may not be 100 percent necessary at this point for health and safety reasons. On the other hand, if they have a full life, close neighborhood and community connections, or simply enjoy being at home, it's worth exhausting every option before pushing them to move out of the home they love.

- *How do others think they're faring?* Sometimes it helps to get a second opinion, either from a family friend or relative or from a professional geriatric care manager who visits older adults' homes and does an informal evaluation. While they may initially resist the notion of a "total stranger" checking them out, this one may be worth insisting on (offer to have a family member pay for it as a holiday gift). You may be surprised to find they're willing to share doubts or vulnerabilities with a sympathetic, experienced stranger that they're loath to admit to their own children or family, easing the family conversations that follow.

- *What do they want?* This may be the most important question of all—and you may be surprised by the answer. While an initial response may be a knee-jerk "I'll cross that bridge when I come to it," many older adults harbor the same fears for their current and future safety and security that their caregivers do, even if pride keeps them from voicing them. Taking the time to sit down with them, draw out their concerns, and find out what they fear most about moving out and what they do want to change about their life—rather than launching into your worries for them, or what you think they ought to do—may give all of you the information needed to make the right decision for everyone concerned.

ª Nell Bernstein, Caring.com, http://www.caring.com/articles/moving -out-relative-question. This article originally appeared on the Caring.com website and is reprinted here with permission.

A 1996 study sponsored by the Robert Wood Johnson Foundation and conducted by the Florence Heller Graduate School for Advanced Studies in Social Welfare at Brandeis University found:[16]

- Older people want to age, and are aging, in place.
- A substantial number of older people live in naturally occurring retirement communities.
- Interest in programs supporting naturally occurring retirement communities as a strategy to promote aging in place is increasing, and the number of programs is growing.

Establishing and maintaining a NORC SSP is not without its challenges. (A neighborhood NORC in Los Angeles was studied by researchers who reported their findings in "Integrating Community Services within a NORC: The Park La Brea Experience.")[17] Recruiting and retaining volunteers is a constant struggle, as it requires seniors to see themselves as partners in service delivery. Securing funding for service provision and administrative staff has also been a continuing problem. Despite the multiple benefits associated with NORC SSPs, significant challenges remain in sustaining these models.

SECTION 202 SUPPORTIVE HOUSING FOR THE ELDERLY PROGRAM (SUBSIDIZED SENIOR HOUSING—NONMEDICAL)

Choices for housing for older adults with few financial resources are quite limited. The Section 202 Supportive Housing for the Elderly program is the only federally funded housing program specifically designed for the older population.[18] It should be noted that there are other federally subsidized housing programs that can and do include older residents. In Section 202 housing, residence is restricted to tenants who are at least sixty-two years old. Resident incomes generally must be below 50 percent of the area's median income. About three hundred thousand Section 202 housing units are available to older residents. In 1999, there were 1,216,000 total units of government-subsidized housing, of which Section 202 housing is a subset.[19]

The US Department of Housing and Urban Development (HUD) funds the construction and operation of Section 202 housing. There continues to be an inadequate supply of this housing; waiting lists for placement are either very long or closed completely. Section 202 housing may have deteriorated, be located in decaying parts of cities, and may not even be accessible to those with disabilities. Some projects, in fact, do not have elevators. Service coordinators are available in less than half the housing sites to help residents access services such as home-delivered meals, transportation, or housekeeping chores. While the number of older people who are eligible and in need of Section 202 housing is increasing, there has not been an increase in the number of units being constructed or rehabilitated. This shortage of affordable housing is a serious problem in an era facing increased numbers of older Americans.

ACCESSORY DWELLING UNITS

An accessory dwelling unit (ADU) is a type of housing either created as part of a single-family home or built separately on a lot. This housing option is sometimes also referred to as a "granny flat" accessory cottage or an elder cottage housing opportunity (ECHO). The older adult homeowner can use an ADU to provide additional income or to house a caregiver. For those on fixed incomes, the additional income from an ADU can be the solution that enables them to remain in their home. In other cases, the older adult moves to the ADU and is able to

ACCESSORY DWELLING UNITS IN SANTA CRUZ, CALIFORNIA

An accessory dwelling unit (ADU) is known by many names: granny flat, mother-in-law unit, in-law suite, carriage house, among others. An ADU refers to a second living unit on a property that includes a kitchen and bath. ADUs provide housing through the use of space either in or next to a single-family dwelling. In most cases, an ADU is a garage conversion, a small backyard cottage, or a guest house–style structure. The city of Santa Cruz started to encourage this type of housing in 2002 as a way of providing affordable housing in the developed core of the city.

Currently, housing prices in Santa Cruz are some of the least affordable in the United States. Only 6.9 percent of its residents are able to easily afford a median-priced home. With over eighteen thousand single-family lots in the city of Santa Cruz, ADUs provide a great opportunity to augment affordable rental housing in the community and offer homeowners a chance to supplement mortgage payments, making their own housing more affordable. In Santa Cruz, ADUs are allowed only on residentially zoned lots of 5,000 square feet or more, and they must meet setback, height, and parking requirements.

The Santa Cruz ADU Development Program has three major components to assist homeowners considering the development of an ADU on their property:[a]

1. A technical assistance program to assist homeowners in designing an ADU for their property. The program includes plans, guides, and training on how to design, permit, and build an ADU.
2. A wage subsidy and apprentice program that provides wage subsidies to licensed contractors employing apprentice workers trained by the Women Ventures Project of the Community Action Board on ADUs built within the city.
3. An ADU loan program offering loans up to $100,000 through the Santa Cruz Community Credit Union.

[a]Accessory Dwelling Unit Development Program, City of Santa Cruz, California, http://www.cityofsantacruz.com/index.aspx?page=1150.

continue to live independently in a smaller residence that he or she can manage with support nearby.

In the middle of the twentieth century, it was not at all unusual for families to rent out an apartment over their garage or a set of rooms in their basement. These features in communities were common. Over the past fifty years or so, many communities have developed more restrictive residential zoning regulations, often resulting in ADUs being prohibited. Zoning ordinances that limit or prohibit ADUs are the principal obstacle to the wide availability of this housing option. Reasons cited for opposing ADUs include overcrowding, decline of property values, reduced parking availability, and increased crime.

SHARED HOUSING

For some older adults, remaining in the home is desired but difficult. Financial constraints can make living alone problematic; some help may be needed with upkeep on the home that has become too much for the older homeowner. Shared housing is an arrangement in which the homeowner provides space for the tenant and receives income and/or needed assistance.[20] Shared housing offers companionship, affordable housing, security, mutual support, and even assistance with home tasks.[21]

Shared living can enhance residents' health and well-being and allow people to remain independent. Shared housing is different from the ADU model in that residents live in the same structure, while in ADUs people live in separate housing structures that are either stand-alone or attached. Lack of privacy can be a downside of shared housing, and, in some communities, zoning laws limit the number of unrelated adults living in the same house.[22]

COHOUSING OR CLUSTER HOUSING

Cohousing is a residential development that is designed to emphasize interaction among residents, while respecting individual privacy. Multiple housing units are built around a common area, creating an intentional neighborhood. For older adults, this design can provide an environment where community plays a critical role in one's ability to continue to live independently.

Cohousing developments often include resident involvement in the planning process, a common area that is shared and jointly owned, a community design that encourages interaction, and some degree of community management.[23] The intentional neighborhood in cohousing developments promotes a sense of interconnectedness among residents and appeals to those who want a lifestyle that encourages community interaction.[24]

Most cohousing communities are intergenerational, but senior cohousing communities are now emerging as well. Starting in 2005, with Glacier Circle in

Davis, California, these developments often incorporate universal design elements, and in some cases, residents agree to assist each other with activities such as shopping, meal preparation, or housework (i.e., instrumental activities of daily living [IADLs]). The atmosphere in cohousing developments can foster a sense of security and safety for residents, since interaction is a norm in these communities. Also, portions of the common areas of the community can be set aside for caregivers' living areas; residents can pool their resources and contract for needed services from a paid caregiver or transportation service.

Costs for cohousing are usually comparable to housing costs in the area and therefore may not be an affordable option. Some communities recognize this limitation and require that a number of affordable units be made available to low-income residents. According to the Cohousing Association of the United States Annual Cohousing Census of 2008, there are only about 115 cohousing communities across all of the states, including fewer than three thousand households.[25]

VILLAGE MODEL

Perhaps the newest development for sustaining independent living is the village model. The village model is a consumer-operated, person-centered approach to aging in place and aging in community. This model seeks to "support the medical, functional, emotional, social and spiritual needs of older adults through the creation of a membership organization."[26] In the village model, residents incorporate as a not-for-profit organization, managed by a board of directors and operated by a combination of volunteers and paid staff or solely by volunteers. Staff oversee, coordinate, and/or administer the delivery of services to members.[27]

Village staff prequalify providers to deliver services at negotiated rates and follow up with members to assess the services received from vendors and volunteers. Services and assistance vary from village to village. Some examples of benefits with village membership include discounts at local health and fitness clubs, transportation to and from various locations, bill paying, household tasks (cooking, cleaning), assisting with groceries and meals, social events, and home health aid. The annual membership fee for a village can range from $150 to more than $500 per person,[28] depending on the menu of services offered and the administrative and operational costs. Some villages have secured grants and gifts to help offset the costs for low-income individuals.

Challenges facing villages include recruiting members and sustaining a professional staff. Because it is a new approach, potential members may be unsure of the model's benefits and may be less willing to pay a membership fee, especially if they are living on a fixed income.[29] Some villages supplement paid services with volunteer-led programs, but there are trade-offs in service quality and liability.

Supportive Housing: When More Help Is Needed

There are several options for older adults who are looking for a setting that includes greater assistance. Supportive housing describes a variety of settings that are designed to provide support, ranging from meals and housekeeping to monitoring health conditions. Supportive housing is a residential setting, not an institutional one. The goal is to promote a sense of independence and autonomy even when care is needed.

Housing that includes services varies from state to state and from community to community. It is important that older adults and their families who are considering supportive options take the time to understand the care and the costs provided in each of these settings. It is also important that families stay engaged in the process before, during, and after the move. Moving is unsettling; moving because more care is needed is even more unsettling.

ADULT FOSTER CARE, ADULT FAMILY HOMES, SUPPORTIVE CARE HOMES, AND BOARD AND CARE HOMES

When care is needed and staying in your own home is not an option, a preferred setting is one that mirrors a private dwelling. An adult foster care home, adult family home, or supportive care home is a private residence in which several older adults (usually no more than six people) receive assistance with activities of daily living, meal preparation, and transportation. The homelike environment of adult foster care promotes a sense of independence and control. There is no official definition of adult foster care, and there are no standard regulations for such homes.

It is difficult to determine an accurate count of these homes because definition, licensing, and regulation vary from state to state. It is estimated that there are nearly nineteen thousand licensed and certified adult foster care homes across the country, serving about sixty-five thousand residents.[30] There are several mechanisms for paying for adult foster care, ranging from private pay (or out-of-pocket payment) for those with financial resources to Medicaid coverage for low-income residents in states with adult foster care covered under a Medicaid Home and Community Based Services waiver. If the state does have a waiver program, expenses related to room and board are not covered by Medicaid, although Supplemental Security Income may be available.

While adult foster care homes are a viable option for many, there are challenges with this option. State laws and regulations sometimes prohibit staff from offering nursing services. A nursing contract might be required for residents who need help managing their medication. It can be difficult to find people to serve as adult foster care providers, and there can be a lack of privacy in group living.

ASSISTED LIVING

About twenty years ago, a new model for housing and care began to be available. Filling a niche for those who could no longer live alone but were not in need of services provided in a skilled nursing facility, assisted living came on the market. Assisted living offers private rooms or apartments with twenty-four-hour supervision that includes a range of care levels but not complex medical care. Residences differ in size and appearance and in the services they offer. Today, the average assisted living resident is over age eighty-five; female (74 percent); in need of assistance with managing his or her medications (81 percent), bathing (64 percent), and dressing (39 percent); and paying privately for care. In 2009, there were over nine hundred thousand people living in assisted living settings.[31]

There is no standard model for assisted living, and there is no federal oversight. With over twelve thousand residences across the United States, models and costs vary widely, based on the services provided. The average monthly fee is between $2,000 and $2,900.[32]

Monthly costs are likely to increase over time as a resident's needs change and additional services are provided. Assisted living can be expensive, and most people are private payers, covering the cost out of their own pocket. Medicare does not cover the cost of assisted living. Over forty states have Home and Community Based Medicaid waivers for a limited number of assisted living residents, so that some low-income eligible older adults can be covered. However, Medicaid will not cover the cost of room and board, only the services component of this housing option.

SKILLED NURSING FACILITIES

For some people with significant health problems, the only solution for the care needed is a skilled nursing facility. These facilities provide both skilled nursing and assistance with activities of daily living—bathing, dressing, eating, and toileting. Most facilities provide dental and mental health services along with therapies, and many also offer additional services such as Alzheimer's disease care units, dementia care, pain management, and palliative care.[33] In 2005, almost 50 percent of residents had dementia, and more than half were bedridden or needed a wheelchair.[34]

The average private-pay cost for a single occupancy room in a nursing home in 2006 was $206 per day (or $75,190 per year). For a semiprivate room, the average cost was $183 per day (or $66,795 per year).[35] It is not surprising that most skilled nursing residents do not pay with personal funds. Only about 22 percent of residents, and 38 percent of expenditures, are covered out of pocket or by private long-term care insurance.[36] About 65 percent of skilled nursing residents are supported primarily by Medicaid,[37] which pays for 45 percent of the cost.[38] Medicare does not pay for long-term care, but it does cover brief stays. After twenty days, beneficiaries must pay a coinsurance ($124 per day in 2007).[39] In 2004, approximately 1.5 million Americans lived in skilled nursing facilities. The majority were older adults: 88 percent of skilled nursing residents are aged sixty-five or older and 45 percent are eighty-five or older. These figures represent only 2 percent of Americans aged sixty-five to eighty-four and 14 percent of Americans aged eighty-five and older.[40] There is controversy about whether skilled nursing occupancy rates will increase in the future. One estimate is that 35 percent of Americans turning age sixty-five in 2005 will live in a skilled nursing facility sometime in their life, 18 percent will stay for at least one year, and 5 percent for at least five years.[41]

Most people view skilled nursing facilities as the setting of last resort and report that, when and if they need care, they want to receive that care at home and in their communities. In many cases, skilled nursing facilities are a short-term solution for someone needing skilled nursing care, medical services, and therapies after a hospitalization. In other cases, it is the only viable option.

Independent Living and Supportive Housing: Continuing Care Retirement Communities

Some people are planners. They may determine that a continuing care retirement community (CCRC) is their best option. This housing alternative features a continuum of care and housing, from independent living apartments and/or homes to skilled nursing facility–level care. There is often an enriched array of social, recreational, educational, and cultural activities. In this "continuum-of-care" system, residents usually enter the facility at the independent living level.

When entering a CCRC, residents sign a contract that the CCRC will provide housing and services for life. Contracts come in several forms: a life care contract, where everything is included and costs should not change over time; or a modified or fee-for-service contract, in which the base fee is lower, but additional fees are charged as additional services are needed. Most CCRCs require a one-time entrance fee and monthly payments thereafter. Fees vary by community and depend on the type of housing and services offered. Initial costs can run from $20,000 to several hundred thousand dollars. The monthly fee is added to that and can range from $650 to over $3,000 each month. The cost of this housing option is an issue for many, so some CCRCs operate on a rental basis and do not require an initial entrance fee.[42]

Hospice

Hospice provides comprehensive care to people facing life-limiting conditions. It is often a very short term approach to care at the very end of life. Hospice focuses

Senior Companion Program. Courtesy of the Corporation for National and Community Service.

on providing quality, compassionate care using a team approach for medical care, pain management, and emotional and spiritual support. Support is provided to the patient and to his or her loved ones. With the belief that people have the right to die free of pain and with dignity and that loved ones should receive necessary support, hospice focuses on caring, not curing. Every type of housing can be the setting for hospice care. Some hospice programs also provide homelike inpatient facilities or are offered in a hospital, a nursing home, or other long-term care facility. Coverage for hospice services is available from Medicare, Medicaid, and private insurance. The number of hospice programs certified by Medicare has grown over the past twenty-five years, from thirty-one programs in 1984 to over three thousand programs in 2009.[43] In 2007, over one million people were served by hospice programs, although most use hospice for a very short amount of time. A Medicare Payment Advisory Commission (MedPAC) report to Congress in 2006 confirmed that the median length of stay of hospice patients was fifteen days.[44]

Conclusion

Even when all of the current housing alternatives are combined, they represent only a very small percentage of living arrangements for older people. As the nation continues to age, housing choices must meet the care needs of a population at different stages of aging. Costs need to be carefully managed and viable business models developed to sustain new approaches for service delivery. Home- and community-based services (HCBS) can be developed and better integrated with housing, particularly for the oldest old and for those who are poor. Rather than isolating older adults from the larger world, costs can be reduced and communities can be enhanced by incorporating older adults and their housing settings into the fabric of the community.

We are a can-do nation. When the baby boomers were born in the middle of the last century, our communities figured out how to build all the schools needed. Now, in the twenty-first century, it is time to figure out how to create the best possible homes and communities for successful aging. We can do it.

Notes

1. Housing policy.org, online guide to state and local housing policy, Center for Housing Policy, National Housing Conference.

2. AARP, "Aging, Migration, and Local Communities: The Views of 60+ Residents and Community Leaders," http://www.walkable.org/assets/downloads/Aging_in_the_Suburbs.pdf.

3. Ibid.

4. Exhibit 1, *A Quiet Crisis in America* (Report to Congress by the Commission on Affordable Housing and Health Facility Needs for Seniors in the 21st Century, Washington, DC, June 30, 2002).

5. Medicare.gov, "Alternatives to Nursing Home Care."

6. Nell Bernstein, "'Boomerang Seniors'—More Aging Parents Are Moving In with Their Kids," Caring.com.

7. Caitlin McDevitt, "Ready to Move, Stuck in One Place," *Newsweek*, October 18, 2008.

8. Seniors Commission Report Exhibit 1: Major Types of Housing Occupied by Senior Householders and Persons (Age 65 and Older) in the United States, 1999.

9. Vera Prosper, "Aging in Place in Multifamily Housing," *Cityscape* 7, no. 1 (2004): 83, http://www.norcs.org.page.aspx?idz160634.

10. "Sun City Arizona AZ: A Great Place to Visit, Play and Retire," http://www.suncityaz.org.

11. Rebecca Cohen, "Connecting Existing Homes and Social Services," http://assets.aarp.org/rgcenter/ppi/liv-com/fs171-homes-services.pdf.

12. United Hospital Fund, "FAQs about NORCs," http://www.uhfnyc.org.

13. NORCs: An Aging in Place Initiative, http://www.norcs.org.

14. Robert Wood Johnson Foundation, "NORCs Offer Opportunities for Delivery of Health and Care Related Services," http://www.rwjf.org.

15. "NORC Blueprint: A Guide to Community Action," http://www.norcblueprint.org.

16. "Promoting Healthy Aging: Aging in Place, NORC Supportive Service Programs, and the 'Community Innovations for Aging in Place' Program," NORCs: An Aging in Place Initiative, http://www.norcs.org.

17. "Integrating Community Services within a NORC: The Park La Brea Experience," *Cityscape* 12, no. 2 (2010).

18. Nancy Libson, "Section 202 Supportive Housing for the Elderly," *2009 Advocates' Guide to Housing and Community Development Policy* (Washington, DC: National Low Income Housing Coalition, 2009).

19. Ibid.

20. "NORC Blueprint."

21. Charles Durrett, *Senior Cohousing: A Community Approach to Independent Living: The Handbook* (Berkeley, CA: Habitat Press, 2005).

22. "The Sharing Solution: Legal Issues to Consider When Sharing a Home," http://www.NOLO.com.

23. Cohousing Association of the United States, http://www.cohousing.org.

24. Durrett, *Senior Cohousing*.

25. Cohousing Association of the United States.

26. Village to Village Network, http://vtvnetwork.clubexpress.com.

27. Jean Accius, "The Village: A Growing Option for Aging in Place," http://assets.aarp.org/rgcenter/ppi/liv-com/fs177-village.pdf.

28. Terri Guengerich, "Neighbors Helping Neighbors: A Qualitative Study of Villages Operating in the District of Columbia" (Washington, DC: AARP Knowledge Management, October 2009), http://assets.aarp.org/rgcenter/il/dcvillages.pdf. (Rates for the DC

Villages offering full-service memberships range from $450 to $530 per person and $600 to $800 per household.)

29. Accius, "Village."

30. Robert L. Mollica, Kristin Simms-Kastelein, Michael Cheek, Candace Baldwin, Jennifer Farnham, Susan Reinhard, and Jean Accius, *Building Adult Foster Care: What States Can Do* (Washington, DC: AARP Public Policy Institute, 2009).

31. "2009 Overview of Assisted Living," National Center for Assisted Living, http://web1.pmds.com /AHCA_eBiz/Default.aspx?tabid=44&action =ShowProductDetails&args=562.

32. Bernadette Wright, "In Brief: An Overview of Assisted Living," http://assets.aarp.org/rgcenter/il /inb88_al.pdf.

33. Ari Houser, "Nursing Homes," http://www .aarp.org/home-garden/livable-communities/info -2007/fs10r_homes.html.

34. Ibid.

35. MetLife Mature Market Institute, "2006 MetLife Market Survey of Nursing Home and Home Care Costs."

36. Houser, "Nursing Homes."

37. Ari Houser, Wendy Fox-Grage, and Mary Jo Gibson, "Across the States 2006: Profiles of Long-Term Care and Independent Living," http://assets .aarp.org/rgcenter/health/d18763_2006_ats.pdf.

38. "National Spending for Long-Term Care" (Georgetown University Long-Term Care Financing Project, 2007), http://ltc.georgetown.edu/pdfs /whopays2006.pdf.

39. Houser, "Nursing Homes."

40. AARP Public Policy Institute analysis of the 2004 National Nursing Home Survey and US Census Bureau population estimates.

41. Peter Kemper, Harriet L. Komisar, and Lisa Alecixh, "Long-Term Care over an Uncertain Future: What Can Current Retirees Expect?" *Inquiry* 42, no. 4 (2005): 335–50.

42. Medicare.gov, "Types of Long-Term Care," http://www.medicare.gov/LongTermCare/Static/CCRC .asp.

43. Hospice Association of America, "Hospice Facts and Statistics," http://www.nahc.org/facts /HospiceStats09.pdf.

44. Medicare Payment Advisory Commission, "A Data Book: Healthcare Spending and the Medicare Program," http://www.allhealth.org/briefing materials/HealthcareSpendingandtheMedicare Program-Medpac2006-660.pdf.

Chapter 6

Community Services

Jennie Chin Hansen and Andrew Scharlach

Introduction

Social and physical environments interact in order to meet basic human needs for physical, psychological, social, and spiritual well-being. Social environments support aging in place by filling gaps between the built environment and the needs and capacities of individuals as they age. Community programs and services can enhance informal social supports and build upon the personal strengths and social resources that older adults bring to their later years.

Emerging trends affect the ability of traditional program and service models to meet the needs of older adults. New services and activities are needed to support the well-being of a more diverse and informed baby boomer cohort, who plan to age in place and are less likely than their grandparents to find fulfillment through playing bingo at the senior center. The nature of community supports is evolving; there are innovative examples that highlight future directions for aging in community. Model programs not only meet the needs of at-risk elderly populations but also enhance individual strengths, social capital, and community capacity.

JENNIE CHIN HANSEN was the president of AARP for the 2008–2010 biennium and currently is chief executive officer of the American Geriatrics Society. She also teaches nursing at San Francisco State University, where she is Senior Fellow at the university's Center for the Health Professions. She serves as a commissioner of the Medicare Payment Advisory Commission and is also a board member of the National Academy of Social Insurance. Previously, she was executive director of On Lok, Inc., which became the model for PACE. She received a bachelor's degree from Boston College and a master's degree in nursing from the University of California at San Francisco.

ANDREW SCHARLACH is associate dean and the Eugene and Rose Kleiner Professor of Aging at the University of California at Berkeley. He also is the director for the Center for the Advanced Study of Aging Services. His most recent book is *Families and Work: New Directions in the Twenty-First Century*. He received his MS in social services from Boston University and his PhD in psychology from Stanford University. He is a Fellow of the Gerontological Society of America and a Diplomate in Clinical Social Work.

The Need for Community Activities and Services

As we age, our physical and social environments take on greater importance than when we were younger. Familiar physical spaces provide a sense of "place attachment," which reminds us of who we are and what continues to be important. Memories of activities that have shaped our lives, as well as emotionally important interpersonal relationships with family and friends who have shared our spaces, reinforce a continual sense of personal identity despite changes in physical functioning. Indeed, community physical and social environments themselves have meaning.[1]

American notions of aging in place tend to focus on helping individuals or couples obtain the services they need to remain in their own homes or apartments as they age. Aging in one's familiar community becomes even more important as we get older. Social isolation is a major problem among the elderly. Older adults' increased time at home can be a result of environmental barriers that increase the cost of leaving one's home, as well as enhanced attachment to the house itself. Forays away from home can embody a risk of experiences that evoke a reduced sense of personal competence, a disablement process that can result in increased vulnerability.[2]

In aging-friendly physical and social environments, social supports and accommodations enable individuals with age-related disabilities to meet basic health and social needs and adapt as those needs change over time. Social supports need to provide opportunities for older adults to develop new sources of fulfillment and engagement. In such an environment, the focus is not only on personal safety but also on human interaction and social integration. By making better use of the potential contributions of older people, communities can tap social capital that is of benefit to the entire community.

Aging-friendly communities focus on five key areas: continuity, compensation, connection, contribution, and challenge.

- *Continuity*: Opportunities to participate in lifelong interests and activities that are self-affirming, including activities that maintain good health and prevent disease and disability
- *Compensation*: Access to services, products, and structures that help to meet the basic health and social needs of individuals with age-related disabilities, including assisted living and technological interventions that support self-care
- *Connection*: Access to sources of social interaction and social support, including built and electronic resources to overcome physical barriers to social contact

- *Contribution*: Opportunities to actively contribute to the well-being of the community, of one another, and of themselves
- *Challenge*: Access to new sources of fulfillment, productive engagement, and interaction, including social, recreational, and educational activities designed to engage and excite older participants[3]

Developmentally appropriate community support services should not just compensate for gaps in person-environment fit, they should also preserve existing well-being. Such services can provide opportunities for exercise and renewed functioning. Opportunities for civic engagement can be introduced. There is substantial potential for enhanced physical, psychological, and social well-being wherever older adults reside. These exist across the continuum of possible built environments—whether they are traditional housing or alternatives, including assisted living, board and care homes, or skilled nursing facilities. Figure 6.1 illustrates the continuum of care across a range of environments.

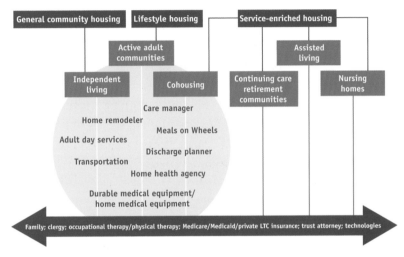

The Continuum of Care

Figure 6.1 Home community-based services. Source: MetLife Mature Market Institute, *Aging in Place 2.0: Rethinking Solutions to the Home Care Challenge*, http://www.metlife.com/mmi/research/aging-in-place.html#insights.

Low-income and ethnic or racial minority communities are especially likely to experience barriers to community support services and may require additional assistance. Barriers include inadequate transportation, insufficient knowledge about available assistance, insufficient financial resources to pay for services, language barriers, lack of culturally appropriate programs, and overt and covert discrimination. Immigrant groups also are apt to experience sociocultural barriers related to cultural norms and traditions. Barriers can include expectations regarding the primacy of family care, reciprocity, and filial obligation, and may result in a reluctance to seek help from nonfamily sources.[4]

Rural communities also pose particular barriers to obtaining the support services older adults need and want. Out-migration of younger people leaves many older people without family members nearby. Lack of family, coupled with greater distances to neighbors and services, can result in increased social isolation. Rural communities are more likely to be underresourced with regard to the basic service infrastructure. Extended distances make services more expensive to provide. Rural elders are less likely than urban elders to be able to access home care and other community support services and more likely to enter a nursing home.[5] Suburban communities also can be problematic, primarily due to transportation barriers, but also due to a lack of affordable housing and of providers of in-home and other support services.

Current Context for Aging in Community

PUBLIC SECTOR INNOVATIONS

Support services for older adults who need assistance are funded in large part by public dollars. Expenses for long-term care totaled more than $200 billion in 2005,[6] of which 70 percent was paid by Medicare, Medicaid, or other government programs. These government programs are heavily biased toward nursing home care, typically requiring more restrictive financial and functional eligibility requirements for home care than for care in nursing facilities. As a result, Medicaid spends nearly five times as much per person for nursing home care as it does for community-based care.[7] The 20 percent of the elderly disabled population who are in nursing homes receive 57 percent of Medicaid long-term care funding.[8] Compared with other industrialized countries, the United States tends to rely more on institutional care and less on community-based supports for people with care needs.

A number of recent federal initiatives have attempted to increase the availability of home- and community-based services as alternatives to nursing home care. The Deficit Reduction Act of 2005 authorized a $1.75 billion Money Follows the Person (MFP) demonstration program that provides enhanced federal funding to enable Medicaid-eligible individuals to move from institutional to community settings.[9] The project has been supplemented by funds from the Patient Protection and Affordable Care Act of 2010, to total $4 billion in funding. The project aims to make "widespread" changes to the long-term care (LTC) support system[10] by "enabling the elderly and people with disabilities to fully participate in their communities."[11] By transitioning roughly forty thousand individuals out of institutions, the Centers for Medicare and Medicaid Services (CMS), which manages the MFP program, expects to identify community-based models that both lower the cost of LTC care and improve quality of life for its beneficiaries. The percentage of Medicaid long-term care spent on community-based care has increased from 24 percent in 1997 to 43 percent in 2008.[12]

In the MFP program, CMS has taken an important first step in emphasizing the value of a community, but all communities are not the same when it comes to the impact on a resident's health, quality of life, and cost of care. As the Mathematica Policy Research noted in an MFP evaluation, "The search for appropriate housing is often complicated by the need to live near service providers and social networks."[13]

In a recent survey of twenty-six state MFP directors, a vast majority believed walkable urban environments could improve a beneficiary's health, enhance the quality of life, and/or lower costs.[14] Yet only a small minority thought MFP funds could or should be used in this manner. Few considered that structural barriers in the senior housing market limit this type of choice from being available in the first place. Still, there is hope that change is in store. Two-thirds of the MFP states have established task forces to address "the chronic shortage of affordable, accessible housing for individuals with disabilities."[15]

PATIENT PROTECTION AND AFFORDABLE CARE ACT

The Patient Protection and Affordable Care Act of 2010 (PPACA) contains a number of provisions enhancing services and supports to make it easier for older adults to remain in their homes. The Community Living Assistance Services and Supports (CLASS) Act established a new national insurance program to help adults with disabilities pay for the services and supports they need, including services such as in-home care and home modifications. Because the program was to be funded through payroll donations and participation would be voluntary, concerns were expressed as to whether premiums would become prohibitively expensive, especially in light of likely adverse selection bias. In 2011, legislation was introduced to repeal the CLASS act.

Individuals with multiple chronic diseases account for up to 85 percent of Medicare spending and typically suffer poorly managed, disjointed care under the current highly fragmented, fee-for-service, traditional Medicare reimbursement system. The PPACA calls for an Independence at Home demonstration program that provides incentives for home-based primary medical care for high-need Medicare beneficiaries with multiple chronic conditions. Targeting intensive, coordinated home care services to those with the greatest need is expected to improve care while reducing expensive hospitalizations and emergency room visits.[16]

Approximately 30 percent of disabled older adults in the United States have unmet needs for basic personal care. (This compares to only about 1 percent in Sweden, to provide a reference point.)[17] Unmet needs are greatest among some of the most disadvantaged members of society, including people who are disabled, poor, elderly, female, immigrants, or racial or ethnic minorities.

In addition, a significantly higher percentage of older African Americans and Hispanics report difficulties with activities of daily living compared to whites.[18] People who never graduated from high school are at twice the risk for physical limitations as high school graduates.[19] In addition, those in the bottom 20 percent of income distribution have impaired physical functioning at a rate of three or four times those in the top 20 percent. Their level of physical functioning deteriorates with age twice as fast as higher earners.[20]

STATE AND LOCAL INITIATIVES

Fiscal and regulatory responsibility for aging services has been devolving from the federal government to state governments, to local jurisdictions, and, finally, to individuals and their families as the government has attempted to limit its financial exposure. A major thrust of recent federal elder care policy has been designed to educate older adults and their families that greater self-reliance will be required in their later years. A centerpiece of George W. Bush's long-term care policy was the Own Your Future campaign to persuade Americans of the importance of planning ahead for long-term care needs.

States have attempted to control costs while meeting the health and social needs of elderly and disabled residents in a variety of ways. Some states have reorganized their financing and delivery systems to improve efficiencies and reduce the bias toward institutional care. Several states were able to integrate administrative and fiscal authority for their long-term care programs into a single state agency. This reorganization has resulted in a substantial reduction in the proportion of state expenditures going toward nursing home care relative to home- and community-based care.[21] Other states have introduced managed care programs, providing all nursing home and community-based services at a capitated rate.[22,23]

Local jurisdictions throughout the United States are adopting aging-friendly infrastructure improvements. Communities also are beginning to improve access and coordination. One-stop-shopping approaches provide consumers with a single phone number, email address, or website to begin the process of obtaining assistance from an array of possible service providers. Examples include the US Administration on Aging (AoA) Eldercare Locator service, multilevel information and referral programs, and concierge services. "No wrong door" approaches provide a coordinated response to consumer needs, building upon interagency collaboration, cross-disciplinary communication, and electronic service records. New opportunities for community participation facilitate personal independence and community engagement. However, public support programs are under increased pressure in the current economic climate.

Caregiving

Caregiving is an essential component of services for older people and can take various forms, ranging from unpaid or "informal" caregiving by family and friends to nonmedical home care to skilled nursing.

UNPAID OR "INFORMAL" CAREGIVING BY FAMILY AND FRIENDS

Family caregivers are defined as those providing unpaid assistance, including personal care, bathing, dressing, feeding, help with medications and other treatments, transportation to doctors' appointments, and arranging for other services. As policy shifts from institutional care toward more home- and community-based services, success depends on friends and family caregivers.[24]

Informal, unpaid support from family and friends is essential for frail older people to be able to age in place. Only 5 percent of older people rely exclusively on paid caregivers. As the need for help with the activities of daily living and the instrumental activities of daily living increases, family and friends are called on to help. Much of what is spent supporting older people is not reported to tax authorities and, as a result, is not reflected in national estimates of long-term care spending. The AARP Public Policy Institute estimates that the value of unpaid caregiving totals some $350 billion annually.[25]

Traditionally, caregiving has been "women's work," and its cost to the caregiver in lost wages, increased stress, and health-related illnesses has been obscured. Many women are putting their career and financial future on hold as they juggle part-time caregiving and full-time job requirements. Twenty-nine percent of the US adult population, or 65.7 million people, are caregivers, encompassing 31 percent of all households. These caregivers provide an average of twenty hours of care per week.[26]

The MetLife Foundation and the Rosalynn Carter Institute for Caregiving are bringing greater attention to these challenges.[27] The MetLife Foundation has sponsored significant research in this field, considering not only the costs to caregivers but also the costs to employers. The Rosalynn Carter Institute for Caregiving synthesizes research in this field, making scholarly information more accessible for larger audiences.

The National Alliance for Caregiving is a coalition that helps to raise awareness and engages in advocacy about caregiving. The US Congress has passed several significant measures, including the Family and Medical Leave Act and federal funding for respite care programs under the Older Americans Act.

HOME HEALTH CARE

In the year 2000, about 12,800 home health agencies served approximately 8,600,000 clients across the United States. In that same year, Medicare paid an estimated 85 to 90 percent of the total cost of home health agency services, amounting to $8.7 billion. The number of home health agencies has increased annually, as well as the number of clients being served.[28]

Costs for home health care vary from area to area. A nurse, therapist, or social worker may cost $70 to $100 an hour. An aide to take care of daily living needs, or the activities of daily living, may cost $10 to $25 an hour. Medicare and Medicaid pay 90 percent of the cost of home health services, with the remainder paid from private funds, including private long-term care insurance. Long-term care insurance policies will pay after Medicare has first contributed its share of the costs.

PRIVATELY PAID NONMEDICAL CAREGIVERS

When a frail older person's determination is to remain at home, the need for care may overwhelm the family. If funds are available, the family can hire someone to come into the home for extended periods of time to provide nonmedical care. If medical care is needed, a nurse or therapist will also be required.

The number of companies offering personal, nonmedical care services is mushrooming across the country. It is evident that there is a growing need for unpaid family caregivers to contract additional help from paid care providers. Many caregivers are now employed full-time or are living a long distance away and find it difficult, if not impossible, to provide such care.

Workforce and Quality Assurance Challenges

Caregiving and other community support for an aging population are limited by a home care workforce that is marked by high turnover, inadequate training, inadequate compensation, limited benefits, and few worker protections. Ninety percent of care providers are women, half are members of nonwhite or Hispanic racial and ethnic groups,[29] and a quarter do not speak English as their primary language.[30] Wages are limited,[31] 40 percent of home care workers have no health insurance coverage, and care providers have one of the highest rates of job-related injuries.[32]

Rise of Personal Responsibility and Technology

Personal responsibility and technology are key themes affecting the relationship among older people, service systems, and the communities within which they live. Older adults and people with disabilities increasingly see themselves as intelligent consumers rather than passive care recipients. Long-term care is being reconceptualized as an array of services and supports that can be obtained in a variety of ways from a variety of sources. Products and services have emerged that are targeted to the baby boomers. These services include transportation services such as SilverRide, a service in the San Francisco Bay Area to help seniors with rides; accompaniment to appointments and personalized trip planning;[33] and gaming devices such as the Nintendo Wii. Technological innovations are well under way, ranging from robotic devices to sensors to telemedicine programs.

Local Community Initiatives at the Interface of Housing and Community Services

Community services can help to bridge the gap between existing physical and social structures. Existing supports for aging in place are fragmented, with distinct financing and administrative silos separating essential domains such as housing, health care, and social supports. There is a lack of integration or even coordination between the built environment and the social environment, or between acute ("medical") care and chronic ("social") care. We need more fully integrated community support services, combining the full spectrum of formal and informal service capacity. Faith-based projects and initiatives can often bridge the gap between formal and informal services. The Center for Faith-Based and Neighborhood Partnerships, within the US Department of Health and Human Services (HHS), works to build partnerships between government and community- and faith-based organizations to better meet community needs.

COMMUNITY INNOVATIONS FOR AGING IN PLACE INITIATIVE: THE ALASKA NATIVE AGING IN PLACE PROJECT

The 2006 reauthorization of the Older Americans Act (OAA) included funding for the Community Innovations for Aging in Place Initiative (CIAIP), which aims to overcome barriers to aging in place by fostering innovative collaborations among community organizations in order to provide more comprehensive and coordinated health and social services to older individuals. Collaborations include partnerships among aging and disability resource centers (ADRCs), area agencies on aging (AAAs), local providers of health and social services, housing entities, community development organizations, and philanthropic organizations. Services provided include care management, evidence-based disease prevention and health promotion services, education, socialization, recreation, and civic engagement opportunities.

The Alaska Native Aging in Place Project is an attempt by the federally recognized Alaska Native Cheesh'na and Mentasta Traditional Tribes to enable tribal elders to age in place. Both tribes are located in a remote area of southeastern Alaska, where temperatures can differ by 150 degrees between the winter and summer ($-62°F$ to $92°F$). The rural environment, primarily subsistence economy, and extreme weather in this area pose unique challenges for tribal elders who wish to remain in their villages as they grow older. As a result, almost one-half of elders over age sixty-five relocate to far-off communities with more skilled care resources, separating family members and disturbing long-standing social support networks. For the Alaska Native Aging in Place Project, the Mount Sanford Tribal Consortium has partnered with local universities, state senior services, and Alaska Native organizations to create a village-based system of care for seniors, which may be replicable in other rural environments throughout Alaska and the United States.[a]

[a]Mount Sanford Tribal Consortium, "Alaska Native Aging in Place Project," http://www.mstc.org.

Rural Initiatives

Rural communities especially benefit from a coordinated approach. The relatively limited availability of organizations and resources in rural America requires multitasking, transdisciplinary work roles, colocation of services, and ongoing partnerships with other organizations, across traditional system barriers and silos. There are five key system components for successfully meeting the needs of the rural elderly: (1) adequate community infrastructure; (2) community-based providers offering a full continuum of primary, acute, post-acute, and long-term care services, supported by an adequate rural health workforce; (3) care coordination systems that offer options within an integrated care system; (4) informed consumers and family members; and (5) partnerships among community service providers.

Promising Model Programs

There are numerous innovative and promising programs operating across the country to provide services for older Americans in their homes and communities. The most important and far-reaching include the following.

CASH AND COUNSELING

The Cash and Counseling demonstration program was originally sponsored by the Robert Wood Johnson Foundation, the Office of the Assistant Secretary for Planning and Evaluation at HHS, and the Administration on Aging. Now operating in fifteen states, the program provides Medicaid consumers with a predetermined monthly allowance, which they can use for virtually any care-related expenses and a wide range of noncare household activities.[34] Within an agreed-upon plan, consumers have total control (and responsibility) for hiring and overseeing care providers, including family members and, in some cases, spouses.

Preliminary evaluations of Cash and Counseling and other consumer-directed models generally find that consumers report fewer safety concerns, fewer unmet needs, and greater satisfaction levels than do those in traditional agency care. These positive results are due at least in part to the fact that independent providers are better able to personalize care and are not constrained by agency guidelines and professional standards that limit work hours and authorized services.[35,36]

PROGRAM OF ALL-INCLUSIVE CARE FOR THE ELDERLY

The Program of All-Inclusive Care for the Elderly (PACE) is based on the belief that "it is better for the well-being of seniors with chronic care needs and their families to be served in the community whenever possible." The origins of the PACE model go back to the late 1960s in the Chinatown–North Beach community of San Francisco, California. Community leaders created a not-for-profit corporation, On Lok Senior Health Services, to build a community-based system of care.[37] (*On lok* is Cantonese for "peaceful, happy abode.") In 1987, federal legislation authorized the replication of the On Lok model; with the help of two foundations, PACE was launched. PACE provides medical and supportive services: adult day care that offers nursing and physical, occupational, and recreational therapies; meals; nutritional counseling; social work and personal care; medical care; home health and personal care; prescription drugs; respite care; and hospital and home nursing care when needed.[38] In 1997, the Balanced Budget Act made the PACE model a permanently recognized provider type under the Medicare and Medicaid programs. Currently, there are PACE or pre-PACE programs in thirty states. The largest of these has more than twenty-five hundred frail elderly enrollees, but most serve a few hundred on average.[39] PACE is able to combine funding from Medicare, Medicaid, and private sources to create a pool of resources to meet each participant's needs. PACE programs have strong incentives to help keep their members as healthy as possible by providing high levels of preventive services, including frequent checkups, exercise programs, dietary monitoring, and programs to increase strength and balance.

The National PACE Association has shown that its program reduces nursing home admissions and their related operational and capital costs. Because of the success of this program over the past forty years, it could be expanded to cover a larger group of the elderly. Present rules require that the person has to be very frail or incapacitated in order to be enrolled in a PACE program. The financial savings to federal and state budgets if the PACE model were expanded invites serious exploration.

Conclusion

A number of challenges face community activities and services of the future. These services cannot be designed based on past characteristics of elderly behavior. Instead, the successful programs of tomorrow must help entire neighborhoods and communities to become more aging friendly, supporting well-being and fulfillment throughout our lives. Adequate service infrastructures are essential. Because costs are such a pressing issue, especially in rural and low-income communities, service models must evolve and change with each community's realities. Across the nation, programs must meet the needs of a more highly educated, diverse baby boomer population composed of people who are more likely to attend a fitness center than a senior center.

Coordination among services also needs to be improved, especially at transition points and across service types and levels of care. Where feasible, health and social services should be accessible from the locations where elders reside, as exemplified by the PACE and naturally occurring retirement community supportive services program (NORC SSP) models. Better use can be made of available and emerging technologies, to assist older adults to age in place or access needed information. Finally, consumers want and need greater involvement in directing their own care, in helping others, and in contributing to the well-being of their communities. Different solutions are needed at various stages of aging.

The ultimate goal of aging in place is about achieving true choice in housing—the ability to live wherever we want, regardless of age or ability. Efforts to provide aging-in-place options, if successful, may prompt resistance from those who fear the specter of aging communities. Such resisters may fear that individuals will continue to reside in their existing communities as they become more impaired and less affluent. Resistance is likely on two fronts: economic-based bias (against people who are less affluent) and function-based bias (against people who are disabled). Community activities and services that facilitate a sense of community may help to ameliorate some of this type of ageism and economic discrimination.

We need to move beyond a focus on meeting individual needs to a broader vision that embraces strategies for enhancing social capital and community capacity. Efforts that build local coalitions, enhance community empowerment, and influence the policy environment are especially beneficial for underserved and vulnerable groups.

In the end, community is more than a physical space or even a social environment. Community helps us to define who we are. Community activities and services that are aging friendly not only provide a context for well-being but also provide a life course filled with possibility. It is in such communities that people of all ages experience themselves and their world in a more positive way.

Notes

1. Philip B. Stafford, *Elderburbia* (Santa Barbara, CA: Praeger, 2009).

2. Lois M. Verbrugge and Alan M. Jette, "The Disablement Process," *Social Science and Medicine* 38 (1994): 1–14.

3. A. Scharlach, "Introduction: Why America's Cities and Towns Need to Be More 'Aging Friendly,'" *Generations: Journal of the American Society on Aging* 33, no. 2 (2009): 5–11.

4. Andrew E. Scharlach, Roxanne Kellam, Natasha Ong, Aeran Baskin, Cara Goldstein, and Patrick J. Fox, "Cultural Attitudes and Caregiver Service Use: Lessons from Focus Groups with Racially and Ethni-

cally Diverse Family Caregivers," *Journal of Gerontological Social Work* 47, no. 1–2 (2006): 133–56.

5. Peter Fitzgerald, Andy Coburn, and Sheryl K. Dwyer, "Expanding Rural Elder Care Options: Models That Work," *Proceedings from the 2008 Rural Long Term Care: Access and Options Workshop*, http://www.ruralcare.org/documents/Rural%20LT%20Care%202008%20FINAL.pdf.

6. Harriet L. Komisar and Lee Shirey Thompson, "National Spending for Long-Term Care," *Georgetown University Long-Term Care Financing Project*, http://ltc.georgetown.edu/pdfs/whopays2006.pdf.

7. Ari Houser, Wendy Fox-Grage, and Mary Jo

Gibson, *Across the States in 2009: Profiles of Long-Term Care and Independent Living* (Washington, DC: AARP Public Policy Institute, 2009), http://www .aarp.org/research/longtermcare/trends/d19105 _2008_ats.html.

8. Carol V. O'Shaughnessy, "National Spending for Long-Term Services and Supports" (George Washington University National Health Policy Forum, Washington, DC, 2010), http://www.nhpf.org/library/the -basics/Basics_LongTermServicesSupports_04-30-10 .pdf.

9. Cynthia Shirk, "Rebalancing Long-Term Care: The Role of the Medicaid HCBS Waiver Program" (George Washington University National Health Policy Forum, Washington, DC, 2006), http://www.nhpf .org/library/background-papers/BP_HCBS.Waivers _03-03-06.pdf.

10. Centers for Medicaid and Medicare Services, http://www.cms.hhs.gov/DeficitReductionAct/20 _MFP.asp.

11. Ibid.

12. O'Shaughnessy, "National Spending for Long-Term Services and Supports."

13. Audra T. Wenzlow and Debra J. Lipson, "Transitioning Medicaid Enrollees from Institutions to the Community: Number of People Eligible and Number of Transitions Targeted under Money Follows the Person (MFP)," *The National Evaluation of the Money Follows the Person Demonstration Grant Program, Reports from the Field #1* (Ann Arbor, MI: Mathematica Policy Research, 2009).

14. Michael Glynn, *Accessibility, Affordability, and Choice: Smart Growth and the "Money Follows the Person" Demonstration* (Ann Arbor: University of Michigan, 2010).

15. Ibid.

16. Patient Protection and Affordable Care Act of 2010, H.R. 3590 (Public Law 111–148, Sec. 3024), 111th Congress (2010).

17. Steven H. Zarit et al., "Patterns of Formal and Informal Long Term Care in the United States and Sweden," *AARP Andrus Foundation Final Report* (State College: Pennsylvania State University, 1998).

18. Dorothy D. Dunlop, Jing Song, Larry M. Manheim, Martha L. Daviglus, and Rowland W. Chang, "Racial/Ethnic Differences in the Development of Disability among Older Adults," *American Journal of Public Health* 97 (2007): 2209.

19. Vicki A. Freedman and Linda G. Martin, "The Role of Education in Explaining and Forecasting Trends in Functional Limitations among Older Americans," *Demography* 36 (1999): 461.

20. John Mirowsky and Catherine E. Ross, "Socioeconomic Status and Subjective Life Expectancy," *Social Psychology Quarterly* 63 (2000): 133.

21. Larry Polivka and Helen Zayac, "The Aging Network and Managed Long-Term Care," *The Gerontologist* 48, no. 5 (2008): 564–72.

22. Ibid.

23. Centers for Medicare and Medicaid Services, "Overview Medicaid State Waiver Program Demonstration Projects—General Information," http://www .cms.hhs.gov/MedicaidStWaivProgDemoPGI.

24. Lynn Friss Feinberg, "Family Caregiving in an Aging America: A National Perspective" (Third National Conference for Caregiving Coalitions, March 18, 2009).

25. *Valuing the Invaluable: A New Look at the Economic Value of Family Caregiving* (Washington, DC: AARP Public Policy Institute, 2006).

26. National Alliance for Caregiving and AARP, *Caregiving in the US*, http://www.caregiving.org/data /Caregiving_in_the_US_2009_full_report.pdf.

27. Rosalynn Carter Institute for Caregiving, "What Makes a Caregiver Program Effective," http:// www.rosalynncarter.org.

28. Jensen Law Office, "Home Health Agency Care," http://www.jensenestatelaw.com/articles /elder-law/60-home-health-agency-care.

29. Lauren Harris-Kojetin, Debra Lipson, Jean Fielding, Kristen Kiefer, and Robyn I. Stone, "Recent Findings on Frontline Long-Term Care Workers: A Research Synthesis 1999–2003," http://www.ohca .com/workforce_center/docs/Recent_Findings_on _Frontline_ LTC_Workers.pdf.

30. Rhonda J. V. Montgomery, Lynn Holley, Jerome Diechert, and Karl Kosloski, "A Profile of Home Care Workers from the 2000 Census: How It Changes What We Know," *The Gerontologist* 45 (2005): 593.

31. US Bureau of Labor Statistics, "Chart Book: Occupational Employment and Wages, May 2007," http://stats.bls.gov/oes/2007/may/chartbook.htm.

32. Debra Lipson and Carol Regan, "Health Insurance Coverage for Direct Care Workers: Riding Out the Storm" (Issue Brief No. 3, Better Jobs Better Care), http://www.bjbc.org/content/docs/BJBCIssue BriefNo3.pdf.

33. http://www.silverride.com.

34. Centers for Medicare and Medicaid Services, "Overview Medicaid State Waiver Program Demonstration Projects," http://www.cms.hhs.gov/Medicaid StWaivProgDemoPGI.

35. A. E. Benjamin, R. Matthias, and T. M. Franke, "Comparing Consumer-Directed and Agency Models for Providing Supportive Services at Home," *Health Services Research* 35, 351–66.

36. Barbara Lepidus Carlson et al., "Effects of Cash and Counseling on Personal Care and Well-Being," *Health Services Research* 42, 467 (2007).

37. National PACE Association, "What Is PACE?" http://www.npaonline.org/website/article.asp?id=12.

38. Ibid.

39. Ibid.

HOMES

Increasingly, health and aging experts are adding another set of societal actions to the compression of morbidity agenda—namely, the redesign of physical environments to facilitate wellness, healthy activity, social engagement, and self-reliance. A place to live that is physically manageable and emotionally uplifting is connected with independence, peace of mind, and self-improvement. Support systems can be added to existing homes or built into new homes to help people remain safe, mobile, self-reliant, fit, and strong.

There are practical steps that will improve aging in place by properly adapting home environments. Home assessments can be used to determine which home improvements are needed to address particular aspects of normal aging. The minimum design standards are called visitability. Universal design is an even higher standard. Single- or multifamily homes can meet the needs of older adults if these homes are properly adapted to people's changing needs over time. The goal should be to support communities in which older people can choose from a variety of types of homes: single-family and multifamily units, rentals, and owner-occupied homes.

New technologies for the home are of great help to older people and their families, but these technologies must be affordable and respectful of an individual's need for privacy.

This part of the book provides case studies of remodeling and new home construction. Trained professionals, such as remodeling contractors, interior designers, and architects, can help families plan and construct needed improvements. With professional advice, a home that is suitable for aging in place can be beautiful as well as affordable.

Chapter 7

The Home Environment and Aging

Esther Greenhouse

Introduction

In adapting homes for aging in place, there are a number of basic concepts that are critical to include:

- An understanding of the physical and cognitive changes associated with normal aging
- Knowledge of the concept of "environmental press," which calls attention to the fit between the built environment and the person, including changes of normal aging
- The concept of universal design in housing environments, particularly with regard to aging
- Visitability as an alternative way of modifying homes and apartments across the country for aging in place
- Awareness of the degree to which assistive technology has influenced aging in place and the impact it will have in the future
- The training that is required to translate the concepts of universal design and visitability into reality—in particular, the Certified Aging-in-Place Specialist (CAPS) certification program and American Society of Interior Designers (ASID) and American Institute of Architects (AIA) programs
- The assessment tools and checklists that are important in evaluating homes with regard to aging in place

ESTHER GREENHOUSE is an environmental gerontologist, a professional who specializes in how the built environment affects the functioning and well-being of older adults. She received her MS and BS degrees from Cornell University's Department of Design and Environmental Analysis, where she has been a researcher and lecturer. A former interior designer, she is an instructor in the NAHB's CAPS program and has been a national speaker for CAPS.

Changes Associated with Normal Aging

Understanding the changes associated with aging—both physical and cognitive—is essential for planning aging in place.

PHYSICAL CHANGES

Data for the average US adult population suggest that there is a steady decline in most measures of physical function after reaching peak values in the mid- to late twenties.[1] For example, a person's maximal ability to perform activities such as running or biking (i.e., aerobic capacity) declines approximately 10 percent per decade after age twenty-five.[2] Strength is initially more stable, with losses of only about 10 percent between age twenty-five and age fifty, but then the changes accelerate, with losses in the range of 15 to 30 percent per decade after age fifty.[3]

Neurological changes can affect the ability to generate force quickly, resulting in a slowing of reaction time with age. Therefore, of particular concern for older adults is the loss of power that is necessary for critical activities of daily living such as climbing stairs, lifting objects, catching oneself during a fall, or getting out of a chair. It is estimated that, on average, a twenty-year-old uses 20 percent of his or her strength to get out of a chair, whereas an eighty-year-old uses 80 percent of his or her strength.[4] Since these represent average numbers, it is important for those who value their independence to try to be on the "positive" side of these averages. When it takes more than 100 percent effort to get out of a chair or when a person's aerobic capacity reaches a critically low threshold of disability, independence is often lost.

As a group, women are more at risk of physical disability with aging because they tend to have lower peak values early in life and tend to live longer than men, prolonging the period of functional loss. Physical activity early in life can increase peak values, and continued activity throughout the life span can change the trajectory of aging in a way that delays or prevents the loss of independence.

It is important to remember that there is a huge variability among individuals at every age. Research over the past several decades has demonstrated the powerful influence of lifestyle factors on the age-associated changes that were once considered to be an inevitable part of aging per se.

Table 7.1 displays the normal physiological aspects of aging and their interaction with the built environment. The table outlines the pitfalls of the traditional home environment with regard to aging in place and points out the improvements that can be made to home environments to assist older people.

COGNITIVE DECLINE

The US Centers for Disease Control and Prevention define cognition as "a combination of mental processes that includes the ability to learn new things,

Age-related physiological changes	Traditional environment	Enabling environmental response
Vision: reduced pupil size, need for more light	Insufficient amount of light provided	Provide light 4× greater than typical; use a variety of light sources: ambient/general as well as task
Reduced light/ dark adaptation	Usually limited options: either intense light or no light; night lights are beneficial, but usually do not provide enough illumination in terms of quantity and area	Provide options for low light levels (particularly blue light to avoid disruption of circadian rhythms) for nighttime use; consider transitional light levels from space to space
Increased sensitivity to glare	Exposed windows at the end of dark hallways can disable with glare; unshielded bulbs and recessed cans cause direct and indirect glare, often making floors look uneven	Avoid light sources at eye level; use bulbs that are shielded by opaque covers
Decreased contrast sensitivity	Lack of contrast between surfaces in critical areas such as kitchens and bathrooms may cause residents to trip or fall	Use contrasting colors, particularly to denote changes in level
Changes in hearing: hearing loss, loss of particular frequencies, decreased ability to discriminate	Traditional doorbells and smoke detectors may not be heard; environments with many hard surfaces may provide a great deal of background noise, particularly for users of certain types of hearing aids	Consider softer surfaces, such as low-pile carpeting; provide visual cues for auditory information: e.g., a visual signal to complement the doorbell or smoke detector
Decreased stamina	Ascending/descending stairs, standing in the kitchen for meal prep, can cause avoidable fatigue	Create opportunities to sit for tasks, such as a seated-height work surface in the kitchen and the bathroom
Decreased balance	Disabling lighting, throw rugs, lack of handrails and grab bars, lack of places to stop and rest, changes in level, all may lead to preventable falls when combined with a decrease in balance	A variety of factors: lighting, handrails, grab bars, minimal level changes, contrasting colors, removal of tripping hazards such as throw rugs, electrical cords, and clutter
Difficulty walking	Ascending/descending stairs, stepping over thresholds, getting in/out of tub or shower with lip, stepping into/out of house	Provide all the necessities on one level: bedroom, bathroom, laundry, kitchen; avoid level changes even with thresholds when possible, at least one zero-step entry to residence
Loss of muscle strength in legs and arms	Toilet low to floor, bookshelves at eye level, lifting required for cabinets/storage	Higher toilet makes sitting and standing easier, build shelves waist to chest level, incorporate assistive devices for lifting
Reduced tactile sensitivity	No redundancies provided	Provide additional information in the form of significant textures and/or nontactile information
Reduced response time	No accommodation	Provide safety features such as water temperature surge protectors

Table 7.1 Aging and the environment. Source: Courtesy of Esther Greenhouse.

intuition, judgment, language, and remembering."[5] With cognitive impairment, mental challenges can affect the ability to perform activities of daily living. The causes of cognitive impairment can be as varied as Alzheimer's disease and other dementias, as well as conditions such as stroke and traumatic brain injury. Some causes of cognitive impairment are related to treatable health issues (e.g., side effects from medication, vitamin B_{12} deficiency, infections, and depression), while other conditions cannot be reversed.

How cognitive decline affects an individual's ability to live independently can vary markedly. Cognitive decline may have an impact on an individual's self-care abilities, even if the home has been renovated and made as accessible as possible. Common problems related to cognitive decline include meeting the needs of activities of daily living, such as meal preparation, medication management, and money management. Memory problems can be problematic in terms of recognizing callers on the telephone or visitors at the door. The intersection of cognitive decline with physical decline can make what once were manageable issues insurmountable, and can fundamentally affect an individual's ability to age in place. As is true of physical decline, cognitive decline is highly variable among individuals.

Environmental Press

In 1973, M. Powell Lawton and Lucille Nahemow's adaptation model[6] explored various facets of "environmental press," proposing that there is a level of fit between a user and his or her environment and that, as functional capacity diminishes, the effects of the environment (press) are more pronounced.[7] Optimum fit is the level at which the environment places demands on an individual within his or her range of abilities:

Good Fit = Independence
Poor Fit = Decline

This concept is of particular importance to people with disabilities or difficulties in functioning. It is of great importance to the elderly because an enabling environment can help them function at the highest

Older man at home. Photograph by Rebecca Robinson.

level possible.[8] An environment that provides obstacles to functioning will actually hasten the decline of remaining abilities.[9]

Falling, with its associated injuries, is an important issue to be addressed in older people's environments. Among people aged sixty-five and older, falls are the leading cause of injury and death and the most common cause of nonfatal injuries and hospital admissions for trauma.[10] Many programs across the country are addressing this issue, with three major prevention strategies: improving balance through exercise; monitoring medication to reduce side effects and drug interactions; and making home environments safer by reducing tripping hazards and adding helpful modifications such as grab bars, railings, and improved lighting.

Universal Design

The early 1980s brought the birth of universal design envisioned by the late Ronald L. Mace, architect and founder of the Center for Universal Design at North Carolina State University. An architect and wheelchair user, Mace was also instrumental in the adoption of the Americans with Disabilities Act (ADA) and the Americans with Disabilities Act Accessibility Guidelines (ADAAG).

According to the center's website, "Ron . . . coined the term 'universal design' to describe the concept of designing all products and the built environment to be aesthetic and usable to the greatest extent possible by everyone, regardless of their age, ability, or status in life."[11] Over the years, his substantial work and significant influence slowly but certainly revolutionized the design and use of many products and aspects of the built environment.

The term "universal design" has become widely used and recognized by both professionals and consumers, but it is often misunderstood. People often equate it with "disability," wheelchair use, and unsightly grab bars, when the point of the concept is embodied in the name itself. People with disabilities, including wheelchair users, benefit from universal design. In addition, universal design also makes daily functioning easier for the general population. Consider the lever door handle, which could be considered the poster child of universal design. Because the lever door handle can open a door with a minimum amount of pressure, a wide range of users and abilities (ranging from mothers carrying a child to people with reduced strength to anyone carrying groceries) benefit daily from its simple, yet powerful design. Kitchen and other home products can also be designed according to the principles of universal design and can help with cognitive as well as physical decline. Such products emphasize perceptible information and instructions such as large-font temperature display numbers on stoves and larger clock faces. These are useful aids for people of all ages.

The key principles of universal design include the following:

- *Equitable use:* Proper site grading, elevated garage floors, entryway weather protection, no-step entry, low thresholds, wide doorways and walkways, minimum-width hallways with sufficient turn radius, smooth, unobstructed traverses, and reachable circuit breakers. Installation of controls, telephone jacks, computer jacks, electrical outlets, wall switches, alarm systems, lighted doorbells, and wide-angle viewers and/or video monitors at proper height.
- *Flexibility in use:* Wall blocking to accommodate future needs, grab bars, shower seats, roll-in showers, center-graded drains, easy-use multidirectional and multifunctional shower controls, transfer access, faucets, vanities, electrical wiring to support medical equipment, and external wiring with easy-access receptacles.
- *Simple and intuitive products:* Products with intuitive features with large symbols for ease of reading along with distinctive color contrast.
- *Perceptible information:* Energy-saving illumination, contrast in flooring, demarking traffic pathways and traffic patterns.
- *Tolerance for error:* Strategically placed fire extinguishers (especially near the stove) and using materials with no/low volatile organic compounds (VOCs).
- *Low physical effort:* Lever-type handles for swinging doors, automatic garage door openers, automatic power door openers (where pragmatic), easy-grip handles for nonswinging doors and cabinets, and automated closet shelving.
- *Size and space:* Full-turn radius of five feet in hallways, bathrooms, bedrooms, kitchen, and walk-in closets. Use of "lazy Susan" products for corner cabinetry. Increased use of open floor plans.[12]

Visitability

Visitability is a movement that asks a practical and fundamental question: what are the minimum features or components needed to make houses accessible to people with mobility impairments?

The concept of visitability has been gaining ground in the past few years. Coming out of disability rights advocacy, primarily under the leadership of Eleanor Smith and the organization Concrete Change, visitability is resulting in thousands of homes that meet minimum levels of accessibility.[13]

Visitability advocates propose that three simple changes to home design can transform the experiences of older adults and people with disabilities who are otherwise isolated by disabling architecture. The three components of visitability are one zero-step entrance, wider doors (at least thirty-two inches) and wider hallways, and at least a half bathroom on the ground floor. The concept aims to do for residential homes what federal accessibility standards have done for commercial buildings, while maintaining flexibility for designers and homeowners.

Voluntary and mandatory visitability programs have begun across the United States since the initial efforts of Concrete Change and Habitat for Humanity in Atlanta in the late 1980s. Research is needed to compare the successes of voluntary and mandatory policies and to identify other design philosophies that have parallel goals to those of visitability. In some cases, such as Pima County, Arizona, visitability laws pertain to all new construction.[14] In other areas, visitability laws only apply to new housing that receives state or federal funding.

There is often a misconception that building for visitability will significantly increase the cost of a home, but this is not necessarily the case. Studies have found that when visitability features are included from the outset, the additional cost per house is approximately $100 to $600, compared to $700 for widening one interior door in an existing home.[15] A home that meets minimum levels of accessibility should be more marketable to an additional pool of possible homebuyers, offering a return on the initial investment. It is important to remember that visitability is a minimum standard. Visitability does not ensure that all needs of frail older people are met or that they will be able to age in place without additional supports. Visitability is, in other words, a helpful start.

Assistive Technology

Products that assist older people have been on the market for some time, beginning with the most basic portable aids like Good Grips ergonomic kitchen tools and cooking products, "grabbers" for reaching items on the floor or on high shelves, and walkers for stability. Environmental aids include grab bars and ramps that can help to maintain or improve daily function. Motorized wheelchairs, scooters, and home elevators or lifts provide another level of support. Personal emergency response systems, which alert a monitoring station in the event of a fall, are also available.

Researchers have described and analyzed national trends in assistive technologies, and a study by Vicki A. Freedman and her colleagues found that shifts of older people toward assistive technologies accounted for half of the decline in the number of people dependent on personal care from 1992 to 2001.[16]

Dramatic increases in the aging population are encouraging the exploration of services and technologies for health monitoring. Companies are acting quickly in moving technology from the laboratory to the home, which has resulted in an explosion of products that range from specific activity checking to full-time monitoring. The LeadingAge Center for Aging Services Technologies (CAST) is working to develop, evaluate, and speed adoption of these technologies.[17] Recent trends in technology are monitored online in the Aging in Place Technology Watch Newsletter, including home automation technology, mobile health applications, caregiver tools, personal emergency response systems, and the like.[18]

The following list illustrates the breadth of offerings available in 2010:

MedMinder (www.medminder.com): An instrumented pillbox to monitor if and when medication is taken

Aerotel Medical Systems (www.aerotel.com): Mobile and home-based devices that monitor critical medical information (e.g., blood pressure, electrical activity of the heart as measured by an electrocardiogram [EKG], blood glucose) and transmit them to remote caregivers

QuietCare (www.quietcaresystems.com): A motion sensor–based system that measures activity levels in the home

People Track USA (www.peopletrackusa.com): GPS-based devices that can summon help or allow family members to locate one another at any time

Bosch Healthcare (www.bosch-telehealth.com): Health Buddy, a management system used extensively by the US Department of Veterans Affairs (VA)

Training

There are a number of major training programs that should be highlighted. These initiatives educate interior designers, builders, architects, and contractors about design for aging in place.

CERTIFIED AGING-IN-PLACE SPECIALIST

In 2000, AARP approached the National Association of Home Builders (NAHB) to create the Certified Aging-in-Place Specialist program, commonly known as CAPS. Since its inception in 2001, thousands of builders, designers, occupational therapists, physical therapists, reverse mortgage specialists, realtors, and many other professionals have become CAPS specialists. CAPS professionals use their knowledge to help make homes accessible for people with disabilities, such as returning war veterans, people with progressive conditions, and those whose abilities have changed due to a fall, a stroke, or normal aging.

Professionals who earn the CAPS designation are required to complete three day-long classes.[19] The first day sets the stage by examining the aging-in-place population, a diverse group composed of three market segments: aging in place without urgent needs, aging in place with progressive condition-based needs, and aging in place with traumatic change needs. Also covered are demographic data, types of design, and sensory and ability changes typical of these groups. The second day emphasizes collaboration between health care professionals, such as occupational therapists (OTs), and building professionals. Instructors use such activities as sensitivity training and group redesign of a floor plan, employing the knowledge gained. The final class is in business management. Upon completion of the CAPS curriculum, designees receive a professional certification, which requires compliance with a code of ethics, as well as continuing education in the form of seminars, classes, trade show and conference attendance, and community service.

AMERICAN SOCIETY OF INTERIOR DESIGNERS: DESIGN FOR ACTIVE AGING

The American Society of Interior Designers (ASID) has taken several proactive steps to ensure that members are well educated to meet the needs of seniors wishing to age in place. It has published a very informative report, "Home for a Lifetime: Interior Design for Active Living," which is an excellent overview.[20] The ASID's educational components include a series of articles and reports that serve as education modules regarding design for various needs and abilities. They cover topics such as universal design, lighting, aging, green design, removal of barriers, wellness and design, and acoustics and hearing. Most of these modules are written by ASID Design for Aging Council members, but they also include information from outside expert sources. For example, the acoustics module contains several links concerning hearing loss and contact information for supportive and professional groups. The links provide specific solutions designers can employ, such as using a flashing light in conjunction with an auditory doorbell. The modules contain explanations of biophysical changes, as well as specifics for appropriate design interventions. For example, while designers should provide seniors with higher light levels to account for decreases in pupil size, the light sources must be shielded to minimize seniors' heightened sensitivity to glare.

AMERICAN INSTITUTE OF ARCHITECTS

The American Institute of Architects (AIA) has a Design for Aging program that publishes articles and guidelines in an electronic format called Blueprints for Senior Living.[21] The program establishes Design for Aging committees at AIA branches throughout the country to educate architects and planners. Continuing education is offered on environments for aging, and awards are made annually to highlight model senior housing solutions. Some of the courses offered in the program include Trending Green in Senior Living, Adult Day Care, Aging in Place and Universal Design, and Supportive Technology and Design for Healthy Aging.

Assessment Tools and Checklists

There are a number of assessment tools that have been developed to aid individuals in assessing their potential home design and day-to-day mobility problems. More such tools are needed. Broad dissemination of these assessments will be very helpful in meeting the needs of those aging in place.

One example tool, the Gerontological Environmental Modifications (GEM)

Environmental Assessment, has been developed by the Division of Geriatrics and Gerontology at the Weill Medical College of Cornell University. The assessment covers a broad range of environmental features, including accessibility, furniture, flooring, and lighting.[22]

The tool consists of a series of yes/no questions. For those answered "yes," the user is given a checklist of possible solutions. For example, the following questions are part of the bedroom evaluation:[23]

Sitting on edge of bed, client's thighs are parallel with floor, with feet firmly on floor Suggestions: Lower bed: remove castors __ cut wooden frame __ order new 3" frame __ Raise bed: new 7" frame __ leg extenders __ other __	Y __ N __ NA __
Client has a handle to help get in and out of bed if needed (T) Suggestions: New handrail __ other __	Y __ N __ NA __

Conclusion

The following chapters include the basic concepts of universal design and visitability and apply them to interior design, renovation, new construction, and technological advances. We address issues of affordability, practicality, and replicability and feature models for aging in place. It is important to know that not every home adaptation must be extensive or expensive. We also address the professional training that is needed and the assessment tools that are most helpful.

Notes

1. M. D. Fitzgerald, H. Tanaka, Z. V. Tran, and D. R. Seals, "Age-Related Declines in Maximal Aerobic Capacity in Regularly Exercising vs. Sedentary Women: A Meta-analysis," *Journal of Applied Physiology* 38, no. 1 (1997): 160–65.

2. A. E. Pimentel, C. L. Gentile, H. Tanaka, D. R. Seals, and P. E. Gates, "Greater Rate of Decline in Maximal Aerobic Capacity with Age in Endurance-Trained Than in Sedentary Men," *Journal of Applied Physiology* 94, no. 6 (2003): 2406–13.

3. F. W. Booth, S. H. Weeden, and B. S. Tseng, "Effect of Aging on Human Skeletal Muscle and Motor Function," *Medical Science Sports Exercise* 26, no. 5 (1994): 556–60.

4. Interview with Dr. Anne Friedlander, former director of the mobility division at the Stanford Center on Longevity; consulting professor, Program in Human Biology at Stanford University; and vice president of ConnectWell.

5. Centers for Disease Control and Prevention,

"Healthy Brain Initiative," http://www.cdc.gov/aging/healthybrain.

6. M. P. Lawton and L. Nahemow, "Ecology and the Aging Process," in *The Psychology of Adult Development and Aging*, ed. C. Eisdorfer and M. P. Lawton (Washington, DC: American Psychological Association, 1973).

7. S. Howell, "Built Space, The Mystery Variable in Health and Aging," in *Advances in Environmental Psychology*, vol. 4, *Environment and Health*, ed. A. Baum and J. Singer (Hillsdale, NJ: Erlbaum, 1982).

8. W. Ittleson, H. Proshansky, L. Rivlin, and G. Winkel, *An Introduction to Environmental Psychology* (New York: Holt, Reinhart and Winston, 1974).

9. L. G. Hiatt, "The Environment's Role in the Total Well-Being of the Older Person," in *Well-Being and the Elderly: An Holistic View*, ed. G. G. Magan and E. L. Haught (Washington, DC: American Association of Homes for the Aging, 1986).

10. National Center for Injury Prevention and

Control, Centers for Disease Control and Prevention, "Web-Based Injury Statistics Query and Reporting System (WISQARS)," http://www.cdc.gov/homeand recreationalsafety/falls.

11. Center for Universal Design, North Carolina State University, "About the Center: Ronald L. Mace," http://www.ncsu.edu/ncsu/design/cud/about_us /usronmace.htm.

12. Center for Universal Design, North Carolina State University, "Welcome!" http://www.ncsu.edu /www/ncsu/design/sod5/cud.

13. Concrete Change, "Home Page," http:// concretechange.org.accuwebhosting.biz.

14. Center for an Accessible Society, "Pima County Visitability Ordinance," http://www.acces siblesociety.org/topics/housing/pimacoruling.html.

15. Concrete Change, "The Costs of NOT Changing," http://www.concretechange.org/construction _nochange.aspx.

16. V. Freedman, E. Agree, L. Martin, and J. Cornman, "Trends in the Use of Assistive Technology and Personal Care for Late-Life Disability, 1992–2001," *The Gerontologist* 46, no. 1 (2006): 124–27.

17. www.aahsa.org/cast.aspx.

18. Brian Dolan, "Revisiting Ten Aging in Place Trends," mobihealthnews.com, http://mobihealth news.com/8490/revisiting-ten-aging-in-place -trends.

19. National Association of Home Builders, "Certified Aging-in-Place Specialist (CAPS)," http://www .nahb.org/category.aspx?sectionID=686.

20. American Society of Interior Designers, "Home for a Lifetime: Interior Design for Active Aging," http://www.asid.org/NR/rdonlyres/4C5EB492 -1BCE-498C-AB8F-5B035C9D2226/0/HomeforaLifetime.

21. American Institute of Architects, "Design for Aging," http://network.aia.org/AIA/DesignforAging /Home/Default.aspx.

22. Rosemary Bakker, "GEM Environmental Assessment," http://www.environmentalgeriatrics.com /pdf/enviro_assessment.pdf.

23. Ibid.

Chapter 8

Technology Solutions

Eric Dishman

Introduction

Since witnessing the terrible impact of my grandmother's Alzheimer's disease on our extended family when I was a sixteen-year-old growing up in North Carolina, I have wondered if there is a better way to help families age in place and whether technology might help. Grandma seemed to lose her soul when the family had to take away her car. She could no longer sell her Avon cosmetics to the neighbors—which was her excuse to get out into the community and socialize. Her collection of doctors never acted as a team, each expert prescribing medications that none of the others knew about, leaving her often in more confusion from the drug interactions than from the disease. Our lives were in constant turmoil as we drove the fifty miles to her home to see if she had left the stove on or the bathtub water running. It was a living hell to get her in the car for a routine doctor's visit—a visit that, frankly, could have been done by phone much of the time.

What might we have done differently? What roles might technology play in enabling seniors to maintain a sense of purpose, a connection to professional and family caregivers, and the freedom to go about their daily lives in their homes and communities, even as age-related conditions threaten everything from muscles to memories? And how might our notions of "neighborhood" and "community" and "health care" change if we could make such inventions widely available and affordable for everyone?

ERIC DISHMAN is director of health innovation and policy for Intel's Digital Health Group. He is founder of the product research and innovation team responsible for driving Intel's worldwide activities and is an Intel Fellow. He has cofounded some of the world's largest research and policy organizations, including the Technology Research for Independent Living (TRIL) Centre, the LeadingAge Center for Aging Services Technologies (CAST), and the Oregon Center for Aging and Technology (ORCATECH). He has a BA from the University of North Carolina in English, speech communication, and drama, and an MS from Southern Illinois University in speech communication.

I care greatly about people, not about technology. Yet I believe that new technologies are needed to help us care for people, especially older people, in the midst of this era of global aging. It is imperative that our society imagine, invent, and invest in a future that brings forth our best technologies to reinvent notions of care for the nearly 1.5 billion people aged sixty-five and above who will inhabit the planet by the middle of the century.[1] Think of these as "gray technologies" intended to address issues related to global aging. Much as society is inventing "green technologies" to address global warming, we need affordable and replicable technologies that enable and require new roles for each of us, our families, and our institutions.

I will share information about these gray technologies and the new relationships and roles they demand, from Intel Corporation's more than ten years of ethnographic and engineering research to bring care to the home and community.[2] I have had the privilege of leading the Intel team of social scientists, clinicians, engineers, and designers who have visited and studied more than one thousand elderly households in twenty countries to inspire and inform our ideas. And we have piloted dozens of prototypes in hundreds of homes over the years, especially with our university collaborators at the Technology Research for Independent Living (TRIL) Centre (www.trilcentre.org) near Dublin, Ireland, and the Oregon Center for Aging and Technology, or ORCATECH (www.orcatech.org), near Portland, Oregon. Across this body of work, three areas of opportunity emerge for technological help:

1. Social engagement and support for seniors facing an epidemic of isolation
2. Prevention of—and early intervention for—illness and injury before it becomes catastrophic
3. Monitoring and management of chronic disease from the home, not the hospital bed

Our research findings come at a critical moment, as those involved in health care reform efforts in the United States and abroad wrestle with how to deliver more and higher-quality care to more people, without increasing costs. It will become increasingly important to make the home a major locus of care, from diagnosis to delivery. We simply won't have the bed space, dollars, or workforce of doctors, nurses, and medical assistants available to address the demands of global aging. We must use technologies and training in our communities to enlist seniors, their families, and neighbors in order to bring health care home. As we explore new technologies, it will be critical to develop affordable assistance to seniors, so that we save dollars that would otherwise have been spent on costly health care interventions.

Technologies for Social Engagement and a Sense of Purpose

From our fieldwork at Intel over the last decade, it has become clear that there is an epidemic of isolation among older people in our society. It comes from multiple factors: the death of friends and family members, the decline in mobility or the inability to drive, the lack of social forums for seniors who live alone, and memory loss that may make name recognition difficult and social engagement embarrassing. This pervasive loneliness is deadly and expensive. Once the social support system has declined, so goes the health of many people. Loneliness—and the lack of purpose that motivates someone to get up in the morning—often spirals into depression and exacerbates other chronic conditions. Without a rich web of neighbors, family members, or friends to help engage the mind and soul of someone living alone, people are forced to rely upon expensive professional care or even institutionalization.

Social health is so important that we often see it as a bigger variable in establishing the overall health and happiness of a household than financial means: being "socially rich" trumps being "financially rich." Seniors who have "porous" social boundaries—those who are open to visits from a wide range of people—tend to do much better than those with "impermeable" boundaries or moatlike behavior—where no one ever knocks on the door or calls. It is in every community's best interest to help maintain and build up social networks for seniors.

Independent living technologies can help us monitor and promote social health, especially for seniors living alone, whose caregiving networks often have no idea just how lonely they can be. We built an early prototype called the "social health support system" (SHSS) at Intel, using off-the-shelf motion sensors and a small device placed on the phone to measure changes in social health.[3] We then used the data collected for applications that enabled seniors—even those in the early stages of memory loss—to stay engaged. This system fed data back to the seniors and, if they chose, to family members and neighbors in their care network about the frequency of visitors to the home and the amount of time that they spent on the phone.

When we first flipped on the SHSS switch in a couple of dozen homes in Las Vegas, Nevada, and Portland, Oregon, the families inevitably called to complain: "Your system is broken—the display says my father hasn't had a visitor or phone call in six days!" Sharing these data between the senior's home and his or her care network provided an immediate wakeup call for family members. These caregivers lived busy, socially saturated lives with cell phones, email, coworkers, and friends surrounding them much of the day. They could not imagine that their parents would go an entire week—sometimes more—without any social contact whatsoever. The technology helped bridge the distance and the generation gap between senior and caregiver, raising awareness and connectivity between the two.

Over many months, these simple technologies showed both the seniors and the caregivers their patterns of "social health"—a behavioral "vital sign"—that forecasted imminent health declines upon registering a major drop-off in social activity compared to the normal amount. Caregivers could check in to see if depression, cognitive decline, or a physical problem was emerging, or at least be more proactive about trying to visit or call. Longer term, as we have been testing these kinds of systems in hundreds of homes, we have seen that social health sensing systems might help detect and differentiate the onset of dementia or other cognitive problems that only such unobtrusive, home-based technologies could pick up.

But could these technologies actually help someone struggling with memory loss to stay socially engaged? We studied many seniors in the early to moderate stages of dementia who were embarrassed or afraid to answer a ringing phone or a knock at the front door because they might confuse complete strangers with long-time friends or even a spouse. We built and tested several graphical interfaces displayed next to the landline phone in these households. One, which a study participant referred to as "Caller ID on steroids," simply displayed the name, photo, brief bio ("this is your best friend of thirty years calling"), and brief history of the prior conversation ("you spoke yesterday about going to the baseball game tonight"). This feature helped the seniors either to remember the caller or to have enough confidence to answer the phone and "fake it" with the "cheat sheet" on their screen until other cues in the conversation would clue them in to who the person on the other end of the line really was.

Another application showed older people how they were doing with a trend line of their social engagement history over the past months. We devised the "social solar system display," which involved placing a photo of the individual at the center of the screen with icons of their key social network (usually no more than six to eight key people) in "orbit" at levels near or far from them based on how much phone time and visits each person had engaged in. One woman in the study jokingly referred to this as the "inheritance detection system," because, as she put it, "the good kids who call Mom are near me on the screen and the bad kids are way out there on the edge." Some of the study participants put sticky notes and other reminders around the house to call or visit a friend, and they could see over the course of a week their success at engaging more as the icons on the edge moved closer to the center.

But technologies offer much more than monitoring social health and reminding people of the names and faces of their loved ones. We need to use them to help connect older people with community members and resources in new ways. For example, our team prototyped a "ride-sharing board" to facilitate social connection and transportation in a rural village in Ireland. Many of the seniors in this community could no longer drive, and without access to public transportation, they felt imprisoned in their homes. There were many other retirees in this community who had cars and drove regularly. So we simply placed global positioning system (GPS) devices on the dashboards of the seniors who still drove and then, with their permission, shared their typical routes (e.g., going to the grocery store in town Tuesday mornings; heading to the pub Thursday evenings) with other seniors who were stuck at home alone. The technology allowed new ways to connect the groups, helping to solve a transportation problem, but, more important, alleviating the crippling loneliness of the homebound and giving the more active elders in the community a sense of purpose and an easy way to "give back" to support others in their town.

As communities enable aging in place, they need to think about what infrastructure is needed to help seniors stay socially engaged and purpose driven. Tomorrow's seniors will demand and require social health technologies to do at least four things:

1. Detect changes or declines in social health as an early warning of more serious problems such as depression or dementia.
2. Provide memory assistance and confidence to those who are challenged to even use their phone or answer their front door.
3. Connect those who are disenfranchised in the community with those who have the ability, time, and desire to "give back."
4. Offer new online forums for sharing one's story, learning new things, or just virtually hanging out with friends or strangers.

BUILDING BRIDGES

The Building Bridges project highlights the opportunity to use social networking technologies for seniors.[a] A phone handset, audio bridge, and online community, combined into an easy-to-use "appliance," opens up new worlds for seniors who are otherwise cut off from each other and society. In this project, seniors schedule live "audio chats"—sort of like the party lines of the early days of telephones—with six to eight remote friends around some topic of the day, such as gardening or sharing stories and digital photos from World War II. Simple touch screen buttons signal to the group that "I want to get a word in"— and the seniors can easily bring in photos or live web cams from around the world, or simply share information about the weather with one another to facilitate conversation. Some have even used this prototype to teach a class on Shakespeare to others "on the network," thus bringing the power of social networking that has been the playground of teenagers and "hipsters" to the needs of an aging population yearning to connect with one another.

[a]J. Wherton and D. Prendergast, "The Building Bridges Project: Involving Older Adults in the Design of a Communication Technology to Support Peer-to-Peer Social Engagement," in *HCI and Usability for e-Inclusion*, ed. A. Holzinger and K. Miesenberger (Berlin: Springer-Verlag, 2009), 111–34.

Building up and bolstering these social networks—online and in person—will help communities save lives and money in profound and surprising ways.

Prevention and Early Intervention for Illness and Injury

As we have studied elderly households, we have gone with people to their doctor's appointments to check up on their diabetes or been with them when they were discharged from the hospital for a painful hip fracture. We have witnessed many unnecessary and costly emergency room visits for what should have been simple phone calls or electronic visits. We have watched as specialists, unconnected by electronic health records or incentives to coordinate care, either over- or mismedicate seniors. We have had to call family members as we, in our fieldwork, have seen early signs of trouble that no doctor or child could witness with an infrequent visit or observation.

Our health systems are imagined, invested in, and incentivized around reactive, crisis-driven response to an illness or injury. As we face global aging and the challenge of paying for this reactive system, we must find ways to change how we deliver care. Communities must begin to shift economic incentives and build infrastructure for prevention and earlier detection. In essence, we need to move from crisis response in a hospital to proactive intervention at home. Technology should be a front-and-center part of that reinvention, particularly technology that is affordable and replicable. A key element to preventive, home-based care for seniors must be systems that provide families, clinicians, and seniors themselves with early awareness of a potential illness or injury before it escalates into a crisis. Early sensor network products—sometimes motion sensors showing patterns of physical activity or bed sensors showing changes in sleep—are already coming onto the market. And our research collaboration with ORCATECH has shown great promise in next-generation monitoring systems to provide early warning based on everything from how fast we walk to the kitchen in the morning to how well or frequently we play an online video game. Monitoring the activities of daily living (ADLs) with inexpensive, unobtrusive sensors and software will provide care teams with what we call "okayness checking" (making sure Mom or Dad's normal routine is doing fine) as well as new "behavioral markers" (which help detect and diagnose the onset of specific diseases).

In one recent ADL-sensing prototype, we placed a simple "shake sensor" on key objects around the apartments of frail seniors who were living alone in an assisted living facility.[4] The data coming from these were helpful to the seniors, their family caregivers (often living hundreds of miles away), and the professional care staff who checked in on them each day. With these "smart tags" placed on key objects, our system could infer whether Mom or Dad was up and out of bed doing their typical

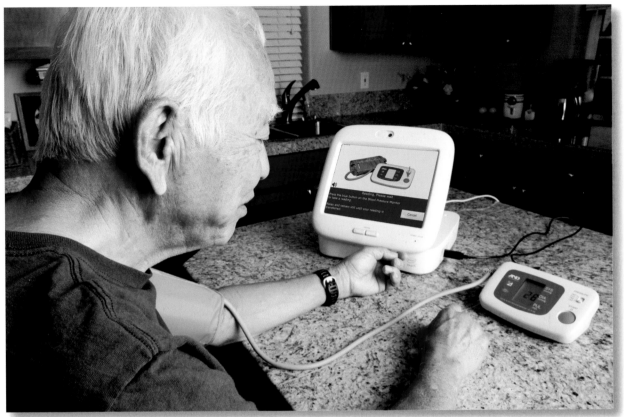

morning routines, getting their regular amount of exercise around the home, fixing meals, or taking their medications. Deviations from these individuals' norms and trend lines showed up as alerts to the seniors (on a simple digital photo display), their chosen family caregivers (via an Internet dashboard), and the staff (with online "autofill" reports).

The seniors in this study relished having a sense of their own progress or an early warning and reminder of declines in key activities they wanted to track, especially exercise and taking medications on time. The family members—whether one or one thousand miles away—got a better sense of the relative "okayness" of their aging parents and knew to check in if Mom seemed inactive or if Dad was missing meals. The care staff was able to better track what ADL assistance was needed (which mattered both for quality reporting and for billing purposes) while spending more time doing hands-on care in the apartment as opposed to documentation and paperwork.

In the future, these technologies will offer more than just monitoring. We have built early prototypes that help seniors with cognitive decline to continue to perform ADLs for and by themselves. The "tea-making assistant" not only prompts a senior to remember to drink some juice or tea upon signs of dehydration but also triggers small "how to" videos created by family members to instruct the senior on making tea in his or her specific kitchen (where the kettle is, how to mix the tea, remembering to turn off the stove). The goal here is to help people complete ADLs on their own as much as possible, without intervening until they really need assistance.

So how might these technologies prevent costly and painful medical procedures in the first place? The "classic" fall at home—which often leads to a major hip fracture or escalates to permanent disability or even death—shows both our society's crisis-driven care paradigm as well as the potential of ADL-monitoring technologies. Falls among seniors in the United States occur in about one out of three people over age sixty-five each year, with costs of the resulting injuries projected to reach potentially more than $50 billion by 2020.[5] Yet our response focuses on reducing falls and fall risks in hospitals, when the majority of those events occur in the home. Could we prevent the majority of falls from ever happening in the first place, perhaps years before they happen?

I am hopeful that we can. Our research collaborators at both TRIL and ORCATECH have been testing a wide range of technologies to look for behavioral markers revealing an increased risk of falling. The "magic carpet" prototype has a grid of inexpensive pressure sensors embedded in a length of hallway carpet or flooring to evaluate changes in seniors' walking speed and stride length to see if we can detect well in advance if they are becoming more unstable on their feet. Another system uses an optical sensor to evaluate "postural sway"—the normal to-and-fro movements all of us have from heel to toe as we stand—which changes as we age. The clinical and home data we have collected so far show different movement "signatures" associated with different medical conditions. This product has helped us to discover the fundamental problems—often muscle mass decline or medication mix—that lead up to a fall and its cascade of drastic consequences and costs.

If we can meaningfully measure changes in motion and steps to discover that someone is becoming more unstable and risky for a fall, what could we do to intervene? The early warning itself might help a doctor to tease out the cause: Dizziness from a medication mix? A cognitive problem showing up? Arthritis setting in? Simply a lack of physical exercise? We believe that many falls occur because of this last reason—lack of exercise—since many seniors lose muscle mass and exercise less as they age. Almost everyone in our studies has heard the news that they should do ten thousand steps a day—which could help dramatically reduce the epidemic of fall-related injuries—but how do we motivate people to do this?

Some years ago, we tested an Internet-connected pedometer that seniors in a continuing care retirement community (CCRC) could wear to help them monitor their daily steps. We weren't getting much sustained interest or walking, except for a few older men who competed with one another. The vast majority of the people in this facility were women who weren't interested in a sports competition. So instead of giving each of them an application to evaluate her own individual steps, we pooled their data into a visualization on a screen at the end of each hallway, showing how the entire group was doing toward a collective goal of hundreds of thousands of steps per week. Pretty soon, neighbors were knocking on the doors of neighbors and urging them to get out and walk, and new habits and social clubs emerged. These self-care technologies and tools—and the online and in-person communities they enable—offer new and creative ways for communities to motivate and sustain good behaviors that will help reduce suffering and expensive medical care over time.

Our communities must get creative in building infrastructure and incentives for preventive care and early intervention if well-supported aging in place is to become a reality for most of us. The biggest challenge is that our society is set up to spend more and more on improved diagnostic scanners or drug therapies for a broken hip, but not on how we might simply prevent the majority of falls from occurring in the first place.

Managing and Monitoring Chronic Disease from Home

The epidemic of chronic disease is omnipresent in the lives of the families we studied, not only in the developed world but in the developing world as well. As a result, communities will need "place shifting" about where chronic care occurs and "person shifting" about who does the lion's share of the care. We will have to learn to care for seniors with chronic disease in the home and with family caregivers and community health workers as much as possible, rather than in overburdened emergency rooms.

Telehealth systems, or what are increasingly becoming known as e-care or electronic care technologies, have been around for decades, but the market for such systems is still quite small. My Intel team has been building and testing e-care prototypes since 1999, with a special focus on seniors managing diabetes, chronic obstructive pulmonary disease (COPD), congestive heart failure, depression, and asthma. The power of these technologies is that they enable many capabilities, discoveries, data types, and interventions that just aren't possible in traditional face-to-face exams.

One of our first prototypes allowed for the capture of classic vital signs like weight, heart rate, blood pressure, and temperature on a regular basis. We had often seen physicians in clinics forced to make fast decisions out of context. Doctors might have to act without *any* data or with, for example, only one blood pressure reading captured in the exam room that was hardly representative of the typical blood pressure trend of that patient the other 99.99 percent of his or her life. The seniors either typed readings into a computer-like hub or, more often, simply used a wired or wireless blood pressure cuff that sent the data automatically to their doctor and alerted the care team when the readings were outside of thresholds the doctor had set. This kind of remote patient monitoring (RPM) is becoming more commonplace, and we find that clinicians like the ability to pinpoint when and where a chronic condition is becoming exacerbated before it turns into an emergency room visit.

Another aspect of e-care technologies that is revolutionizing chronic care is the ability to personalize a care plan for seniors. In another of our systems, the doctor or nurse could set up alerts ("your weight has gone up too rapidly, please call the clinic"), reminders ("please don't drink grapefruit juice when you take this medication"), or even just-in-time patient education (a video on how to use a blood pressure cuff or a recipe for low-salt foods) based on vital signs and survey responses the seniors were taking from home. These seniors had multiple chronic conditions and radically different knowledge about—and abilities to care for—their own conditions, so customizing the care plan was crucial.

With many of these e-care systems, the clinicians can then "reach out" anytime via secure messaging to check in with the seniors or their family members, or via a video "virtual visit" to do an exam immediately. Even the simple connected camera helped the care team get a better sense of the context of care (is Mom's home that is usually neat suddenly a mess today?) as well as the overall wellness (is Dad looking pale and gaunt compared to normal—does Dad just not look "right"?).

One of the biggest challenges in chronic care management is helping seniors to manage often complex medication regimens. Many people we studied took ten or more medications a day, which is a challenge to remember even without cognitive difficulties. Telehealth technologies can help the whole care team, including all the specialists involved in the care of Mom or Dad, know exactly what medications are involved. They can prompt that patient to take just the right pill at just the right moment. Waking up each morning with an alert to today's medication plan, as well as the ability to get customized education (photos of pills, survey questions about side effects, suggestions for what foods to eat), was a lifeline for many of the seniors in our home pilots.

If aging in place is to become feasible, we will need to use the telehealth technologies that are already here—and invent more for tomorrow—to deal with the global epidemic of chronic disease. E-care offers effective, ethical, and economic ways to augment and offload the traditional hospital or clinic visit by:

- Collecting real-world and eventually real-time vital signs and other health data from the home

- Personalizing surveys, educational content, reminders, and alerts for patients based on their own needs, experience with different technologies, and preference for privacy and ease of interruption
- Enabling medication reconciliation, reminding, and self-management in the home of those with even complex regimens
- Facilitating virtual visits and remote encounters that don't require travel to a sometimes crowded and germ-infested clinic

Increasingly, global aging trends will require that these e-care systems feed data and knowledge back not only to highly trained medical experts but also to seniors and patients themselves—and their family and friends who help care for them— who must be trained and empowered to be part of coordinated care teams in the community.

Conclusion and Challenges

I opened this chapter talking about my grandmother's Alzheimer's disease and by saying that I care more for people than technology, yet I have focused much of my time on technology to help us imagine how it might help us cope with and embrace aging. Why are so many of my examples from research and prototypes instead of products? Well, first, I should confess to being a researcher at a technology company: that's what I know about. There are early products on the market, but it's not my place to advertise or represent particular technologies. But even with those, we have to admit that the availability, access, and affordability of these kinds of solutions are still quite limited. I believe that we face significant challenges in this area for a number of reasons.

First, I believe there is an inherent "ageism" in our society. Ageism, which was first identified by the incredible gerontologist, Robert Butler, who died in 2010 and to whom many of us owe our careers in aging, keeps us from focusing on aging in place. We've created a culture obsessed with youth and repulsed by the old, especially when it comes to new technology. To embrace the need for aging-in-place technologies means first embracing the fact that aging, illness, injury, and, yes, death are something to be reckoned with, not ignored. Time is probably on our side on this one, as baby boomers face and embrace these issues and transform what it means to be "old" as they have so many other notions in society like "family" and the "workplace."

Second, we are mired in a self-reinforcing health care economy that is premised entirely upon face-to-face visits as the way to pay the health care bills. Unless and until the financial incentives change to actually diagnose, treat, and care for people in their homes and communities—instead of in hospitals and clinics—

gray technologies for chronic care and independent living will be slow to advance. Health care reform in the United States and in many other countries is slowly changing this system. With significant health care reform, it is possible that e-care can become a viable part of both in-home and in-clinic care. As market conditions improve, there is hope that more and more private and government payers will search for new ways to care for more people with fewer dollars.

Third, our regulatory and legal frameworks are notoriously out of date and unprepared for a twenty-first-century health care system that needs to treat seniors wherever they live, work, and play. The convergence of medical devices with consumer electronic and everyday computing devices has left agencies like the Food and Drug Administration (FDA) with unclear guidelines about how to regulate the manufacture and marketing of these independent living systems. In turn, the marketplace lacks confidence in pursuing these innovations. Furthermore, health privacy laws, liability laws, and outdated procedures for licensing health care providers in and across states and countries are slowing the pace of gray technology innovation, since they have not been designed for a globally connected world of devices, consumers, and care providers. Nonetheless, recent meetings held by the FDA in the United States and the explosion of conferences on "m-health" (mobile health) are showing signs of progress that agencies and institutions are prepared to rethink their policies.

Fourth, given many of the issues cited previously, there is a decided lack of research infrastructure and funding for individuals, universities, and companies to explore gray technologies. To develop true knowledge transfer from academic and corporate labs like my own at Intel to full-fledged, scalable production, we need more than small-grant, niche programs focused on aging in place. For example, working with TRIL and ORCATECH, our extended team has outfitted approximately five hundred elderly homes with broadband and clinical assessment tools in order to test these technologies. National cohorts of ten thousand or more households are needed to produce the evidence to support our hypotheses more convincingly. There are promising signs that the Centers for Medicare and Medicaid Services (CMS) in the United States and the Ambient Assisted Living Joint Programme in the European Union will invest in a research infrastructure that will ignite the knowledge gains and products in independent living.

Fifth and finally, our biggest challenge to achieving a robust industry of gray technologies for global aging is an imagination problem, not a technology problem. Our society is held within the powerful gravitational grip of our history of medical care as it has been done now for almost two hundred years. We have come to naturalize and normalize a reactive model of care wherein frail and sick seniors— and patients of all ages—travel to expensive, centralized medical complexes to be put back together again by amazing health care experts and expensive medical technologies. Everywhere you look in pop culture, from television to music to movies, we reinforce this dramatic and dominant "medical miracles" mind-set.

It is hard to challenge our imagination and mind-set to look at health and long-term care differently and to rethink what it means to be a patient, a provider, a caregiver, and a community. It is difficult to reform our principles to focus on prevention rather than intervention, coordinated care rather than specialty care, home-centric treatment rather than hospital-centric treatment, and self-care rather than expert care. We will have to be sure that these technologies are affordable and respectful of an individual's privacy. Individuals and their families will need to find the balance of peace of mind, privacy, and cost appropriate to their needs, even as those needs change over time. At the end of the day, taking aging in place to its logical conclusion means that we, as patients, as retirees, and as family caregivers, are going to have to use the latest technologies to take on new roles and responsibilities to make ourselves and our communities healthier.

Aging, like global warming, requires a new social covenant that we must each undertake in our everyday lives. Gray technologies will, hopefully, be the tools to help us get there. This is hard work, it is necessary, and it is starting to happen.

Notes

1. UN Population Division, *World Population Prospects: The 2008 Revision*, http://www.un.org/esa/population/publications/WPA2009/WPA2009_WorkingPaper.pdf.

2. For more information about the broad range of research studies at Intel, see http://www.intel.com/about/companyinfo/healthcare/people/index.htm.

3. For a good overview of this social health work, see Margaret Morris, "Social Networks as Health Feedback Displays," *IEEE Internet Computing* 9, no. 5 (2005): 29–37.

4. S. Reder, G. Ambler, M. Philipose, and S. Hedrick, "Technology and Long-Term Care (TLC): A Pilot Evaluation of Remote Monitoring of Elders," *Gerontechnology* 9, no. 1 (2010): 18–31.

5. http://www.cdc.gov/injury/index.html.

Chapter 9

A Contractor's Perspective

Greg Miedema

Introduction

I am not an expert on aging nor am I an academic researcher. I'm a professional remodeling contractor who has adapted a number of homes. I have had training in contracting and remodeling and am a Certified Graduate Remodeler. I have found that remodeling solutions share common themes and broad guidelines. At the same time, these applications need to suit individual households. Ability levels and needs become more diverse as we age, and remodeling solutions need to reflect a wide range of experiences.

We have a huge stock of existing dwellings and residences throughout the United States. We simply cannot, on a wholesale basis, replace what we have physically or functionally. We often need to remodel. The new home building industry is already committed to various product segments (starter homes, custom homes, multifamily homes), and while aging-in-place concepts are beginning to be integrated into new construction, there are still many homes that need to be adapted as our society ages.

Home modifications need not be drastic, dramatic, or financially exhausting. The diversity among older people demands a diverse range of solutions. Not everyone wants or needs the highest level of modifications. And not every home needs them.

I recently assessed a multilevel home for an older couple. While installation of grab bars and handrails may seem complex, for about $1,500 we put in accessories

GREG MIEDEMA is president of Dakota Builders, Inc., in Tucson, Arizona. He was named Remodeler of the Year in 1998 and again in 2005. Active in the community, he serves as a volunteer for the Salvation Army and on community building projects in the Tucson area, and he is board chair of Rebuilding Together. He serves on the board of the Southern Arizona Home Builders Association (SAHBA) and is a Certified Graduate Remodeler (CGR), Certified Graduate Builder (CGB), Certified Green Professional (CGP), and Certified Aging in Place Specialist (CAPS).

that left the residents confident in their ability to carry on the activities of daily living without assistance or fear of falls.

Adaptations can be staged with changing conditions of life. A few handholds, lever handles, and latches may suffice temporarily, gradually shifting to zero-step shower conversion, widened doors, and other features as needed. All of these adaptations achieve the same goal—independent living with dignity and comfort.

Old People's Solutions

Aging-in-place remodeling is often perceived as an "old person's solution." "I'm too young to worry about that now" is a common reaction to suggestions about lifelong features in homes. As we start making these features more standard, universal, and contemporary, these objections will diminish. When we start referring to housing options as "more comfortable" instead of "because you are getting older," they will be more universally accepted. We need to start offering solutions for comfort now, putting the focus on ease for people of all ages.

Widening a doorway is not just for "when you need a walker," it's also helpful in carrying laundry, groceries, and children. Putting blocking in a bath or shower is not only required for "when you need help bathing," it's also for a sensible handhold in a wet area, perhaps when you have a sprained ankle after a soccer game, or for leaning into the tub while bathing the kids. Blocking is very simple to do; it involves bracing wood between wall studs behind the wall for better support for towel bars or handholds inside the room. Another example is the lever door latch. First designed for ease of access by people with disabilities, it is now a standard offering.

Fortunately, many trends in both remodeling and new construction are already moving into the market. Some are so integrated we don't realize they were originally designed for older people. Single-handle faucets, lever door latches, and easy-to-use appliances are sensible and comfortable and not only "for the old." The recent trend toward more open floor plans and the development of the "great room" are other examples of lifestyle trends that have the benefit of helping us to get around more easily. Minimizing subdivisions in the home, reducing the number of hallways, and making rooms like the kitchen more open have value in accommodating a variety of abilities.

Cultural Norms about Homes

The US real estate, financial services, and construction industries have been successful in promoting different types of housing for different stages in our lives.

We first might purchase a starter home; then, as we reach our peak earning years, the move-up home comes into view. As our children leave home for college or to start their own families, we might move to downsize or to move up into luxury living for two. There are even particular stages of homes in a continuing care retirement community.

But is there really a need for the same people to be forced to find so many different houses in their lifetimes in order to meet their needs? Why can't the "starter home" be the "ender home," by including wider hallways, wider doors, grab bars, sensible lighting, and even transitions? That model would mean moving only when we want to move and not because our houses are no longer the right fit.

Major economic forces may have begun to reshape the homebuying market, as we no longer expect a profitable return on equity every ten to fifteen years. Without that financial incentive, the move-up, luxury, and retirement home stages of our lives may not be sensible. Owning a home remains the goal for most Americans, and a mortgage debt repaid becomes a lifetime savings account. But perhaps it's time to think about investing in homes that suit us throughout our lives, which would conserve resources, maintain familiarity, and stabilize our neighborhoods at the same time.

Practical Challenges

There are certainly physical and building code challenges to successful remodeling for aging in place. Some terrain is not appropriate for single-level living or even zero-step entries. In areas where basement or crawl space construction is the norm, creativity is required to provide an accessible entry. When ground clearance precludes a zero-step entry, a solution ought to be possible without rewriting the entire city building code. Ageless and barrier-free housing should be encouraged by making standard building codes more flexible.

In the same vein, to slap a low-threshold entry and a lever latch on every home and call it "Done!" detracts from real solutions for real people in real houses. Many locales have established visitability ordinances, which help with ensuring basic access. These ordinances can and should be built upon to require, for example, that bathrooms are adaptable and functional for a variety of users.

Remodeling solutions require trained professionals. The combined skills of a remodeler and other aging professionals may be required. Before solutions are hammered out literally, we need to hammer them out virtually. With the proper interpersonal and communication skills, along with tools for documenting and assessing needs, remodeling can be a manageable process for families at any stage of life.

Zero-step entry. Courtesy of Traditions of America at Silver Spring, 2009 NAHB Best of 50+ Housing Silver Award Winner. Photograph by John Lewis.

An Aging-in-Place Home Walkthrough

A "walk" through a home will identify the most desirable areas to adapt and modify for aging in place.

THE ENTRANCE

The first step is simply about entering the home. A front door must accommodate a wheelchair. Wood frame homes are easiest to change, as they require only some framing and reframing, but even masonry homes are adaptable. The challenge is to define the degree of difficulty, think creatively about solutions, and weigh the benefits. Porches and outdoor decks can be made accessible in order to provide pleasant outdoor space.

DOORS

Once inside, doors are key. There is little to be gained by modifying an interior space if you cannot move easily in and out of the rooms. Even two or three inches on a door can make the difference between full use of the home and being restricted in the space. In non-load-bearing walls, increasing door width can be as easy as removing the "cripple" or "trimmer"; in a load-bearing wall, metal brackets can be added to serve the same purpose. Light switches and outlets are often located next

Accessible kitchen
—cabinet detail.
Courtesy of the Na-
tional Association
of Home Builders
Remodelers.

to a doorway. Although a concession may have to be made on the trim or casing reveal, that is a relatively minor compromise.

Evaluating the need for a door altogether is also an important step. Using pocket doors—those that slide into a wall cavity—can also make for easier entry. It's important to understand the dexterity of the user when considering pocket doors. Splitting a doorway into two doors, as with the use of a double-hung door, is another way to widen a door yet make the door leaves easier to operate. For example, if an opening of forty-eight inches is desirable, two twenty-four-inch doors can be used as a pair; not only are they more durable as a set (less likely to warp or to strain a hinge) but they also are easier to step (or use a wheelchair) in between.

THE MOST USED ROOMS: KITCHEN AND GREAT ROOM

We need to think next about the most used rooms in a house. The kitchen, often designed as part of a great room, falls into that category. Depending on the user,

Accessible kitchen —oven and sink detail. Courtesy of the National Association of Home Builders Remodelers.

multilevel counters and raised or lowered appliances/appliance stations may be appropriate. A raised dishwasher is not only easier for someone in a seated position to use but also requires less bending and strain for someone with a back condition. A sink with knee space may be necessary for independent use of the kitchen and can be accomplished outright or by the use of foldaway doors. Extended tops on islands and peninsulas add workspace for those in a wheelchair or who otherwise need to sit for extended periods.

As we design seated work areas, we need to consider where the light switches should be located and how the lighting is focused in the kitchen. Plenty of undercabinet and task lighting may be needed. Platforms for washers and dryers and front-loading washers are popular now. These features are essential for wheelchair users, and they have the added benefit of being easier for everyone to use.

BATHROOMS

Bathrooms are also rooms on the "must do" list. We need to think first about the room entry. How wide can we make the door and not compromise adjacent space? Once inside, can we function, maneuver, turn, and reach all of the fixtures? One of the most common projects in remodeling is the tub-to-shower conversion, often in the master bath but occasionally in the hall or guest bath as well. Remodeling the master bathroom offers quite a few inherent advantages. Because there is likely already a door from the hall or adjacent area into the bedroom, the door into the bathroom can be more flexible. For example, this door can be a pocket door or a double door. The tub-to-shower conversion is easier, and a low-slope floor can be drained with a center or offset drain, a front trench drain, or both. A bench can be built in or an accessory mounted on the wall with appropriate blocking. Handheld shower accessories are almost standard, with no bearing on the user's ability.

The advent of the comfort-height commode is yet another example of designers and manufacturers moving one step closer to usability by all. Knee space for a sink can be accommodated in much the same manner as for a kitchen sink; remove the base cabinet, use a wall-mounted sink, foldaway doors, or, depending on the mobility of the user, maybe even use a pedestal sink. Thought should be given for adequate and reachable storage in all cases.

Accessible shower design. Courtesy of the National Association of Home Builders Remodelers.

LIGHTING, OUTLETS, AND ELECTRICAL SWITCHES

In every room, attention should be paid to lighting, outlets, and electrical switches. Lowering the switches and raising the outlets requires minimal effort but makes activity easier for anyone with range-of-motion limitations. Closet redesigns can be simple and cost effective.

The Costs of Remodeling

With every need and every solution, there must be consideration of cost. As we know, assisted living is extremely expensive and can be required for a number of years. By comparison, home adaptations are relatively affordable alternatives for

Accessible closet design. Courtesy of the National Association of Home Builders Remodelers.

many Americans. For affluent homeowners, although an extensive adaptable bath remodeling project might start at $15,000 to $20,000, extensive remodeling still might represent the most cost-effective solution. A simple tub-to-shower conversion, leaving the rest of the bathroom "as is," can be completed for $5,000 or less. As we add a lever faucet handle, grab bars, and perhaps a comfort-height commode, a bathroom can be renovated for under $6,000. Such a renovation can make the difference between moving and maintaining a degree of independence and dignity in one's present home.

The MetLife Mature Market Institute is an important information and policy resource center on issues of aging, long-term care, and the mature market. In September 2010, the institute released a report titled *Aging in Place 2.0: Rethinking Solutions to the Home Care Challenge.*[1] This study reported that many advocates and experts envision a future aging in place in which home design, medical and home monitoring equipment, and comprehensive care services are unified into an efficient monitoring and management system. (Chapter 8 highlights some of these new technologies.) The MetLife study offers practical suggestions on priorities for various home modifications and their estimated costs.[2] The study's prioritized renovations are listed below.

FIRST PRIORITY
Falls prevention. Cost: $1,000 or less.

- Removing throw rugs, especially in the bathroom
- Installing grab bars and grips in the bathroom
- Making sure that handrails on both sides of steps are sturdy
- Good lighting and switching, especially at stairs, halls, and entries

- Securing or removing carpets at stairs
- Soft path lighting for nighttime mobility

SECOND PRIORITY

Entryway, easy movement, and use-of-home features. Cost: $4,500 to $30,000.

- Removing, if possible, or reducing the number and/or height of steps and possibly increasing the horizontal depth of steps for easy side stepping with both hands on one rail
- A clear, no-step path to the bedroom and bathroom
- Rearrangement or repositioning of furniture, entertainment systems, and spaces

THIRD PRIORITY

More substantial remodeling and equipment. Cost: $8,000 to $75,000.

- No-step shower or bath lift mechanism, seated sink, and assistance space at the toilet
- Seated/multilevel food preparation areas
- Sun- and rain-protected outdoor areas
- Backup power sources for power outages

It is easy to see how low-cost interventions such as removing throw rugs and adding grab bars have clear payback in terms of avoidance of falls, resulting in fewer hospitalizations and medical costs. According to the MetLife report, more substantial renovations can average $9,000 to $12,000 per one-story residence. This kind of investment might take longer to recoup, but even if one hospitalization or one serious fall with medical and health care consequences is avoided, the savings might appear relatively early.[3]

Conclusion

My goal is to make sure that a forced move from one's familiar surroundings is not driven by age or disability. As we face the realities of our existing housing stock and struggle with current and future economic trends, it will often be important that people stay in their homes for most of their adult lives. When financial challenges arise, several generations of a family may move in together, which further reinforces the case for the broadest adoption of accessible features. Multigenerational housing will put more pressure on builders and remodelers to develop solutions and features that are more affordable and practical and therefore appeal to a broad range of users. Making accessible features the norm, rather than the exception, is the challenge.

Notes

1. MetLife Mature Market Institute, *Aging in Place 2.0: Rethinking Solutions to the Home Care Challenge*, http://www.metlife.com/mmi/research/aging-in-place.html#insights.

2. Ibid., 25–26.

3. Ibid., 26.

Chapter 10

A Case Study

Interior Design for Aging in Place

M. Robbins Black

Introduction

In my interior design practice, I have seen a dramatic shift in the ways in which people think about and plan for aging in place. I often talk with people who are thinking about certain key aspects of their homes and apartments. First, they are interested in feeling safe and secure, protected from falling and other hazards of the built environment. Second, they want to feel that they have choices as they plan for the future. Many people prefer to age in place for as long as possible; others imagine new options in housing as they age. Third, they long for a beautiful living environment that is within their price range. Price ranges vary, of course, but the desire for a pleasing environment is universal. Finally, there is a strong awareness of environmentally conscious design choices, ranging from better insulation (leading to lower heating costs) to Energy Star appliances to environmentally safe building materials.

Yet it is difficult for us to plan for the future, even given our wishes for a secure homelike setting. "I cannot think about that now" was my seventy-seven-year-old friend's reply to her sons when they encouraged her to move from her two-story town house to a single-level residence. Her knees were bad and the stairs were long and laborious, but she could still manage. The thought of packing and deciding what to take and what to sell or give to family or charity was too much for her, so she did nothing.

She subsequently had serious health problems, and as a result, she fell. She stayed in a hospital and rehab unit for six months. She could not return to her house in its present condition. It needed a costly chairlift, the sliding glass door through the courtyard to the garage was too heavy for her to open, and the threshold was

M. ROBBINS (ROBIN) BLACK is a registered interior designer in San Antonio, Texas. She spent ten years with the firm of Ford, Powell, and Carson Architects, based in San Antonio, before forming her own firm. She received a bachelor of interior design degree from Auburn University after spending two years studying liberal arts at the American College in Paris.

Casa Finale living/ dining room. Courtesy of M. Robbins Black. Photograph by Al Rendon.

awkward under the door. A deck was needed for the transition from the garage to the back door, as the shifting soil had made the concrete pads uneven. Because of the depressed housing market, selling her two-story town house and moving to a different home was not a good option. Her family had no choice but to install a chairlift, replace the sliding glass door, and build a deck in preparation for her return home. They had to organize all of this work while she was in the hospital, and they felt additional stress as they left her bedside to oversee the contractors doing the remodeling. The process was difficult for everyone—and more expensive than anyone anticipated. While the immediate problem was solved, nobody thought it was an ideal process or result. Many families do not have the financial resources to achieve such solutions and have few options for caring for older relatives. The result can be premature institutionalization, desirable to no one.

A Personal Account

The following is a personal account of how my husband (who is an architect) and I approached our own aging in place. I offer our story as a way of thinking through the issues and ideas involved. Some people will age in place in their current home,

NATIONAL ASSOCIATION OF HOME BUILDERS INTERIOR DESIGN ELEMENTS

To help builders, designers, and architects understand how to design for aging in place, the National Association of Home Builders has created a list of practical design features that can "make the home safer, with less maintenance and more barrier-free."[a]

Changes in the kitchen for easier meal preparation and eating:

- Lever-handle faucets with pullout spray
- Raised dishwasher to avoid back strain (a good idea for front-loading washers and dryers, too)
- Rolling island that can be placed back under the counter
- Revolving corner shelves and pullout shelves
- Lower, side-opening oven
- Pullout cutting board
- Adjustable-height sink
- Side-by-side refrigerator with slide-out shelves and a water/ice dispenser
- Cooktop with controls at front
- Larger, friendlier cabinet and drawer pulls

Changes in the bathroom—the number one place for accidents in the home:

- Two or three attractive-looking grab bars in shower

- Lever handles on faucets
- Slide-bar-type handheld shower, for sitting or standing
- Shampoo nooks inset in the wall
- Curbless showers—nothing to step over and can be rolled into if a wheelchair becomes necessary later
- Tub and shower controls moved closer to entry point
- Antiscald, temperature- and pressure-balanced tub and shower valves for safer bathing
- Entry doors at least thirty-two inches
- Thirty-two- to thirty-six-inch pocket doors
- Higher toilets with nonslam seats and lids

Moving around within the house:

- Improved lighting with recessed fixtures in common areas and hallways
- Lever handles on doors and windows
- Lowered light switches and thermostats; raised outlets
- Planning for future elevator by stacking closets
- Adding blocking in walls for future chairlift at stairs
- Wider doors that accommodate wheelchairs and walkers

[a]Dan Bawden, "What Is 'Design for Independent Living,' Anyway?" http://www.nahb.org/generic.aspx?genericContentID=114505.

others will age in place in a new apartment, and still others may move in with family members. I hope that my account will provide useful thoughts for any of these circumstances and for a range of financial realities.

Some years ago, my husband and I realized that a move from our large, inaccessible home was inevitable. The long flight of stairs from the garage was one of the deciding factors. After looking at countless one-story homes, we found a

Casa Finale screened-in porch. Courtesy of M. Robbins Black. Photograph by Al Rendon.

1953 single-story, 2,500-square-foot house near our old neighborhood. There is a detached apartment created from a garage in the back. Long-range plans call for using the apartment for a caretaker. Presently, it is my office.

In our new house, which we promptly named "Casa Finale," we were committed to using sustainable, green, and accessible features as we began to remodel. We wanted to create a handsome, functional home filled with our edited furnishings, art, and collections, with a backdrop of our choices of materials, colors, and light fixtures.

CIRCULATION

We wanted to create an accessible home that had rooms open to each other. To do this, we opened up the den to the kitchen using a counter with drawers. This counter provides easy-to-reach storage. The result is unencumbered open circulation.

The back patio, viewed through two pairs of glass sliding doors in the den, was turned into a screened-in porch with an exterior concrete block fireplace. This exterior room then became part of the interior.

Casa Finale natural lighting in kitchen. Courtesy of M. Robbins Black. Photograph by Al Rendon.

BATHROOMS

The vanities and sinks in our bathrooms are at a height of thirty-six inches so that we do not have to stoop as we age. The tub was taken out of the hall bathroom and in its place is a five-foot shower with a bench, handheld shower, shampoo shelf, and grab bar. We installed low-flow toilets with nonslam lids, one being a comfort-level toilet.

NATURAL LIGHTING

Our idea was that if we were to be homebound later in life, it would be with windows, good lighting, and views. By bringing "the outside in" through the addition of double-paned windows in the dining room and in a bedroom, we also made the interior of our small home appear larger. Views of the front, back, and side yards from the den afford panoramic views of the outside.

A privacy issue from living room to den was solved by a pair of pocket louvered doors between the two rooms that are drawn at dusk. When they are open, we can look all the way through our house. Big trees and the yard give us the feeling of

Casa Finale lighting in living room. Courtesy of M. Robbins Black. Photograph by Al Rendon.

living outdoors. Flowering crape myrtles in a curved pattern at the end of the yard and the big trees shield us from the street.

ARTIFICIAL LIGHTING

There is ambient and task lighting throughout the house. Sconces have frosted glass covering the light source. Every room except the living room has ceiling fans, but none have the light kits, which cause glare.

Track lighting throughout the house provides the ambient light that softly lights the rooms, while higher levels of light are used for the art and bookshelves. The tracks and track heads were recycled from other houses.

The bathrooms have lights on either side of the mirror above the pedestal sink to evenly light the face. A fan/light combination adds more ambient light. All of the lights in the house are on separate switches and on dimmers so each room's lighting can be dialed up or down.

Task lighting and ambient lighting are both used in the kitchen. There are two halogen wall sconces over the windows along the sink counter. The light over the sink is a recessed downlight, and light in the room can be brought up or down with dimmers. This area is the best workplace in the house.

COLORS AND MATERIALS

We chose muted colors for the counters, flooring, and wall coverings and used semitransparent stains on doors and floors. There is a contrast in color from the wall to the floor; light baseboards supplement the contrast so that, as our eyes age, we are better able to discern the difference from floor to wall.

WINDOWS AND DOORS

Louvered pine doors from a Habitat for Humanity ReStore outlet replaced the existing narrow doors. Louvered doors allowed for airflow into closets. All entry doors were replaced with the same French doors, all keyed alike, and all of our

GREEN DESIGN AND AGING IN PLACE

Robert Pfauth, an architect based in Jacksonville, Florida, speaks and writes on green design and the elderly. He points out that sustainable design can be particularly beneficial to older people for the following reasons:

- Seniors can experience heightened sensitivity to temperature extremes, and so building heating, ventilation, and air-conditioning systems must provide flexibility while also conserving energy. Natural ventilation is a key aspect of enabling temperature control.
- In terms of indoor air quality, sustainable building design pays careful attention to the products that are used, guarding against airborne toxins and other pollutants.
- To assist seniors with vision impairments, diffuse daylighting is the recommended course. This can lower utility costs as well as creating visually therapeutic environments. Use of natural light as much as possible is critical.[a]

Sustainable design, green design, urban planning, universal design, and aging in place are all inherently tied to one another. This synergistic design approach provides a more effective finished product that combines usability with aesthetic appeal, sustainability, and urbanism.

Because the basic principles of good design apply to all these fields, there are many aspects of green design that are appropriate to universal design and designing for aging in place and vice versa. They are compatible and complementary.

Green designers use the environmentally friendly concepts of reduce, reuse, and recycle. In this time of concern about the ecosystem, more consumers want building materials and design products that won't hurt the environment. Universal design and aging in place take these concepts one step further by employing materials and design products that won't hurt the occupants. Cork and bamboo flooring, for example, are not only fast-growing and renewable resources but also termite resistant, thus eliminating the need for chemical treatments, which might affect the aged, especially those with respiratory diseases, asthma, or even just allergies. Plus, they have the added benefit of being "easy on the joints."[b]

[a]Robert Pfauth, "Incorporating Green Principles Can Benefit Elder-Friendly Design," http://www.di.net/articles/archive/2376.
[b]Leslie Shankman-Cohn, "Design for Aging and Green Design: They're More Alike Than You Think!" http://www.asid.org/designknowledge/aa/inplace/active/agingandgreen.html.

CHARITABLE SUPPORT FOR HOME AND NEIGHBORHOOD IMPROVEMENT

Habitat for Humanity seeks to eliminate poverty housing and homelessness from the world and to make decent shelter a matter of conscience and action. This organization invites people of all backgrounds, races and religions to build houses together in partnership with families in need. www.habitat.org

The Home Depot Foundation's mission is to ensure that every veteran has a safe place to call home. www.homedepotfoundation.org

Lowe's Charitable and Educational Foundation funds nonprofit organizations and public agencies that support our charitable goals. The foundation's primary philanthropic focus centers on K–12 public education and community improvement. Within these areas, Lowe's Foundation is committed to supporting projects that have the greatest impact on our communities and align with our core business—home improvement. www.lowes.com/cd_Charitable+and+Educational+Foundation

The Walmart Foundation's various grant programs support initiatives focused on enhancing opportunities in education, workforce development/economic opportunity, health & wellness, and environmental sustainability in an effort to create opportunities so people can live better. The Walmart Foundation's National Giving Program supports nonprofit organizations that implement programs in multiple sites across the country or have innovative initiatives that are ready for replication nationally. www.walmartstores.com

operable doors were equipped with lever handles. Widening the doors to thirty-six inches allows for wheelchair access for aging in place, which was as important as letting light into the house.

SUSTAINABLE MATERIALS

Sustainable, renewable, and safe materials were used throughout. The kitchen cabinet and drawer fronts were made from bamboo or stainless steel. Existing wooden 1953 kitchen cabinets were painted and reused. Rubber tiles were used for the kitchen floor. The counters are sealed limestone, and the two bathroom floors have slip-resistant limestone floors.

We recycled as we remodeled the house. We researched carefully the products that went into our new home. We were conscious of old lead paint on exterior screens and exterior trim, as well as volatile organic compounds (VOCs) that were formerly used in paint. We used paint that was free of VOCs, water-based glue for the rubber floor, and water-based sealers on the oak floors.

We consulted several resources to help us with our planning, including Home Depot and the Home Depot Foundation.

EXTERIORS

The exterior aluminum siding was removed from the house and recycled. Insulation was installed, over which the final exterior material—cedar shingles—was applied. The front porch, sidewalk, and back patio were paved with Arkansas River stone for slip-resistant surfaces.

The previous owners had left a collection of operable exterior security lights, so that our outdoor path from the carport through the breezeway to the covered back patio was well lit.

APPLIANCES

The appliances are Energy Star. The washer is front loading, with low water use, and the dryer is on a pedestal for comfort. The dials in the gas cooktop are centered so as not to burn an arm or hand reaching for dials at the back of the stove. The majority of the cabinets have rollout drawers for ease of visibility. We have lightweight pots and pans as well as plates. There is a pullout spray on the kitchen faucet as well as a single-lever control.

Conclusion

Our home was chosen to be one of six houses on the 2009 AIA Homes Tour in San Antonio. We were pleased about this recognition because, in our new home, we applied what we had learned in studies for our degrees in architecture and interior design and in our years of practice. A large amount of knowledge about aging in place and sustainability came from the continuing education courses in health, safety, and welfare that I am required to take to stay in compliance with the Texas Board of Architectural Examiners. Continuing education as a registered interior designer is also required to remain in good standing with our professional organizations, the American Institute of Architects (AIA), the American Society of Interior Designers (ASID), and the International Interior Design Association (IIDA).

We believe that good interior design can make a significant difference in all homes and apartments—large or small, old or new, shared or single occupancy. We also believe that good design does not need to be expensive or overwhelming and that by following basic design ideals we can successfully create healthy options for aging in place.

Chapter 11

Multifamily Housing

Hipolito Roldan

Introduction

Multifamily housing" is defined as an accommodation that houses more than one family in separate units that can be either owned or rented by the occupants. Multifamily housing includes duplexes, units in high-rise and low-rise buildings, garden homes, townhomes, lofts, and homes in mixed-use buildings. This housing type includes co-ops, condominiums, tenancies in common, and rentals. Market-rate multifamily housing is distinguished from "affordable housing," which is defined as costing no more than 30 percent of its occupants' income.[1]

Multifamily housing meets the needs of a range of households, including those who seek services that are more affordably provided in higher-density settings, those who want to avoid the expense of single-family home maintenance and upkeep, and those who seek housing management. Multifamily rental housing is valuable for those who cannot qualify for a mortgage loan, those unwilling to take on the risks of homeownership, and those who have just moved to an area or plan to move again soon. Multifamily housing also is well suited to meeting national goals of energy independence and sustainable development by encouraging retrofitting of older properties, building and preserving developments at higher densities closer to transit nodes, and building in more compact patterns within walking distance of shopping and other amenities.

Like older people in single-family homes, seniors in multifamily housing are exercising a preference to age in place. It is estimated that 67 percent of elderly householders in multifamily housing remain there until death (38 percent) or until

HIPOLITO ROLDAN is chief executive officer of the Hispanic Housing Development Corporation in Chicago, Illinois. He has developed over twenty-eight hundred affordable apartments and town houses in thirty-five developments for families and elderly residents of several Hispanic communities in Chicago. In 1998, he received a John D. and Catherine T. MacArthur Fellowship for his work in community development. He was also a contributing author to the book *Casa y Comunidad*. He holds a BA from St. Francis College and an MA from Long Island University.

experiencing sufficient impairment to enter a hospital (4 percent) or a nursing home (25 percent).[2]

Approximately 25 percent of those aged fifty-five and older live in multifamily housing and occupy 16 percent of all rental multifamily housing. Multifamily housing may be particularly beneficial to older residents because of the accessibility requirements of Section 504 of the Rehabilitation Act, the Fair Housing Amendments Act, and the Americans with Disabilities Act Accessibility Guidelines for public spaces in multifamily projects.[3]

According to the Joint Center for Housing Studies at Harvard University, two million rental housing units disappeared between 1993 and 2003, many of which were leased at lower market rates or subsidized affordable rental rates.[4] Although perhaps a number of these projects should have been torn down, the costs of replacement may be prohibitive. Government-subsidized housing developments are targeted to individuals and families whose household income is below a specified level and who rely on public funds for construction, operation, or rental subsidies.[5] Between high construction and land costs, it is difficult to build moderately priced housing at reasonable costs in the cities and suburbs without government subsidies.[6] It is important that the United States rethink the best way to deliver housing subsidies to help low-income Americans afford rental housing and to meet the housing needs of the growing number of seniors.

There are significant differences between multifamily housing and senior housing. The physical design, location, staffing, services, and operating philosophy of multifamily housing are not often planned to accommodate the specific needs of frail older people.[7] Multifamily housing for seniors should offer elevators, have wider hallways and doors, and offer amenities that include on-site medical services and dining. Most important, building managers should be prepared to support elderly residents. For example, some building managers will move older residents ever closer to the first floor as units become available to assist in their ability to continue to age in place. Some offer health and social services within the building or nearby. Greater attention should be paid to exploring the enhancement of multifamily housing for elderly people. Careful consideration should be given to locating multifamily projects in neighborhoods of single-family homes so that residents who have spent many years in the neighborhood can remain connected to the families, friends, and even social adversaries who help to stir the soul.

A Case Study

In 1998, a descriptive, exploratory study was conducted that considered a number of indicators of a multifamily development's capacity to enable elderly tenants to age in place successfully.[8]

Three groups of indicators were explored:

Group 1—support indicators: operating attitudes and policies: These measures include the presence of laundry facilities and a community room in the development. The manager's attitude toward tenants aging in place in multifamily housing should also be taken into consideration.

Group 2—activities and services: These factors assess whether aging-related frailty is regularly supported and include such measures as whether supportive services are provided and whether a resident services coordinator is available in the development. Data also include whether a dining/meal program is provided and whether transportation services are offered.

Group 3—safety and convenience features: These indicators address physical aspects of the development and the neighborhood in which it is located. Items include the building security system, handrails (or the lack of handrails) in the hallways, and the availability of nearby amenities.

As is noted in this important work, a significant number of older people are living and aging in place in age-integrated multiunit housing developments. Multifamily residences have become a major but largely unacknowledged and unexplored retirement housing option. Most elderly tenants moved in while younger and chose to stay, while others moved in at an older age to be near friends or family or to take advantage of the building's location.[9]

Future Trends

In a 2011 appearance before Congress, a representative of the National Apartment Association testified that the United States is on the cusp of a fundamental change in our housing dynamics. Changing demographics and new economic realities are driving more people away from the typical suburban house and causing a surge in rental demand. "Tomorrow's households are more interested in urban living and less interested in owning. They want smaller spaces and more amenities. Unfortunately, our housing policy has yet to adjust to these new realities."[10]

Today, nearly eighty-nine million Americans, almost one-third of all Americans, rent their homes. As predicted by Dr. Arthur C. Nelson, director of the Metropolitan Research Center at the University of Utah, half of all new homes built between 2005 and 2030 should be rental units, or an estimated three hundred thousand units a year. Of that number, almost half will be inhabited by older people.[11]

However, it is unlikely, at the time of this writing, that there will be an adequate supply of suitable multifamily housing. Although the data are difficult to sort in this complex and largely unexplored multifamily market, luxury apartments, condos and co-ops, and townhomes for wealthy Americans aged fifty-five and older should be a healthy market. Providing services for aging wealthy Americans should also be a growing field, whether in senior housing or in age-integrated multifamily developments.

The University of Michigan Health and Retirement Study describes the immense differences in income and wealth among older Americans.[12] The 20 percent of people at the lowest end of the economic scale have negative or minimal net worth, while those in the top 20 percent have an average of $800,000 to $1.5 million. The top 20 percent have income from assets that include stocks, bonds, checking accounts, certificates of deposit (CDs), rental properties, and business and farm holdings. These nonhousing assets may be needed to purchase a new home for numbers of suburban baby boomers who are aging in the homes that may now be larger than they need or want.

For all but the top 20 percent, the value of their home is the most important part of their wealth. According to the Health and Retirement Study, the average household income for the middle 20 percent of people aged sixty-five to seventy-four ranges from $17,000 to $42,000.[13] Access to housing wealth is important for middle-income Americans. Those unable to sell their homes may need to convert their single-family residences into multifamily housing.

Even more problematic is the availability of housing and services for older people who are poor. According to the Joint Center for Housing Studies, in 2009, an unprecedented 19.4 million Americans spent more than half of their income on housing. By 2009, there were 10.4 million extremely low income renters and only 3.7 million affordable and available units. Because income gains have lagged housing costs for decades, "affordability pressures" are making their way up the income scale.[14]

Multifamily housing for the very poor is chaotic and scarce. As of 2009, there were 1.1 million public housing units and 2 million privately owned, publicly subsidized units, an overall loss of 700,000 from peak levels. Older subsidized properties need remodeling, financing for new construction is quite challenging, eligibility requirements are confusing, and wait lists are steadily growing. There is also a dearth of affordable housing with services and a dearth of research about which types of housing and services are significant as older people decline in physical and mental functioning. There could be efficiencies in the delivery of services where there are concentrations of older people such as in vertical naturally occurring retirement communities (NORCs), but further cost-benefit analysis is needed. Without extensive study, we cannot make the case that aging in place in multifamily housing with services will save on expensive institutional care.

Conclusion

It is crucial that adequate financing be put into place for the construction of multifamily housing. In the past, multifamily housing finance for all but the wealthiest older Americans has depended on two government-sponsored enterprises (GSEs): the Federal National Mortgage Association (Fannie Mae) and the Federal Home Loan Mortgage Corporation (Freddie Mac). The recent default rate of GSE-backed multifamily loans is less than 1 percent, while defaults on single-family homes have soared. The Federal Housing Administration (FHA) and Government National Mortgage Association (Ginnie Mae) are federal agencies that also have been essential for multifamily housing finance. There must be a stable and liquid secondary market in order for Americans to have decent rental housing on fair and reasonable terms.

Notes

1. Richard M. Haughey, *The Case for Multifamily Housing*, 2nd ed. (Washington, DC: Urban Land Institute, 2003), 1.

2. Vera Prosper, "Aging in Place in Multifamily Housing," *Cityscape* 7, no. 1 (2004): 82.

3. Julia Beamish and HyunJoo Kwon, "Multifamily Housing for Baby Boomers: The Appeal of Universal Design" (Universal Design Summit 4, Virginia Tech University, Blacksburg, October 10, 2010).

4. *Meeting Multifamily Housing Finance Needs during and after the Credit Crisis: A Policy Brief* (Cambridge, MA: Joint Center for Housing Studies, Harvard University, January 2009).

5. Prosper, "Aging in Place in Multifamily Housing," 84.

6. Les Shaver, "Disappearing Act: Apartment Buildings and Rental Homes Vanish One by One, with No Replacements in Sight," *Multifamily Executive*, October 10, 2006.

7. Prosper, "Aging in Place in Multifamily Housing," 83.

8. Ibid.

9. Ibid.

10. Arthur C. Nelson and Peter Evans, Testimony before the House Committee on Financial Services on "The Future Role of FHA and Ginnie Mae in the Single Family and Multifamily Mortgage Markets," May 25, 2011.

11. Ibid.

12. *Growing Older in America: The Health and Retirement Study* (Washington, DC: US Department of Health and Human Services).

13. Ibid.

14. "America's Rental Housing: Meeting Challenges, Building on Opportunities," *State of the Nation's Housing 2011* (Cambridge, MA: Joint Center for Housing Studies, Harvard University, 2011).

Chapter 12

A Case Study

The Freedom Home

Keith Collins

Introduction

For many years, my business partners, Michael Shrenk and George Aucott, and I have built houses throughout the state of Florida. We grew our company, New Millennial Homes, by focusing on affordability. We began to hear a common question from our clients that went something like this: "How can I have a place to live that not only suits my current needs but can be flexible as my needs and physical conditions change?" We knew little about the so-called adapted housing industry, although each of us had thought a bit about our own homes as we cared for ourselves, our aging parents, and, in Mike's case, his critically ill wife and aging mother.

In August of 2005, we noticed an article in *Planet Realtor* (a publication for real estate professionals in Tampa, Florida) that noted that there are more disabled residents in the Tampa Bay area than anywhere else in the nation. The article also pointed out that these residents face the difficult challenge of finding homes that are both accessible and affordable. Mike and I did a little research, using data from the US 2000 Census, and we learned that one in ten people in the United States has a disability.[1]

We reflected on these data and matched them with what we were hearing from our older clients. We began to recognize that the upcoming retirement of the baby boomers would only add to this trend. We learned that over the next twenty years the physical needs of the boomers were predicted to change dramatically. We located a study conducted by AARP reporting that 90 percent of people over the

KEITH COLLINS received the AARP/National Association of Home Builders Livable Communities Award in 2008, in recognition of the Freedom Home. This award program was developed to recognize forward-thinking builders, remodelers, and developers whose cutting-edge designs make life easier, safer, and more comfortable for American families. He is chief operating officer and director of New Millennial Homes in Tampa, Florida, is a veteran of the US Marine Corps, and has completed extensive continuing education courses in construction management, contracting, and planning.

Freedom Home exterior. Courtesy of New Millennial Homes.

age of fifty wanted to stay in their current home as long as possible. Yet 25 percent of those who wanted to stay in their homes believed that they would be forced to move because their present home would not be able to adapt to their changing physical needs.[2]

As we probed further, we learned that the Tampa-based James A. Haley Veterans Hospital is one of the top polytrauma centers in the world and is one of the four hospitals in the country to receive wounded service personnel critically injured in combat areas abroad. Many were returning with special needs and permanent disabilities, and finding few choices to allow them to live comfortably and with dignity at home. We could not find standard, affordable home designs for people with disabilities. Custom homes were being designed and built, but with higher price tags. Remodeling wasn't always the best option. The needs of disabled veterans particularly spoke to us because my business partners and I are all veterans, and we have faced physical challenges and injuries in our lifetimes, either personally or in our families.

Since 2006, we have considered these related needs of disabled Americans, wounded and disabled veterans, and the coming needs of aging baby boomers to introduce a quality and affordable home that can meet the needs of all people. We became the first builder in the country to introduce and build a standard home that we called the Freedom Home.

The Freedom Home Concept

Our priority for the Freedom Home was that it needed to be attractive, affordable, and life-enhancing. Our goal was the creation of a barrier-free home that was in compliance with the Federal Housing Administration (FHA), the US Department of Veterans Affairs (VA), and the Americans with Disabilities Act (ADA), while being adaptable to changing physical mobility circumstances. We worked specifically on the needs of returning service personnel as part of the Warrior Transition Program under the auspices of the US Department of Defense and the VA. Our work has embraced the needs of individuals who are blind, have spinal cord injuries, and/or are quadriplegic or paraplegic. By focusing on these physical limitations, we developed a design that also would meet the needs of individuals facing the challenges of normal aging, such as difficulty climbing stairs, getting in and out of bathtubs, and seeing better in the dark.

We knew that the Freedom Home concept must include a full range of living options—houses, duplexes, townhomes, condominiums, and apartments. In developing the Freedom Home, we have relied upon our twenty-five years of building in constantly changing neighborhoods and real estate markets. In the last twelve years, we have built over two thousand affordable homes for families with diversified needs and requirements. Additionally, our involvement with remodeling homes and rehabilitation of neighborhoods has given us insight into the rationale, concepts, characteristics, and process of building homes for those who are aging. We have worked to make our homes barrier-free, universal in design, adaptable, affordable, and multigenerational. We focused on simple, affordable, replicable, and applicable solutions. We have been conscious about the fact that, if people can live in their homes independently, we all will save money in terms of institutional care that otherwise would be needed. Figure 12.1 illustrates a typical floor plan of the Freedom Home.

We have created the Freedom Home in various sizes to serve different family realities. The Freedom Home begins at 952 square feet and has two bedrooms and two bathrooms. Our largest home is 3,200 square feet with four bedrooms and three bathrooms. The cost of this larger model ranges from $75 to $90 per square foot. Our most popular homes are in the 1,200- to 1,500-square-foot range at a cost of $40 to $50 per square foot and in the 1,500- to 2,500-square-foot range at $60 to $70 per square foot. (These prices are net of land costs.) According to information

BEDRM 2

BATH 2

MASTER BEDROOM

HALL

W/D

M. BATH

SHOWER AREA

BEDRM 3

RFG

LIVING

KITCHEN

DW

DINING

PORCH

RAMP

OPT. DOOR AT M. BEDROOM

CARPORT

OPT. CARPORT

The Freedom Home

NEW MILLENNIAL HOMES

FLOOR PLAN - (ELEV. A)
1200 LIVING SQ. FT. / 1297 TOTAL SQ. FT.

*All dimensions are approximate and reflect block construction

NMH

Figure 12.1 Freedom Home floor plan. Courtesy of New Millennial Homes.

on the Tampa Realtor website, these prices are approximately half of the price per square foot found in comparable custom homes in the area.[3]

We also knew that paying attention to cultural differences and distinctions would play a major role in the success of the Freedom Home. Diverse cultures view home settings and use in different ways. For example, in our experience, Latino families often prefer bright vibrant color schemes, in houses with many small bedrooms because multiple generations may be living together. They often seek a large den or living room and a big kitchen, as well as ample porch and patio areas for expanded living. Asian families are sometimes concerned with the proper feng shui in deciding which way the front of the house faces. Our American Indian clients have been interested in incorporating décor and materials blending earth, water, sky, and wind. We have found that, by attending to these cultural differences, we can design homes that best meet the unique needs and preferences of our clients—and still remain affordable.

The Life Span Approach

We have worked to develop a life span approach in developing the Freedom Home. This is drawn from the work of Ronald L. Mace, who wrote about universal design and housing for the life span of all people.[4] The concept is simple and pragmatic—that we design a home to last through an individual's entire life span. This means accounting for normal aging, such as a broken ankle at any age, or a more permanent disability. We began with the very simple premise that people need to be able to get through their front door and then be able to maneuver throughout their home without barriers, limitations, or obstacles. This is the concept of visitability—a zero-step entry, bathrooms on the ground floor, and thirty-two-inch entry doors.

This may seem daunting, but if these factors are considered throughout the home design process, they are manageable. In the Freedom Home, we have built these considerations into our design. The "look and feel" of the house is not institutional, because accommodations are planned at the outset of the design and not as an afterthought. Early thinking about accessibility also saves money, because changes are not required later in the planning process or in a remodel.

Conclusion

As we prepare for the aging-in-place preferences expressed by the baby boom generation, it will be critical to design homes that are affordable, accessible, and attractive. We believe that these qualities for new homes will be good for people of all abilities. We also believe that it is both feasible and advisable that we develop models that are replicable across the county. In the coming years, it is our hope that our Freedom Home model will be joined by many others that enable Americans to have home environments that support them to be independent, regardless of any disabilities they might have. As my partner Mike Shrenk has said, "Your home should give you freedom, and should be a house that works for you."

Wally Dutcher, US Navy veteran, spokesman for the disabled, and consultant for Freedom Home Concepts. Courtesy of New Millennial Homes. Photograph by Keith Collins.

Notes

1. US Census Bureau, "Census 2000 Gateway," http://www.census.gov/main/www/cen2000.html.

2. AARP, "Home and Community Preferences of the 45+ Population," http://www.aarp.org/home -garden/livable-communities/info-11-2010/home -community-services-10.html.

3. "Tampa Market Trends," Trulia.com, http:// www.trulia.com/real_estate/Tampa-Florida /market-trends.

4. Center for Universal Design, North Caro- lina State University, "Center for Universal Design NCSU—Home," http://www.ncsu.edu/www/ncsu /design/sod5/cud.

NEIGHBORHOODS

Research indicates that some aspects of community development may offer important health benefits, while others may result in health problems for the most vulnerable segments of the population. Further research is needed to understand the linkages between the built environment and health.

All across America, neighborhoods are aging, and we need to go beyond piecemeal ideas to create more comprehensive municipal responses to aging. Capable leadership, an asset inventory, and a strategic planning process that involves widespread community participation are proven aspects of this process. Chattanooga, Tennessee, is an example of ways in which local communities can create significant change.

Most people in the United States live in the suburbs and will continue to live in the suburbs. Retrofitting existing neighborhoods can be accomplished through adaptive reuse, by redevelopment, or by removing structures to bring back green space. Neighborhoods can overcome the seemingly immutable physical features that otherwise render them socially disconnected, geographically isolated, underprotected, and underserved. Such seemingly unchangeable barriers as the street layout, distance from necessary stores and services, and even criminal incidents can be overcome with an intentionally designed overlay of community services that pull together aging neighborhoods.

Planners, designers, and developers believe that there may be a growing market among baby boomers for the walkable urban form of neighborhood. The work of the New Urbanists has advanced smart growth principles, which are highly applicable to the creation of communities for Americans of all ages. There are hurdles, however, in the lack of flexibility in traditional zoning, the absence of adequate financing, and the additional management required for walkable urban communities.

There are abundant opportunities for newly designed communities not only in revitalized urban areas but also in the less dense first-ring suburbs and in the green-grass exurbs. In such places, there is physical space to build entirely new concepts of communities, as well as homes of various sizes, price points, and configurations, designed for people who are seeking to age in place. A mix of ages and homes can be consciously woven together as communities of cohesion and support.

Chapter 13

Healthy Communities

Lawrence D. Frank

Introduction

Sparked by staggering obesity rates and the awareness that major health benefits stem from moderate levels of physical activity such as walking, public health professionals are making the built environment their business.[1] A significant amount of recent research has focused on the relationship between neighborhood design and the health of young people and working-age adults.[2] There has been less research to date on the health effects of homes and communities on older adults. Urban planners, engineers, architects, and landscape architects have a growing awareness that communities can affect the health of those who live in them.[3]

One of the cornerstones of healthy aging is the concept of *place*. When we think about aging in place, we often think first about the individual's residence. If we shift our focus from the individual dwelling to include the community, we pave the way to think more broadly about the services and neighborhoods that could benefit people of all ages. A recent book, *In the Neighborhood*, documents the loss of social fabric in physically isolating American suburbs over the past half century.[4] Elderly people spend more of their time at home and in their immediate neighborhoods than younger Americans, and as a result, they are more affected by the opportunities and constraints created by the design of their community.

DR. LARRY FRANK is the Bombardier Chairholder in Sustainable Transportation at the University of British Columbia and Senior Non-resident Fellow of the Brookings Institution. He has written two books, *Health and Community Design: The Impacts of the Built Environment on Physical Activity* and *Urban Sprawl and Public Health*. He received his PhD in urban design and planning from the University of Washington College of Architecture and Urban Planning and his MS in civil engineering transportation studies from the University of Washington School of Civil Engineering.

Community Design and Health

The connections between community design and health are complex. Research is needed to determine cause and effect and to develop community planning guidelines that will make a difference. Our travel patterns, physical activity levels, and diet are tied to where we live, and these realities affect our health. How we travel also has an impact on the amount of air pollution and greenhouse gas emissions we generate. The social environment within a neighborhood impacts our sense of safety and walkability. Fear of crime and traffic can render an otherwise walkable place unwalkable for an older adult.[5]

More walkable places are associated with increased physical activity and lower obesity rates in the general population.[6–8] However, causal evidence remains fleeting because of the effects of underlying attitudes and preferences that also shape behavior.[9] Our behavioral relationship with our physical environment is impacted by income, ethnicity, gender, and age.[10] One recent study showed significant differences in perceptions of neighborhood walkability across age ranges and included older Americans.[11]

From a public health perspective, it is critical to understand the underlying disparities and risks that exist across age, income, and ethnicity. It is important to create places that are walkable and where there are opportunities to be active and to have access to healthy foods. Older adults face the challenge of reduced mobility, which can limit their ability to carry out activities of daily life and meet their needs in their local community. Minority and lower-income older adults who live in unwalkable areas are particularly vulnerable because they often have fewer travel options. As a result, they are more reliant on the amenities that are provided near their homes.

A community that is walkable for older adults benefits everyone.[12] Distances to destinations, qualities of pedestrian facilities, crosswalk timing, visibility, paving materials, presence of street furniture and places to sit, speed of nearby traffic, and other factors impact where older Americans will be able to walk.

One of the most critical aspects of healthy aging is the ability to maintain independence and self-reliance. A considerable body of evidence exists about the importance of self-reliance in maintaining dignity and a sense of self-worth.[13] A walkable environment with shops and services nearby, connected with good pedestrian facilities, serves older Americans well. More walkable environments also provide access to opportunities for social interaction, which have been associated with protective health benefits.[14]

Healthy aging is not the only reason to retrofit existing communities. An age-friendly environment is one in which young, old, and those in between are able to interact. In many ways, young and old people share common relationships with the built environment. Both groups have less car access and are more sensitive than working-age adults to the physical design of the communities in which they reside.[15]

Measuring Walkability

A walkable community is one in which there is proximity to both recreational and other destinations and where direct, connected, and safe pathways are provided.[a] A large body of evidence has been amassed on the relationship among proximity, connectivity, and health-related outcomes in the general population. Some recent evidence is specifically focused on older Americans. Figures 13.1 and 13.2 contrast two overriding concepts of community design—proximity and connectivity, both critical walkability elements.

Proximity measures the degree to which complementary land uses (live, work, play) are intermixed and compact. Figure 13.1 shows examples of this pattern. The image on the left shows a disconnected pattern where housing, work locations, and retail and other services are located far away from one another. The example on the right shows intermixed uses where people can live, work, play, and shop in a connected and compact community. The irregular lines (called network buffers) on each example depict what a person can reach within a kilometer (about a half mile) of his or her home.

Figure 13.2 conveys connectivity, or the directness of the route one can travel between two locations. To date, connectivity has largely been measured based on roadway geometry; it is also very important to factor in the presence or absence of sidewalks. A lack of sidewalks in rural and suburban settings makes it difficult for

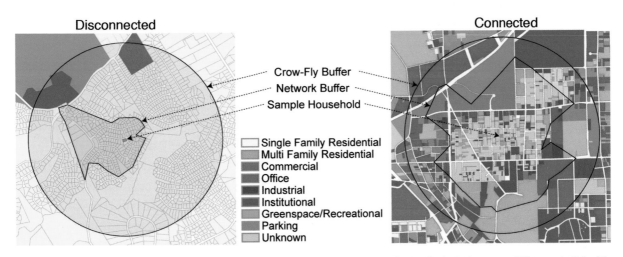

Figure 13.1 Proximity and connectivity. Source: Reprinted from Lawrence D. Frank, Martin A. Andresen, and Thomas L. Schmid, "Obesity Relationships with Community Design, Physical Activity, and Time Spent in Cars," *American Journal of Preventive Medicine* 27, no. 2 (2004): 89. Copyright © 2004, with permission from Elsevier.

Figure 13.2 Adapted from Figure 7-1 in Lawrence D. Frank, Peter O. Engelke, and Thomas L. Schmid, *Health and Community Design: The Impacts of the Built Environment on Physical Activity* (Washington, DC: Island Press, 2003). Copyright © 2003 Lawrence D. Frank and Peter O. Engelke. Reproduced by permission of Island Press, Washington, DC.

pedestrians. Walking on a busy arterial with limited sidewalks can be terrifying for anyone—especially an older adult. Without good sidewalks, even a well-designed street grid can fall short in providing pedestrian access.

Case Study: Walkability Analysis

Figure A compares two very different communities near Seattle, Washington, using a walkability analysis. On the left is the more central and walkable Queen Anne neighborhood, and on the right, the more auto-oriented Redmond neighborhood.

Several factors explain the differences between Queen Anne and Redmond. Older, more central areas like Queen Anne were developed at a time when the ability to walk was a requirement. After World War II, cars became more common, and many new neighborhoods tended to be less walkable. Each of the walkability values for the older Queen Anne neighborhood is higher than those for the newer Redmond neighborhood; some are dramatically different. Queen Anne has a higher level of residential density with multi- and single-family dwellings interspersed, making it possible for an older adult to smoothly transition from a single-family home into a condo or apartment. Queen Anne is also more mixed use and connected so that key destinations are nearby and within a direct and walkable

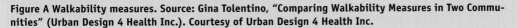

	QUEEN ANNE			REDMOND	% DIFFERENCE
Net Residential Density (dwelling units/acre)	14.96			6.83	119%
Mixed Use Index (range of 0-1)	0.29			0.17	72%
Intersection Density (per square km)	94.69			41.27	129%
Retail Floor Area Ratio	0.61			0.09	563%

Figure A Walkability measures. Source: Gina Tolentino, "Comparing Walkability Measures in Two Communities" (Urban Design 4 Health Inc.). Courtesy of Urban Design 4 Health Inc.

distance. Queen Anne also has a well-developed and interconnected sidewalk system.

The greatest contrast between these two communities is with respect to the retail floor area ratio (FAR), a measure that captures the relationship between retail floor space and the amount of land area in retail use. Deep building setbacks from roadway edges, usually in the form of large-surface parking lots, denote a low FAR. A high FAR value is given when retail is located next to the curb and when buildings occupy most of the site. Note that the FAR is nearly five times higher in Queen Anne than in Redmond. When buildings are located closer to the street, the walking distance to and between shops and services is reduced and the need to navigate dangerous parking lots eliminated. This latter point alone can determine if an older adult will walk to a nearby store. A higher retail FAR also can be important for community building. A recent study concluded that a higher retail FAR was a significant predictor for a stronger sense of community.[c] This same study concluded that higher levels of auto-oriented retail (such as strip commercial development) can reduce the sense of community.

[a]Lawrence D. Frank, Peter O. Engelke, and Thomas L. Schmid, *Health and Community Design: The Impacts of the Built Environment on Physical Activity* (Washington, DC: Island Press, 2003).

[b]Lawrence D. Frank, James Sallis, Brian Saelens, Kelli Cain, Terry Conway, and Paul Hess, "The Development of a Walkability Index: Application to the Neighborhood Quality of Life Study," *British Journal of Sports Medicine* 44 (2010): 924–33.

[c]Lisa Wood, Lawrence D. Frank, and Billie Giles-Corti, "Sense of Community and Its Relationship with Walking and Neighborhood Design," *Social Science and Medicine* 70, no. 9 (2010): 1381–90.

Built environment measures	Variable definition	Data source	Method derived
Net residential density	Number of dwelling units divided by land area within a 1 km network buffer around each place of residence and employment	1990/2000 US census and/or region-specific parcel data from metropolitan planning organization (MPO) or county assessor	Total dwelling units in buffer/total residential acres in buffer
Intersection density/street connectivity	Number of 3+ legged intersections within a 1 km network buffer around each place of residence and employment	MPO-regional road network data set	(1) Identify street-level network junctions; (2) identify junctions as intersections; (3) join intersections to buffers around trip ends; (4) count intersections in buffer, divide by buffer area
Retail floor area ratio	Floor area of retail divided by land area in retail use within a 1 km network buffer from each place of residence and employment	Region-specific parcel data from MPO or county assessor	Retail floor area divided by total parcel area
Mixed-use index/land use mix	Evenness of distribution of square footage of floor space across land uses within a 1 km road network buffer from each place of residence and employment	Region-specific parcel data from MPO or county assessor	Calculated using entropy index method, as described by Cervero and Kockelman (1997)
Walkability index	Index of the above four walkability measures	Attributes previously calculated above	Sum of normalized values of the above attributes

Table 13.1 Walkability table. Source: Adapted from context in Lawrence D. Frank, James Sallis, Brian Saelens, Kelli Cain, Terry Conway, and Paul Hess, "The Development of a Walkability Index: Application to the Neighborhood Quality of Life Study," *British Journal of Sports Medicine* 44 (2010): 924–33.

Walkable Variables

A set of variables that have been used extensively in the scholarly literature to measure the overall degree to which a place is "walkable" is described in Table 13.1. By collectively examining the variables of net residential density, land use mix, street connectivity, and retail floor area ratio, we create a common measure we have called walkability.[b]

Walkability and Health

There is an extensive body of evidence on walkability as a predictor of physical activity and obesity.[16] A 5 percent increase in walkability in King County (Seattle region) was associated with a 32 percent increase in the minutes of walking and biking.[17] More research is needed to determine if there is a causal link among walkability, physical activity, and obesity. For example, the Transportation Research Board and Institute of Medicine's 2005 report found significant relationships between physical activity and various measures of the built environment, but concluded that there is an absence of evidence to support a causal link.[18]

Physical activity is measured in a variety of ways. One study using objectively measured physical activity showed that people in the most walkable areas of the Atlanta region were 2.4 times more likely to get the recommended thirty minutes of moderate physical activity per day than those in the least walkable areas of that region. The same study found that more than twice as many (37 versus 18 percent) of those located in these walkable areas obtained the recommended physical activity levels.[19]

While more contested, obesity has also been widely linked with walkability, with summary studies canvassing and synthesizing numerous papers now published showing largely consistent results.[20] One study found that land use mix or the presence of shops and services was a very significant predictor of obesity. This study found that a typical white male weighed about ten pounds more in the most sprawling neighborhoods than in the least. This study also showed that each additional hour spent in a car was associated with a 6 percent increase in the odds of being obese. Each additional kilometer walked per day correlated with a 4.8 percent reduction in the odds of being obese.[21]

WALKABLE NEIGHBORHOOD STUDY

A recent study of the residents of Atlanta, Georgia, found that only 4 percent of the sample reported walking over a two-day period. Fifty-seven percent of the sample were overweight, and 20 percent were obese. Those with one or fewer cars were almost three times more likely to walk, those with a degree were almost twice as likely to walk, and those living in a highly walkable neighborhood were two times more likely to walk than those in a low walkable neighborhood.[a] Some other results from the study of Atlantans included:

- Increased walkability was related to a 32 percent reduction in the odds of being overweight.

- Those who walked were 49 percent less likely to be overweight.
- Women and those with a degree were less likely to be overweight.
- Younger participants were more likely to be categorized as obese, as were nonwhites and those with no college degree.
- Those who met the physical activity guidelines were 45 percent less likely to be obese.
- Those who visited a fast food outlet at least once in the two-day survey period were 1.8 times more likely to be obese.

[a]Lawrence Frank, Michael Greenwald, Steve Winkelman, James Chapman, and Sarah Kavage, "The Built Environment and Obesity," *Preventive Medicine* 50 (January 2010): S99–S105.

The National Institutes of Health funded the Neighborhood Quality of Life Study, which recruited 2,199 people (1,287 in King County and 912 near Baltimore, Maryland). People living in more walkable neighborhoods engaged in substantially more physical activity than those in low-walkable neighborhoods. People living in more walkable neighborhoods were less likely to be overweight or obese than those in less walkable neighborhoods. Overweight and obesity were more common in lower-income neighborhoods.[22] For people who are poor, an unwalkable area was found to be the worst case condition.

Seniors in Towns

There has been recent debate about whether seniors are moving back into towns and cities. In Seattle, there seems to be a significant shift in where older people are projected to live. Figure 13.3 displays a higher proportion of people aged sixty and older in the census tracts within the central area of the city of Seattle. In this instance, seniors are found to be living in town. Increased darker shading of census tracts for 2011 indicates a higher proportion of elderly residents.

Central locations can offer considerable benefits to older Americans, including increased access to retail and other services, increased levels of physical activity, and reduced likelihood of being obese.[23-25] Additional research suggests beneficial mental health for older men who live in more walkable areas.[26]

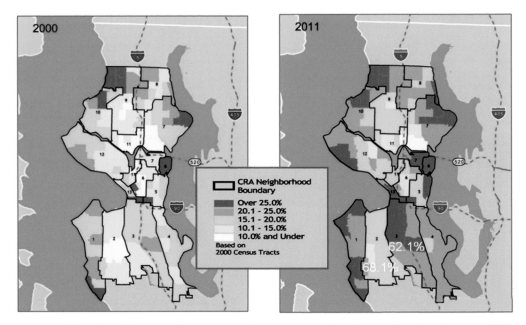

Figure 13.3 Seattle residents aged sixty and over by census tract. Data Source: Geolytics, Inc. from 2000 Long Form and 2006/2011 Estimate and Projections.

CHANGING TRAVEL AND HEALTH CHARACTERISTICS OF THE ELDERLY

Travel patterns in the elderly have been the subject of limited research to date, and the primary focus has been on access to opportunities and safety.[a,b] However, as we age, considerable changes take place in our ability and desire to travel to destinations outside of the home. These changes have important policy implications for community design. Table A provides a summary of the travel patterns of older Americans.

As Table A shows, older people travel less. The percentage of older people with a driver's license, total number of trips, transit use, and miles driven all decline with age. Willingness to walk holds constant until about age seventy-five and then declines based on perception of traffic and sidewalk availability. These changes through the aging process indicate the need to evaluate different mobility characteristics of older Americans as they age. Doing so will help us to understand not only revealed activity and travel patterns but also the trips they wanted to make but did not.

[a]Genevieve Giuliano, "Land Use and Travel Patterns among the Elderly," in *Transportation in an Aging Society: A Decade of Experience* (Washington, DC: Transportation Research Board, 2004), 192–212.
[b]Sandra Rosenbloom, "Mobility of the Elderly: Good News and Bad News," in *Transportation in an Aging Society: A Decade of Experience* (Washington, DC: Transportation Research Board, 2004): 3–21.

Variables	25–64 years old	65–74 years old	75–84 years old	85+ years old
Percentage with no driver's license	6.8%	13.5%	23.1%	57.6%
Percentage with a medical condition impacting travel	3.6%	12.4%	23.2%	33.6%
Percentage with no household vehicles	4.2%	7.9%	16.9%	18.2%
Total trips daily per person (all modes)	3.6	2.8	1.8	1.0
Percentage traveling by transit (1+ bus or rail trips over two-day survey period)	5.0%	2.2%	1.2%	1.3%
Miles traveled as driver	28.9	17.2	8.8	2.5
Percentage of people whose willingness to walk is affected "very much" by traffic	28.6%	28.8%	23.6%	22.1%
Percentage of people whose willingness to walk is affected "very much" by sidewalk availability	35.3%	35.8%	30.6%	46.2%

Table A Travel patterns of the elderly. Data Source: L. D. Frank (PI) and J. Chapman (Co-PI), SMARTRAQ Study, funded by the Georgia Department of Transportation, http://www.act-trans.ubc.ca/smartraq/pages/reports.htm.

Walkability, Air Pollution Exposure, and the Elderly

Not all aspects of walkable environments are necessarily beneficial to health. Recent evidence shows that increased levels of walkability can be associated with increased levels of exposure to certain harmful air pollutants known as small particulates.[27] Older adults are sensitive to adverse health effects, including cardiovascular and other circulatory impacts of small particulates. Young people also suffer from exposure to harmful air pollution, including developmental problems with lung formation and function.[28]

Seniors are most susceptible to exposure to small particulates, which are often concentrated very close to the edge of roadways. Concentrations of particulates decline quickly away from roads, leaving many areas that are walkable with cleaner air.[29] Research also suggests that elevation above street level is associated with reduced concentrations of harmful pollutants. The key point is that as walkability is increased in communities, we need to mitigate exposure to air pollution.

Conclusion and Policy Considerations

Strategies are needed to ensure that Americans of all ages can live in communities that promote physical activity and active living.[30] Americans, young and old, need regular social interaction, access to healthy foods, and safety from traffic. They need access to public transportation. They also need to live where exposure to air pollution is not a health threat. Senior living facilities and schools should be located carefully and, in particular, should not be adjacent to major transportation corridors. Lending policies should provide incentives to developers to create healthier communities. Housing needs to be affordable.

Evidence is emerging that the physical design of communities plays a central role in the health, well-being, and overall quality of life of older Americans. But the study of the built environment's relationships to the health of older Americans is in its infancy. Further research is needed to evaluate the relative health risks and benefits with more or less walkable places. Factors to be studied include access to healthy foods and physical activity, as well as air pollution, noise, crime, traffic, and obesity. We need to document the relative health care and service delivery costs of walkable versus more auto-dependent areas. We must develop indicators and guidelines for housing, transportation, and social needs of the elderly that are measureable, actionable, and replicable.

As we consider aging in place, we need to be aware that some communities are healthier for aging than others. Community environments that are polluted and that require dependence on others to access services and amenities tend to be less healthy. Places where walking is either difficult or impossible are not only less healthy places to age, they have significant costs and negative impacts on society as a whole. We can create measurable and performance-based transportation funding that will make communities healthier—models for this have been proposed by organizations such as Transportation for America and Smart Growth America. We can also pass legislation that will fund walkability and affordable housing in our communities. Our goal, as we develop these and other solutions, is for all Americans to age in a healthy place.

Notes

1. World Health Organization, *Preventing Disease through Healthy Environments* (Geneva: World Health Organization, 2006).

2. Committee on Physical Activity, Health, Transportation, and Land Use, Transportation Research Board and Institute of Medicine, *Does the Built Environment Influence Physical Activity? Examining the Evidence* (Washington, DC: Transportation Research Board, 2005).

3. Lawrence D. Frank and Sarah Kavage, "A National Plan for Physical Activity: The Enabling Role of the Built Environment," *Journal of Physical Activity and Health* 6 (2009): S186–S195.

4. Peter Lovenheim, *In the Neighborhood: The Search for Community on an American Street One Sleepover at a Time* (New York: Penguin Books/Perigree Trade, 2010).

5. G. O. Cunningham and Y. L. Michael, "Concepts Guiding the Study of the Impact of the Built Environment on Physical Activity for Older Adults: A Review of the Literature," *American Journal of Health Promotion* 18 (2004): 435–43.

6. Howard Frumkin, Lawrence D. Frank, and Richard Jackson, *The Public Health Impacts of Sprawl* (Washington, DC: Island Press, 2004).

7. Brian E. Saelens, James F. Sallis, and Lawrence D. Frank, "Environmental Correlates of Walking and Cycling: How Findings from Transportation, Urban Design, and City Planning Literature Can Inform Physical Activity Research," *Annals of Behavioral Medicine* 24, no. 3 (2003): 80–91.

8. James F. Sallis, Lawrence D. Frank, Brian E. Saelens, and M. Katherine Kraft, "Active Transportation and Physical Activity: Opportunities for Collaboration on Transportation and Public Health Research," *Transportation Research Part A: Policy and Practice* 38 (2004): 249–68.

9. Tim Schwanen and Patricia L. Mokhtarian, "What Affects Commute Mode Choice: Neighborhood Physical Structure or Preferences toward Neighborhoods?" *Journal of Transport Geography* 13 (2005): 83–99.

10. Lawrence D. Frank, Jacqueline Kerr, Rebecca Miles, and James F. Sallis, "A Hierarchy of Sociodemographic and Environmental Correlates of Walking and Obesity," *Preventive Medicine* 47 (2008): 172–78.

11. Ryosuke Shigematsu, James Sallis, Abby King, Terry Conway, Brian Saelens, Lawrence D. Frank, Kelli Cain, and James Chapman, "Age Differences in the Relation of Perceived Neighborhood Environment to Walking for Transportation and Leisure," *Medicine and Science in Sports and Exercise* 41, no. 2 (2009): 314–21.

12. Lawrence D. Frank, Peter O. Engelke, and Thomas L. Schmid, *Health and Community Design: The Impacts of the Built Environment on Physical Activity* (Washington, DC: Island Press, 2003).

13. Kate Lothian and Ian Philp, "Care of Older People: Maintaining the Dignity and Autonomy of Older People in the Healthcare Setting," *British Medical Journal* 322 (2001): 668.

14. Frumkin et al., *Public Health Impacts of Sprawl*.

15. Sandra Rosenbloom, "Mobility of the Elderly: Good News and Bad News," in *Transportation in an Aging Society: A Decade of Experience* (Washington, DC: Transportation Research Board, 2004): 3–21.

16. Neville Owen, Ester Cerin, Eva Leslie, Lorinne DuToit, Neil Coffee, Lawrence D. Frank, Adrian Bauman, Graeme B. Hugo, Brian Saelens, and James Sallis, "Neighborhood Walkability and the Walking Behavior of Australian Adults," *American Journal of Preventive Medicine* 33, no. 5 (2007): 387–95.

17. Lawrence D. Frank, James Sallis, Terri Conway, James Chapman, Brian Saelens, and William Bachman, "Many Pathways from Land Use to Health: Walkability Associations with Active Transportation, Body Mass Index, and Air Quality," *Journal of the American Planning Association* 72, no. 1 (2006): 75–87.

18. Committee on Physical Activity, Health, Transportation, and Land Use, *Does the Built Environment Influence Physical Activity?*

19. Lawrence D. Frank, Thomas L. Schmid, James F. Sallis, James E. Chapman, and Brian E. Saelens, "Linking Objective Physical Activity Data with Objective Measures of Urban Form," *American Journal of Preventive Medicine* 28, no. 2 (2005): 117–25.

20. Mia A. Papas, Anthony J. Alberg, Reid Ewing, Kathy J. Helzlsouer, Tiffany L. Gary, and Ann C. Klassen, "The Built Environment and Obesity," *Epidemiologic Reviews* 29, no. 1 (2007): 129–43.

21. Lawrence D. Frank, Martin A. Andresen, and Thomas L. Schmid, "Obesity Relationships with Community Design, Physical Activity, and Time Spent in Cars," *American Journal of Preventive Medicine* 27, no. 2 (2004): 87–96.

22. James F. Sallis, Brian E. Saelens, Lawrence D. Frank, Terry Conway, Donald Slymen, Kelli Cain, James Chapman, and Jacqueline Kerr, "Neighborhood Built Environment and Income: Examining Multiple Health Outcomes," *Social Science and Medicine* 68, no. 7 (2009): 1285–93.

23. Laura D. Kubzansky, S. V. Subramanian, Ichiro Kawachi, Martha E. Fay, Mah-J. Soobader, and Lisa F. Berkman, "Neighborhood Contextual Influences on Depressive Symptoms in the Elderly," *American Journal of Epidemiology* 162 (2005): 253–60.

24. Ethan M. Berke, Thomas D. Koepsell, Anne V. Moudon, Richard E. Hoskins, and Eric B. Larson, "Association of the Built Environment with Physical Activity and Obesity in Older Persons," *American Journal of Public Health* 97 (2007): 486–92.

25. Lawrence D. Frank, D. Rosenberg, A. King, and J. Kerr, "Physical Activity and Obesity Relationships with Community Design in Older Americans," *Journal of Health Policy* 7 (2010): S82–S90.

26. Ethan M. Berke, Laura M. Gottlieb, Anne V. Moudon, and Eric B. Larson, "Protective Association between Neighborhood Walkability and Depression in Older Men," *Journal of American Geriatric Society* 55 (2007): 526–33.

27. Julian D. Marshall, Michael Brauer, and Lawrence D. Frank, "Healthy Neighborhoods: Walkability and Air Pollution," *Environmental Health Perspectives* 117 (2009): 10.

28. W. James Gauderman, Hita Vora, Rob McConnell, Kiros Berhane, Frank Gilliland, Duncan Thomas, Fred Lurmann, Edward Avol, Nino Kunzli, Michael Jerrett, and John Peters, "Effect of Exposure to Traffic on Lung Development from 10 to 18 Years of Age: A Cohort Study," *The Lancet* 369, no. 9561 (2007): 571–77.

29. Alex A. Karner, Douglas S. Eisinger, and Deb A. Niemeier, "Near-Roadway Air Quality: Synthesizing the Findings from Real-World Data," *Environmental Science and Technology* 44, no. 14 (2010): 5334–44.

30. L. D. Frank and H. McKay, "Time to Walk the Talk: Embracing the Built Environment to Promote Physical Mobility," *British Journal of Sports Medicine* 44, no. 9 (2010): 615.

Chapter 14

Local Community Action

Ron Littlefield and Robert H. McNulty

Introduction

As the largest generation in the history of the United States approaches traditional retirement age, the needs of aging residents will have to be addressed quickly and effectively by thousands of communities. A survey undertaken in 2005 by the MetLife Foundation, the National Association of Area Agencies on Aging, the International City/County Management Association (ICMA), the National Association of Counties, the National League of Cities, and Partners for Livable Communities revealed that, of ten thousand governmental jurisdictions surveyed, 54 percent had not even discussed their community's ability to accommodate aging residents with regard to transportation, housing, social services delivery, and health care.[1] Communities across the nation must address antiquated zoning laws and poor to nonexistent public transportation serving the needs of elders. Communities must transform their perception of older residents as liabilities and instead reframe them as vital assets.

RON LITTLEFIELD was sworn in to his second term as mayor of Chattanooga, Tennessee, on April 20, 2009. He brought with him many years of experience in city government and urban planning. He was a realtor, specializing in commercial and industrial development, in both Tennessee and Georgia, from 2000 to 2005. He has been an instructor at the University of Tennessee at Chattanooga, as well, teaching a summer postgraduate course on metropolitan politics and policies. He has a BS in business administration from Auburn University.

ROBERT H. MCNULTY founded Partners for Livable Places (now Partners for Livable Communities) in 1977, which is a national leader in revitalizing American cities. He served as a research assistant at the Smithsonian Institution and as director of environmental programs at the General Services Administration. He was an adjunct professor and acting director of the Graduate Program in Historic Preservation at Columbia University's School of Architecture. He contributed a chapter on the quality of life to *Interwoven Destinies* and was coeditor of the *State of the American Community Report* in 1994. He graduated from the business school at the University of California at Berkeley and received his law degree from Boalt Hall at the University of California at Berkeley.

Achieving a Livable Community

There are several important questions to ask when trying to create a community in which the elderly are fully integrated and well cared for: What public services are required? Where should services be located? How can cross-generational contacts be made on a daily basis? What special recreational, educational, and cultural opportunities are needed? How can the poorest and oldest members of society be supported? How can streets and squares become safer and more accommodating? How can a community be made more affordable? And, most important, how can older people be engaged in the planning of such a community?

Every community—whether urban, suburban, or rural—poses challenges for older residents. However, when some of the simple needs of daily life are within walking distance or within the reach of public transportation, the need for intensive social services may be reduced. Many elderly people can experience a higher quality of life if they fully participate in the daily activities of the community. As higher quality of life is achieved, one could expect to find the costs to society related to the health and well-being of older adults significantly reduced.

Key Challenges and Action Steps to Building a Livable Community for All Ages

Asset mapping—a process based on the practice of asset-based community development (ABCD)—can be an effective tool to empower older adults and to build livable communities. An asset-based approach to solving community problems focuses on the skills, connections, and other special capacities of the community. Not-for-profit organizations, universities, and/or local governments can support an asset-based approach through research, technical assistance, and funding.

During the asset-mapping process, a group of trained community citizens conducts an inventory of a community's assets through written surveys and face-to-face interviews. A professional partner helps create a detailed map of these assets. Geographic information system (GIS) technology and expertise can be critical resources to this process. Assets evaluated include the following:

Housing
Planning and zoning
Transportation
Worker retraining and the economy
Health and community wellness
Culture and lifelong learning

Seniors at an ABCD planning meeting. Courtesy of www.pedbikeimages.org/Dan Burden.

Public safety

Civic engagement and volunteer opportunities

Community leadership

An exhaustively researched asset map helps stakeholders better identify connections and partnerships. The process of research itself develops relationships that match overlooked assets with community needs. The talents and experience of older residents are often among the most overlooked assets in a community.

Once a community has taken a complete inventory of its resources, leaders can more effectively work toward a livable community for all ages. This chapter presents an outline for community change and then describes a case study—Chattanooga, Tennessee—in which these principles have been implemented.

Housing

The needs and expectations for housing change with age, and housing options within our communities must reflect this evolution. Most older Americans will continue to live in the home in which they raised their families, but as people age, their activities, family composition, and financial resources change. They need to be able to find housing of the type and location that best suits their changing situation.

A livable community provides a range of housing types at various levels of affordability. In addition to assisted living and skilled nursing facilities, there should be a range of housing types available. The options should include supportive housing arrangements that are affordable for people of low and moderate incomes. Most communities, however, face major economic and political challenges to providing a diverse housing stock, which includes apartments, home-sharing options, and other more compact housing. In fast-growing communities, rapidly rising real estate values can displace low- and moderate-income residents, who often happen to be older adults. Older renters tend to pay a disproportionate share of their income on housing, forcing them to cut back on other basic necessities such as medicine and food.

Older homeowners may also struggle with rising property taxes. Numerous tools are available to state and local governments to reduce the property tax burden on older and poorer homeowners. Some local governments exempt all or part of the assessed value of older adult homeowners' property from school taxes. Local governments can also limit or freeze increases in property assessment values. Alternatively, localities can develop tax assistance programs to provide grants for low-income households.[2]

Planning and Zoning

Community planning should be a transparent, participatory process. All too often, citizens and neighborhood leaders are not engaged in land use planning unless a significant development proposal affects their own neighborhood. Planning concepts also tend to be expressed in highly technical terms, making constructive participation from citizens even more difficult. Many older citizens are the most experienced and influential civic leaders and can help local governments and planners educate their fellow citizens about the need for more flexible land uses and zoning.

Local governments can educate citizens about the needs of a maturing population through the comprehensive planning process. In most states, local governments are required to develop and update master land use plans every five to ten years. Governments can use this process as an opportunity to educate citizens about the changes facing their community. Visualization tools, such as detailed aerial maps and charrettes, have been successful in engaging citizens from a wide range of backgrounds, including older adults.

Transportation

Most adults fear the prospect of giving up their car keys—and for good reason. To live independently, older Americans must be able to maintain a mobile lifestyle, and in most communities today, that means owning and driving a car. Unfortunately, that is not an option for all residents. In addition, driving can be made even more difficult through signage and road design that confuses and endangers drivers of all ages and abilities. When visiting the doctor or getting a bag of groceries becomes an ordeal, quality of life is compromised. Enabling older adults to remain mobile and engaged in their communities requires transportation planning and repurposing of streets to include pedestrians, bicyclists, transit users, and automobiles.

Senior participants in independent transportation network, Portland, Maine. Courtesy of ITN America. Photograph by Stewart Smith.

INDEPENDENT TRANSPORTATION NETWORK, PORTLAND, MAINE

The Independent Transportation Network (ITN), a not-for-profit organization started by a community leader in Greater Portland, Maine, provides adults aged sixty-five and above and those with visual impairments with a highly flexible, consumer-oriented suite of services. Fees are based on the distance of the trip, whether the ride is shared, and whether the reservation was made in advance or on the same day. Fares are usually about half the cost of a taxi.[a]

Volunteer drivers receive either a cash reimbursement or an equivalent credit for every mile they drive. Volunteers may save these credits for their own transportation needs when they limit or stop driving, or they may donate them to family members or low-income older adults.[b]

[a]AdvantAge Initiative, *Best Practices: Lessons for Communities*, pp. 34–36, http://www.vnsny.org/advantage/tools/advantage_best.pdf.
[b]Ibid.

DRIVING

Although older drivers are involved in fewer crashes than other age groups, they also generally limit their trips as they age, which can increase isolation. Older drivers tend to experience difficulties driving at night, reading traffic signs, and turning at busy intersections. All drivers—but particularly older drivers—benefit from improvements to the driving environment.

Small modifications in roadway design and signage can greatly improve safety for all motorists, especially older adults. State and local transportation departments have found that relatively minor improvements have measurably reduced crashes. Improvements include brighter stoplights and pavement markings, larger lettering on street name signs and directional signs, protected left-turn signals, and converting two-way-stop intersections to four-way-stop intersections.

Next to driving themselves, the most preferred mobility option of older adults is to ride in cars driven by friends, relatives, or other trusted companions.[3] Volunteer driver programs can provide such mobility options.

PUBLIC TRANSPORTATION

Older adults represent a large and primarily untapped market for transit and other community transportation. Only 3 percent of all trips taken by Americans aged sixty-five and older are by bus or train.[4] Older individuals also have different travel patterns than many "traditional" transit users who commute primarily to and from work. For older individuals who are not familiar with transit services, assistance in understanding and using these services is needed. Individuals with health impairments or disabilities often have difficulty using fixed-route transit systems because of factors such as poor pedestrian accessibility or the lack of accessible design features at bus and rail stations.[5] Cost can become an issue for those on fixed incomes.

Transit providers can use a range of tools to adapt services to customers' needs. These include allowing same-day scheduling for patrons of paratransit services through computerized scheduling and dispatching systems; extending service hours to weekend and evening times; providing neighborhood circulator services such as smaller shuttle buses serving senior centers; and purchasing low-floor buses, which are easier for older adults to board.

WALKABILITY

Americans of all ages would walk more if the physical infrastructure were more conducive to walking.[6] One of the most effective methods for improving a community's walkability is to perform a walkability audit. This tool provides an opportunity for a group of decision makers, citizens, planners, or other stakeholders to experience a pedestrian environment together. A local presenter may start out with a visual introduction to walkable environments, providing local and national examples. The group leader then accompanies the group along a selected route, pointing out good and bad conditions and encouraging participants to do the same. Participants may fill out an assessment to identify specific gaps in the pedestrian network, such as missing curb cuts or broken sidewalks. Challenges to walkability

Seattle Sound Steps half marathon, Seattle Parks and Recreation, Seattle, Washington. Courtesy of Sound Steps.

ACTIVE LIVING TOUR, RICHMOND, VIRGINIA

One approach to educating participants in creating sustainable communities is to expose them personally to examples of both good and bad practice. Such an approach was used in Richmond, Virginia, through an "Active Living Tour." During the tour, city staff, citizens, and media traveled by bus around the city to study examples of good and bad walkability, including the East End neighborhood. Within a few weeks of that tour, city staff had improved one of the audited sidewalks along an arterial road. Audit data helped feed into the planned redevelopment of the 25th Street Corridor and strengthened the case for reducing building setbacks and other pedestrian-friendly guidelines. In addition, the audits led to a partnership with the Richmond chapter of the Safe Kids Coalition, and city engineers have assessed sidewalk conditions around thirty elementary schools.[a]

[a]International City/County Management Association, *Active Living for Older Adults: Management Strategies for Healthy and Livable Communities* (Washington, DC: ICMA Press, 2003); James Emory, program consultant.

include ensuring safety for older people and providing rest stops for those who can walk only very short distances at a time.

Worker Retraining and the Economy

Communities must not make the mistake of overlooking the talents and skills of older adults. In a recent report, the US Bureau of Labor Statistics (BLS) found that, between 1977 and 2007, employment of workers over the age of sixty-five increased by 101 percent.[7] The BLS expects this trend to continue. Between 2006 and 2016, the number of workers between the ages of fifty-five and sixty-four is projected to grow by 36.5 percent. In addition, employment of those aged sixty-five and up is expected to increase by more than 80 percent.[8] Many older people will likely seek part-time employment during daytime hours and will need flexible and inexpensive transportation options to get to work.

Communities can take a number of steps to enable older residents to remain in their positions or take on new jobs. Nontraditional recruiting techniques such as partnerships with national organizations that focus on older Americans can be effective. Other ideas include flexible work arrangements such as part-time work schedules or telecommuting. An attractive mix of benefits and incentives for older workers can include increased time off for medical care, employee discounts, and pension plans that allow retirees to return to work. Employers can provide employees with financial literacy skills to ensure they have a realistic plan to provide for retirement security. Challenges include how to modify tasks that are physically demanding as people grow older and how to retain experienced workers when budgets are under severe stress.

Health and Community Wellness

A livable community for all ages has a high capacity to both address and prevent health problems. The capacity to address health problems must include accessible hospitals and clinics, transportation services to and from health care facilities, and home- and community-based care services. Although some frail residents may need institutional care, many other older residents should be able to receive services in their homes and communities.

The capacity to protect and improve residents' health and wellness requires an environment that encourages physical activity. Preventive health programs such as health fairs and free screenings can be helpful. Creative efforts are needed to engage older adults in the civic and cultural life of the community. Such services must support people at a range of age and disability levels and be affordable for low- and moderate-income individuals.

NUTRITION

Establishing and supporting farmers' markets and community gardens can be an effective and flexible way for local governments to make fresh, healthy, and locally grown food available to residents. Farmers' markets can often support themselves with vendor fees.[9] Local governments can provide support by designating public land for a market, allowing the use of food stamps, promoting markets, and helping with setup, cleanup, and maintenance. Community gardens can provide exercise, social connection, and a source of locally grown food.

FITNESS

Local governments can also play a critical role in developing programs that encourage active living among older adults. Many municipalities offer exercise

RESERVE JOB PLACEMENT PROGRAM, NEW YORK, NEW YORK

ReServe enhances the lives of older adults and strengthens their communities by recruiting professionals aged fifty-five and over who have finished their primary careers and matching them with part-time, modestly stipended positions in not-for-profit organizations, government agencies, and public institutions. In these settings, older professionals can put their skills, experience, and social capital to work. All ReServists are paid $10 per hour and work approximately fifteen hours each week. ReServists represent a wide variety of professions, including social workers, attorneys, health care professionals, and marketing specialists, among others.[a]

[a] http://www.reserveinc.org.

Chattanooga farmers' market, Chattanooga, Tennessee. Courtesy of the City of Chattanooga.

classes that are tailored specifically to older adults, such as swimming programs and osteoporosis prevention classes. Local governments can encourage walking by sponsoring group programs and distributing pedometers, enabling participants to track their exercise. City governments can promote area trails by distributing maps and other materials that make these amenities easy to find and use.

SENIOR FARMERS' MARKET NUTRITION PROGRAM, RENO, NEVADA

The city of Reno, Nevada, is a lead partner with the State of Nevada Commodity Food Distribution Program in supporting the Senior Farmers' Market Nutrition Program. This program, funded through a US Department of Agriculture grant, provides eligible low-income seniors with vouchers to use at accredited farmers' markets throughout the community. The city of Reno enlists seniors in the program and offers group transportation to the farmers' markets. High school volunteers have also participated, helping seniors do their shopping and carrying their vegetables and fruits.[a]

[a]National Association of Area Agencies on Aging and the MetLife Foundation, *The Maturing of America: Getting Communities on Track for an Aging America*, p. 8, http://www.n4a.org/pdf/MOAFinalReport.pdf.

HEALTH CARE

Vaccinations and preventive screenings at health fairs and other venues are key to healthy communities. Some local governments partner with pharmacies, shopping malls, and other businesses to provide screenings in places patronized by older adults. Creating or augmenting medical transportation services requires a highly coordinated effort among local governments, health providers, transportation planners, transit agencies, aging and disability advocates, human services organizations, and community groups. Rarely are the services coordinated. Community-wide partnerships are needed to identify funding sources, such as federal transportation programs and local foundations. This initiative is particularly important in serving frail older people who are poor.

Examples of effective and creative partnerships to improve access to medical transportation include working with the local transit agency to adjust routes

Get Online Partnership, Chattanooga, Tennessee. Courtesy of Choose Chattanooga.

and encouraging transit fleet sharing among health institutions, human services providers, and other organizations.

Culture and Lifelong Learning

Lifelong learning and participation in cultural and recreational activities are important for older adults' health and for communities' quality of life and economic competitiveness. Communities can use existing cultural assets such as public libraries and local academic institutions to provide new lifelong learning opportunities. By encouraging partnerships between repertory theaters, artists, community organizations, and agencies serving older adults, local governments also create new opportunities to fund and increase the relevance of arts and cultural programs in the community.

Older adults are often the most generous and impassioned patrons of arts programs. As the baby boom generation ages, the demand for arts and cultural activities will grow. Communities can take steps to prepare for these growing audiences by training artists in residence and other professionals about the unique needs and abilities of older adults. Communities also can engage older adults in planning programs, taking an asset-based approach that taps older adults' unique strengths. Intergenerational oral history programs can be one of various creative ideas.

Computer skills are increasingly vital to accessing community information and participating in the workforce. Many older adults wish to keep up with the digital age so that they can e-mail children and grandchildren, get information without going to a library, read the daily newspaper in large-font size, or get up-to-date medical information. Technology can also enable older adults to work in part-time, consultative, and other more flexible employment arrangements. Local governments can help create computer centers that are conducive to the learning styles of older adults.

Public Safety

Both the perception and the reality of a safe environment are important in enabling residents to remain active and engaged in the community. More than one-third of older adults interviewed in a national survey identified crime as a problem in their neighborhoods.[10] Fears about neighborhood safety can stem from other concerns, such as a lack of communication between citizens and law enforcement agencies or cultural differences between older adults and other community residents.[11]

Not just an issue of the public realm, safety is also a concern within individual households. Elder abuse at the hands of relatives or caregivers is often not reported or detected. Older adults who are physically or mentally abused, or financially exploited, often do not know where to turn. Collaboration between social services agencies and law enforcement officials is critical to detecting and preventing elder abuse.

CIVIC INVOLVEMENT

Neighborhood Watch programs organize citizens to work with law enforcement to keep trained eyes and ears on their communities. These programs can be used as a civic engagement tool for older adults who often have the most knowledge of their neighborhoods and play vital roles as "eyes on the street."

Many local governments help older adults feel safer and more secure through programs that match them with neighbors, friends, or other volunteers. Mail carrier alert programs match older residents with friends and neighbors, whose contact information is provided to local postal service administrators. If a mail carrier notices that a resident's mail has not been collected, the third party is contacted so that he or she can check up on the resident. Police departments can work with aging advocates and adult protective services agencies to improve detection and reporting of elder abuse. Programs must balance care for the elderly with respect for privacy and confidentiality.

Civic Engagement and Volunteer Opportunities

A livable community for all ages engages older adults in meaningful work for the common good. Retired individuals have opportunities to use the skills and experience they've developed over time to serve their communities directly and to take on leadership roles. Intergenerational connections should be routine. Older adults can function in their communities as mentors, tutors, coaches, teachers, and role models, as well as in other roles that benefit children and youth.

Retirees have the skills, ideas, connections, and time to put toward the betterment of their communities. This trend is growing; many members of the baby boom generation have expressed a desire to volunteer upon retirement.[12] Outdated models of volunteering constitute a critical challenge, however. Most community organizations and not-for-profits are not prepared to manage large numbers of volunteers and mobilize their full range of skills.

INTERGENERATIONAL PROGRAMS

Older adults prefer working with children and youth more than any other volunteer activity.[13] This intergenerational work has a strong impact; young people who participate in intergenerational programs show measurable improvements in school attendance and attitudes toward school.[14]

Intergenerational learning can occur and develop in a variety of forms. Tutoring and mentoring programs have become increasingly common in urban areas, for example. Experience Corps, a national program with local affiliates in nineteen cities, mobilizes adults aged fifty-five and above to work as tutors, mentors, and classroom assistants in elementary schools that serve predominantly low-income families.

SOCIAL WELFARE PROGRAMS

San Diego County, California, has enlisted older adults to tackle some of the biggest social and economic issues facing the area. A school for foster care children, for

example, provides nearby housing for older adults, who receive reduced rents in exchange for mentoring the children. Another program employs older adults in part-time jobs as mentors to families who are transitioning from welfare to work. Many welfare case managers consider the senior mentoring program the most effective welfare-to-work program in the county.

SENIOR ACADEMIES

Senior academies are programs that teach older people how to effect change in their communities through greater civic involvement. These "schools in service" incorporate structured educational and hands-on community experiences. Key community partners may include local elected officials, community-based organizations, local universities, and regional councils of government.

Community Leadership: A Case Study

Community leadership must be inclusive, issue based, institutionalized, and continuously renewed. Systemic change doesn't happen without a broad base of support from neighborhood groups, elected officials, public servants, businesses, not-for-profit organizations, and other community networks. Leaders must also be drawn from many different parts of the community.

A prime example of extraordinary leadership and community action in addressing the needs of an aging population is the story of Chattanooga, Tennessee. The story of Chattanooga outlines many of the principles of the "all person friendly" community and represents an example of putting these principles into action.

THE CHATTANOOGA EXPERIENCE

The aging of a city's population calls for an overhaul of community infrastructure and resources. Having successfully met this challenge, Chattanooga, Tennessee, proudly presents itself as "the most transformed city in America." Although Chattanooga's history and development pattern is similar to that of other cities, the "uncommon story" is how it has dealt with economic change and how it is preparing to deal with population changes of the future.

Throughout the 1950s and 1960s, Chattanooga was often listed among the top ten industrial cities, but this success eventually gave way to an unfortunate accolade. In October of 1969 on an evening news broadcast, Walter Cronkite announced to the country that Chattanooga, Tennessee, had been named the "dirtiest city in America" by the US Department of Health, Education, and Welfare (now the US Department of Health and Human Services). It was a wakeup call for the community.

With renewed verve and dedication to reverse the environmental damage industry had caused, Chattanooga proceeded to clean its air and water, to rebuild its downtown, to rediscover its riverfront, to build parks and playgrounds, to extend sidewalks and trails, and to restore the integrity and charm of its neighborhoods. Once dirty and depressing, the city became clean and green—now often listed among the most livable cities in America and on track to become a world-class model of sustainable development. The city has now turned to preparing for an aging and retiring population.

As Chattanooga began its transformation forty years ago, only the older parts of the city had sidewalks. Most parks were for "stick and ball" sports as opposed to passive enjoyment. The concept of greenways and trails was alien to the community. In 1981, Chattanooga began a relationship with Partners for Livable Places (now Partners for Livable Communities) to pursue a broader agenda. This agenda asserted that quality-of-life amenities played a critical role in the economic health of the community. A community-wide coalition was established to undertake a visioning and planning effort to change the very character of Chattanooga.

In the course of this undertaking, the late James Rouse, a world-class

developer of Harbor Place in Baltimore, Maryland, and Faneuil Hall in Boston, Massachusetts, was invited to speak to a gathering of leaders of the struggling city. In a large meeting at Chattanooga's historic Tivoli Theatre, someone in the audience asked Mr. Rouse how to make the city grow. His response was straightforward and elegant: "It's really quite simple. Just make the city the best that it can be for the people who already live here and the rest will take care of itself."

Turning talk into action, the city proceeded to act on this idea. Many spectacular changes to the city's built environment have taken place, such as the development of an aquarium and the installation of new parks along the shoreline of the Tennessee River as it wends its way through downtown Chattanooga. A south-bank riverwalk was extended to connect with other trails and greenways. More than a century old, the Walnut Street Bridge was converted to a pedestrian-only bridge with a wood plank walking surface. All development was done with the mind-set of making the city the best it could be for all the people—including the aged and disabled.

In the late 1980s, Chattanooga public officials were challenged by a local group of disabled citizens to spend a day in a wheelchair. The effect was an immediate

Chattanooga District Tennessee Senior Olympics. Courtesy of Alexian Brothers Senior Ministries, Photograph by David Humber.

and long-lasting commitment to remove barriers and improve access throughout the city. Handicap-accessible design elements were incorporated into the riverwalk and Walnut Street Bridge construction plans. Previously missing sidewalks were extended and wheelchair ramps installed throughout the city.

The city's Parks and Recreation Department has developed a variety of passive parks to appeal to the entire population. Two state-of-the-art recreation centers are centrally located with indoor pools and programs for older citizens. For the more adventurous, Outdoor Chattanooga offers a wide assortment of facilities and programs to challenge and entertain people of all ages. Chattanooga's Department of Education, Arts and Culture maintains two civic centers for a wide variety of gatherings, classes, and special events, in addition to a senior center located inside a center city mall.

Chattanooga has continuously reviewed and amended its planning procedures and zoning regulations to encourage the infilling of vacant lots and to increase the density of neighborhoods. Old industrial areas of downtown have been redeveloped as communities with a wide range of residential options, including townhomes, condominiums, apartments, and single-family homes on small lots. Special financing incentives have encouraged the use of vacant parcels in older downtown neighborhoods. These activities not only spur economic activity but also create more walkable neighborhoods.

Chattanooga built two new downtown elementary schools in recent years. Both are magnet schools that encourage younger couples to choose the central city to raise their families in the context of a rich urban community. Chattanooga also offers extended opportunities for older individuals to continue to grow intellectually through free or reduced-cost programs at local community colleges or at the University of Tennessee.

The city's Department of Neighborhood Services and Community Development, well staffed with highly trained neighborhood specialists, ensures that a wide variety of services are offered to meet the special needs of each community. The department also administers the city's community development program, including a variety of home remodeling, renovation, and weatherization programs. The city's 311 call center offers a single point of access for reporting and requesting city services.

Chattanooga's increasingly rich community of cultural facilities, including theaters, a performing arts center, museums, and the aquarium, offers opportunities for volunteer or part-time service. In the schools, recreation centers, parks, playgrounds, and civic programming, mentoring is encouraged.

Not forgetting the problems of its past, Chattanooga has adopted a broad and ambitious policy of environmental improvement and sustainability. That standard of environmental excellence and the focus on quality of life as an economic development strategy has worked well. Chattanooga's focus on clean environments and quality of life were recently cited by two major companies as their reason for choosing the city. Alstom Power is investing more than $300 million in renovating a large old riverfront facility into a clean and green manufacturing site for high-tech components for the nuclear industry. Volkswagen is investing more than $1 billion in a brand-new Leadership in Energy and Environmental Design (LEED)–certified manufacturing complex.

The important point is this: If the dying and decaying "dirtiest city in America" can transform itself into a city that regularly finds itself on the top ten list of most livable cities, then any city can do it. Every city, large or small, has qualities that made them attractive places in the first place. All that is required to become a livable community for all ages is to recognize the trends that are reshaping the future, focus on those elements that will be important over the next ten to twenty years, listen to citizenry from all generations, and make the city the best that it can be for the people who live there.

Notes

1. National Association of Area Agencies on Aging and the MetLife Foundation, *The Maturing of America: Getting Communities on Track for an Aging Population*, http://www.n4a.org/pdf/MOAFinalReport.pdf.

2. Adopted from M. Scott Ball, *Aging in Place: A Toolkit for Local Governments* (Atlanta: Community Housing Resource Center, 2001), 9–10.

3. Ibid.

4. Jon E. Burkhardt, Adam T. McGavock, and Charles A. Nelson, "Executive Summary," *Improving Public Transit Options for Older Persons* (Transportation Cooperative Research Program Report 82, 2002), 1.

5. Anita Stowell Ritter, Audrey Straight, and Ed Evans, *Understanding Senior Transportation: Report and Analysis of a Survey of Consumers Age 50+* (Washington, DC: AARP Public Policy Institute, 2002), 32–33.

6. Partners for Livable Communities, *A Blueprint for Action: Developing a Livable Community for All Ages*, http://www.n4a.org/pdf/07-116-n4a-blueprint4actionwcovers.pdf.

7. US Bureau of Labor Statistics, *Spotlight on Older Workers*, http://www.bls.gov/spotlight/2008/older_workers.

8. Ibid.

9. International City/County Management Association, *Community Health and Food Access: The Local Government Role* (Washington, DC: ICMA Press, 2006), http://bookstore.icma.org/freedocs/E43398.pdf.

10. Center for Home Care Policy and Research, "A Tale of Two Older Americas: Community Opportunities and Challenges" (2004), 7.

11. For example, Community Partnerships for Older Adults, "'Peace Making Circles' Overcome Generational and Cultural Barriers in Milwaukee," *Community View* newsletter, December 2005, http://www.partnershipsforolderadults.org.

12. Partners for Livable Communities, *Blueprint for Action*.

13. Richard Adler, *Engaging Older Adults in After-School Programs* (San Francisco: Civic Ventures, 2002), 10.

14. Joanne D. Meier and Marcia Invernizzi, "Book Buddies in the Bronx: Testing a Model for America Reads," *Journal of Education and Students Placed at Risk* 6, no. 4 (2001): 319–33.

Chapter 15

Retrofitting Suburbs

Ellen Dunham-Jones and June Williamson

Introduction

What is suburbia? It is many different things, and for the majority of aging Americans, it is "home." Yet the low-density, auto-dependent, and use-separated physical characteristics of the suburban form can inhibit successful aging in place. It is vitally important, then, that suburban areas be redeveloped, reinhabited, and regreened, in other words retrofitted. Retrofitting is important in order to more sustainably meet the needs of long-lived individuals while extending the usefulness and attractiveness of societal investments for younger generations. We argue that this can be best accomplished by looking to obsolete real estate—such as vacant big-box stores, moribund malls and strip centers, and empty office parks—to create enriched places that can provide support for a healthier, happier, more self-reliant experience of aging in the suburban landscape.[1]

Pursuing such a strategy allows us to provide for the needs of older Americans and to improve the economic and environmental health of existing communities while also tapping into the substantial market clout of the baby boom generation. The boomers' needs and preferences have driven massive suburbanization in the United States for the past six decades. Born between 1946 and 1964, they were the children for whom the postwar neighborhoods of suburban yards and swing sets

ELLEN DUNHAM-JONES is professor in the Architecture Program at the Georgia Institute of Technology and a registered architect. She coauthored *Retrofitting Suburbia: Urban Design Solutions for Redesigning Suburbs*. She received her AB in architecture and planning and her master's in architecture from Princeton University.

JUNE WILLIAMSON is associate professor of architecture at the City College of New York/CUNY and a registered architect. She has been a visiting professor at Columbia University, Georgia Institute of Technology, University of Utah, and Boston Architectural College. She coauthored *Retrofitting Suburbia: Urban Design Solutions for Redesigning Suburbs*. She received her BA from Yale University, her master's in architecture from MIT, and her master's in urban planning from the City College of New York.

were designed. As they grew older, they tended to stay away from the center city, moving into garden apartments, then starter homes, then new ever-larger move-up homes. With families of their own, they juggled the demands of home and work on increasingly congested arterial roads and supported the malls and big-box power centers that leapfrogged the older subdivisions. As empty nesters, some of them moved downtown, but the vast majority continue to live in suburbia[2] and say they want to stay in suburbia to age in place.[3] The big question is how to overcome the mismatch between the child-focused and auto-dependent suburban landscape and the needs of a rapidly growing older population that, sooner or later, will have to give up the car keys?

The conventional answer for many seniors has been to move into retirement homes. Sometimes these are tall buildings in urban locations, but more often they are self-contained complexes with a suite of community amenities, surrounded by landscaped parking lots sitting isolated in unwalkable areas. Perhaps because the boomers are watching their parents and grandparents struggle with these choices, or perhaps because of their generational commitment to remaining youthful and independent, only 9 to 20 percent of boomers say they want to live in an age-restricted environment.[4] As a result, retirement community models are changing.

Consumer research shows that today's fifty-five-plus market strongly values proximity to shopping, nature, and their children; low-maintenance and energy-efficient homes; walk/jog paths; and the amenities associated with a village center. They value these features at double the rate that they value clubhouses and one and a half times the rate they value golf courses. They are eager to remain engaged by volunteering and continuing to learn in their multigenerational communities, stay physically active, and be able to safely walk to a mix of uses.[5] Public health research reinforces the benefits of such choices, and, from an architectural standpoint, we can imagine designing them into new retirement communities that function more like a traditional town, incorporating lessons from naturally occurring retirement community supportive services programs (NORC SSPs).[6] But the question remains, how do we successfully incorporate these new models into suburban development patterns as they currently exist? Table 15.1 describes the changing models of retirement communities, past, present, and future.

The answer lies in recognizing that it isn't only the people in suburbia who are aging. So are the buildings and infrastructure. For various reasons, primarily having to do with the economics and regulations of real estate development, suburban building types from the last sixty years were not built to last. Retail buildings have a particularly short life span, often less than twenty years. Coupled with high vacancy rates due to the effects of the economic crash of 2007–2009 and large amounts of land paved over for parking, this means that there is an abundance of redevelopable property in existing suburban communities already served by

	Past	Present	Future
Generation	Greatest Generation 1911–1924 GI generation 1900–1924	Silent generation 1925–1945	Baby boomer generation 1945–1965
Community type	Active adult community	Age-targeted active adult community	Multigenerational community
Location	Primarily in Sun Belt states, including Arizona, California, Florida, and Texas	Prevalent in traditional Sun Belt states and at the periphery of major metropolitan areas	Diversity in locations from secluded country locations to dense urban settings
Retirement focus	Forebears unlikely to have provided a model of retirement. Easy and affordable living	Flexibility and freedom to pursue interests	Health, well-being, and personal enrichment redefining mature. Who said anything about retirement?
Perspective	Solitary passage, age segregated	Our time, retirement from work only, cocooning	Intergenerational, back to a simpler life, personal authenticity
Financial resources	Social Security, modest home equity	Social Security, declining pension funds, 401(k), greater home equity	Primary income, 401(k), home equity, inheritance
Mind-set	Accepted aging as natural part of life cycle, happy to be alive	A well-deserved respite	Unlikely to accept aging as a part of life. Not winding down but rewinding
Lifestyle	Passive	Passive to active	Active
Major focus	Lifestyle driven	Primarily lifestyle driven with greater consideration for product	Heavy emphasis on product and how product will fit lifestyle: community that is consistent with my values
Product type	Basic small single-story attached or detached home on small low- or no-maintenance lot; value box, little variation	Small single-story attached or detached home on small low- or no-maintenance lot; higher-quality, mass-produced product	Increasingly varied, from downtown condominiums to large country estates. Customization (jewel boxes), high-level finishes, bigger homes appear to prevail
Key amenities/ activities	Golf, shuffleboard, clubhouse, pools, bingo	Eateries, learning/business center/ clubhouse, social/entertainment, fitness center, parks, golf, pools, trails, lakes, team sports	People, places/third places, town centers, learning centers, well-being venues, nature and water (active and passive)
Model	Del Webb's Sun City concept	Shea's Trilogy concept	Opportunity to create definitive concept

Table 15.1 Changing models of retirement communities. Source: Courtesy of Gregg Logan, RCLCO.

infrastructure. These areas provide prime opportunities for retrofitting suburbia to better meet the needs of the next generation of older adults.

Retrofitting: Examples of Reinhabitation, Redevelopment, and Regreening

Retrofitting takes many forms, depending on the circumstances. We have found it useful to distinguish among three general strategies. *Reinhabitation* involves the

Victorian Homes town houses for seniors on site of former strip shopping center in Levittown, New York. Photograph by June Williamson.

adaptive reuse of existing structures for more community-serving purposes, often as "third places." If home is the first place, and work the second place, the third place is where you go to hang out and build community. *Redevelopment* entails replacing existing structures and/or building on existing parking lots, generally with a compact, walkable, connected mix of uses and public spaces that supports a less auto-dependent and more socially engaged lifestyle. *Regreening* requires demolition of existing structures and restoration of land to green space, as parks, community gardens, and/or reconstructed wetlands. Regreening is sometimes a phasing strategy for eventual partial redevelopment.

In Levittown, New York, retrofitting has meant introducing housing choice in an otherwise famously homogeneous place by subsidized redevelopment of a small commercial property as town houses for seniors. Levittown also allows for mother/daughter use permits so that an in-law apartment (or accessory dwelling unit) can be created. Two-family senior residences (a form of shared housing) are permitted so that elderly homeowners on fixed incomes may rent out parts of their homes to unrelated adults. In Phalen Village, in a lower-income, low-density part of St. Paul, Minnesota, regreening has occurred: demolishing a dead strip shopping center and restoring the wetland lake that preceded it while providing the adjacent fifty-

Apartments over retail on site of former strip center parking lots in Mashpee Commons on Cape Cod, Massachusetts. Courtesy of Mashpee Commons LP.

five-plus housing cooperative with boardwalk access to a new nature preserve. In Mercerville, New Jersey, and numerous other places, vacant retail space has been reinhabited by health and fitness centers, many of them targeting programs for older people. Retrofits like these are converting grayfields into healthier, more sustainable, and more livable places. These places facilitate walking instead of driving, social interaction instead of isolation, and the health benefits associated with improved air quality and water quality and tempered thermal conditions.[7]

These benefits are manifest in varying degrees in the over eighty examples of suburban retrofits across the country that we have studied.[8] They demonstrate surprising potential for significant change, in some cases simply by building on top of large-surface parking lots. The owners of Mashpee Commons in the town of Mashpee, Massachusetts, on Cape Cod, incrementally developed mixed-use buildings with shops facing sidewalks along a grid of streets on top of the former parking lots of a 1960s strip center. It is now an attractive, walkable New England village with civic anchors and approvals to add two additional compact residential neighborhoods connected to the downtown that will include senior-oriented affordable patio housing. Douglas Storrs, one of the developers, notes, "Thirty-percent of the occupants of those apartments have consistently been seniors. They love the convenience of living here and the increased opportunities for social interaction that they find lacking in suburban residential neighborhoods."[9]

1975   1995   2015

Figure 15.1 Belmar, Lakewood, Colorado. These maps trace the history of the Villa Italia Mall in Lakewood, Colorado, from its peak as a regional mall through its decline and redevelopment as Belmar, a walkable, mixed-use downtown with great connectivity and a mix of housing types, including "lock and leave" patio homes targeted at retirees.

Some of the most dramatic retrofits have involved the demolition and redevelopment of dead malls into new downtowns. Two notable projects near Denver, Colorado, are Belmar in Lakewood and CityCenter Englewood, each with different strengths that reveal the range of possibilities. CityCenter Englewood is the more affordable of the two. A former department store has been reinhabited by the new city hall at the west end of the site adjacent to a new light rail station and public green, while the rest of the large three-story mall has been replaced with rental apartments, a gym, and services oriented to public art-adorned streets that lead to big-box discount retail at the site's east end. Belmar, though pricier, contains a wide range of housing types along with retail, restaurants, and office uses that help it function like a real downtown. The development, featuring high-quality, energy-efficient construction, has replaced a 103-acre superblock with a twenty-three-block, walkable downtown. See Figure 15.1.

New construction is inherently expensive, and many not-for-profit and low-profit community-serving uses that enhance seniors' lives are more likely to reinhabit surplus space rather than redevelop it. We've found numerous examples of vacant big-box stores reused as community centers, schools, churches, and libraries. A portion of Crestwood Court, a mall in St. Louis, Missouri, has become ArtSpace, where theater groups, dance troupes, and artist studios have taken over empty stores. The new owners of two former strip malls in Phoenix, Arizona, made them a hip destination, renamed La Grande Orange, by painting them with bright colors, converting a former post office into an upscale restaurant, and putting in a gourmet grocery store with table service. These examples provide "third places," neither home nor work, that are used for social interaction. Because suburbia has tended to focus on life within the privacy of the home, it has not had a rich supply of third places. Retrofits are overcoming this deficit as more and more suburbanites, including older adults, find themselves seeking opportunities to be social outside the home.

Older adults have also been well served by the growing number of suburban retrofits that increase access to health care and medical services. A former grocery store in Savannah, Georgia, was reinhabited by a women's medical center, even making use of the high voltage from the freezer section to power the magnetic resonance imaging (MRI) machines. Smaller clinics are popping up in shopping centers around the country, while the entire second floor of the Hundred Oaks Mall in Nashville, Tennessee, has been reinhabited by the University of Vanderbilt's Medical Center.

The Case for Change

There are many reasons why it is desirable to retrofit suburban development patterns and reduce dependency on automobiles. In addition to easing aging in place, other compelling reasons include mitigating climate change,[10] reducing dependence on foreign oil, controlling household transportation costs, and diminishing the negative health consequences of sedentary lifestyles, as well as realizing the positive benefits of directing growth to enhancing existing communities instead of consuming greenfields at the metropolitan periphery. But is it practical? We think so. Our studies of existing and emerging retrofits reveal that the strong market for these changes is due in large part to the dramatic shifts in

CHANGING SUBURBAN HOUSEHOLDS

Despite the popular perception of suburbia as dominated by families full of kids—that's not the case. Continuing a downward trend since 1970, the 2008 *American Community Survey*[a] data on suburban households reveal that only one-third of households had children under the age of eighteen, and only one-quarter fit the stereotypical suburban image of a married couple with children. Their numbers are exceeded by the number of married couples without kids (29 percent), most of whom are "empty nester" preseniors. The largest and fastest-growing category of suburban households are the "nonfamilies" at 30 percent, 80 percent of whom are single people living alone, more than a third aged sixty-five and older. In fact, almost 40 percent of suburban residents are aged forty-five or older, up from 34 percent in 2000. The percentage of suburbanites over age sixty-five will continue to expand for the next twenty years as the baby boomers cross that threshold.

It is also worth noting that suburbia is not as affluent or racially homogeneous as the stereotypical perception. Since 2005, more of the nation's poor have resided in suburbs than in central cities, and in 2008, for the first time in history, a majority of all racial/ethnic groups in large metro areas lived in the suburbs.[b]

[a]US Census Bureau, *American Community Survey*, http://www.census.gov/acs/www.
[b]Brookings Institution Metropolitan Policy Program, *The State of Metropolitan America: On the Front Lines of Demographic Transformation*, pp. 51, 85, 92, 100, http://www.brookings.edu/metro/StateOfMetro America.aspx.

Common suburban obstacles to aging in place	Retrofits to zoning code and public works standards to ease aging in place
The large lots that provide privacy and outdoor space can become difficult to maintain with age and result in fewer group activities and necessary uses being located within a walkable distance from the home.	Revise zoning to encourage smaller-lot, higher-density, and mixed-use infill and redevelopment in targeted locations. Consider requiring new developments to meet LEED-ND standards.
Homes on large lots with social spaces oriented to the backyards instead of toward front porches or stoops provide less opportunities for social engagement with neighbors and the health benefits that accrue from communal networks and social capital.	Encourage new development and remodeling and additions to engage the street. Encourage the regreening of "missing teeth" parcels into community parks and gardens.
The single-use zoning that separates residential and commercial uses further contributes to reliance on the automobile to leave the neighborhood for everyday trips.	Revise zoning to allow for a mix of uses at higher densities so as to encourage redevelopment of underperforming properties where desirable.
Lot-size minimums and restrictions on rentals and multifamily housing preserve a consistent character and income level between homes, but make it difficult to downsize within the same neighborhood, afford high property taxes on a fixed income, build senior housing, or justify transit service where densities are too low.	Revise zoning to allow accessory dwelling units (ADUs) and backyard cottages to be added to residential properties. Employ form-based zoning (instead of use-based zoning) to allow for contextual integration of senior-oriented housing types (town houses, patio homes, cottage courts, senior housing, cohousing, etc.).
The "loops and lollypops" cul-de-sac road layouts that limit cut-through traffic and are perceived to reduce crime actually lengthen trip distances, making it difficult for residents to access transit or communal amenities like parks, community centers, or libraries. At the same time, they reduce the number of residents that emergency and social service providers can efficiently and affordably serve.	Increase connectivity by whatever means possible. New streets, paths, or parks are sometimes possible in the buffers between developments or the setbacks between properties. Establish a master street plan, set block-size minimums, or establish a connectivity index based on minimum intersection density for new development as a means to improve street network efficiency.
The lack of transit, lack of sidewalks and nearby destinations, and wide roads that encourage speeding discourage walking, contributing to sedentary lifestyles and reduced longevity.	Establish Complete Streets standards and require use of the new Institute of Transportation Engineers (ITE) manual *Designing Walkable Urban Thoroughfares*.
The "drive 'til you qualify" model of providing affordable housing pushes many seniors on tight budgets to peripheral locations, isolating them from family, friends, doctors, and familiar locales. Rising fuel prices compound their budgetary constraints.	Establish minimum requirements both for high-quality public space and for a percentage of affordable units within new and redeveloped walkable centers.

Table 15.2 Retrofitting common obstacles to aging in place in suburbia. Source: Courtesy of the authors.

suburban demographics—especially the aging of the population and the consequent reduction in the percentage of households with children and increase in single-person households.[11]

Retrofit Case Studies

How do retrofits happen? In many cases, a private developer takes the first step. However, communities are often better served by taking the lead and coordinating changes to regulations in accordance with their own vision of the future. A proactive planning department might initiate a revisioning process with local stakeholders, including the health department. This process is typically followed by changes to zoning laws and public works standards using the appropriate strategies shown in Table 15.2.

Infrastructure changes often necessitate customized public-private partnerships to work out the funding for redevelopment. These are time-consuming challenges but can be facilitated by greater coordination at the regional level. Several suburbs have formed regional alliances to better argue for transit investments, tax revenue sharing, and/or consolidated services.

Case Study 1: Columbia Pike, Arlington County, Virginia

The retrofitting of five miles of Columbia Pike is an exemplary model of this process. A historic toll road, it is now an aging commercial strip corridor in Arlington County, Virginia. After extensive community meetings and a weeklong urban design charrette, the county adopted a form-based code in 2003 to provide incentives to developers to replace the existing low-rise buildings with mid-rise buildings located in a series of walkable, mixed-use nodes along the road. The buildings are taller at the center of the nodes and taper down when abutting single-family houses.[a] Tax revenue from the increased density will support streetcar service along the corridor. These improvements are making Columbia Pike safer and more livable for all residents, but especially for older citizens.

Takis Karantonis, executive director of the county-funded Columbia Pike Revitalization Organization (CPRO), says, "Aging populations are more locally oriented and community driven, and they stay local." He sees "seniors demanding a high-quality urban realm with attractive usable town squares, walkable sidewalks and benches, the reduced crime that comes with well-populated places, bus stops with real-time info, and a preference for streetcars over busses—due to the lurching associated with rapid acceleration and deceleration." In the end, he says, "All the senior groups expressed a strong preference for walkable urbanism."[b]

Access to senior services and adequate affordable housing emerged as top priorities and are being combined in innovative ways. Subsidized taxi service will continue to be provided to two new, green, intergenerational senior centers for county residents who live beyond walking distance. However, the main goal

The proposed Arlington Mills Community Center and Senior Center is being redeveloped with a mix of uses in accordance with the Columbia Pike form-based code. Underground parking and a landscaped public plaza will replace the former front parking lot and also serve an adjacent five-story building with a mix of market-rate and affordable housing units. Courtesy of Davis, Carter, Scott Ltd.

is to bring services to residents, instead of the other way around. This will be accomplished by linking the senior centers to the walkable, redeveloped nodes and by building affordable housing on the site of a former strip mall.[c] At the same time, the CPRO hopes to establish a concierge system within existing affordable rental complexes along the corridor to deliver services to their aging residents and mitigate displacement due to gentrification.

[a]The regulating plan and form-based code used to direct redevelopment along Columbia Pike were produced by an advisory working group composed of county staff and community members based on work done by Geoffrey Ferrell of Ferrell Madden Associates with Dover, Kohl and Partners and Steve Price. Details are available online at http://www.columbia-pike.org/?page_id=298.

[b]Takis Karantonis, telephone interview with Ellen Dunham-Jones, July 14, 2010.

[c]The Walter Reed Community Center and Senior Center is approximately five blocks from the Town Center node on Columbia Pike and offers adult day health care as well as activities for all age groups. With its green roof, daylighting, and green materials, it meets the energy efficiency ranking of LEED Silver. The Arlington Mills Community Center and Senior Center is located directly on Columbia Pike in the Neighborhood Center node.

Case Study 2: Thornton Place in Northgate, Seattle, Washington

Northgate in Seattle, Washington, also successfully combines redevelopment, reinhabitation, and regreening approaches and integrates senior housing into a newly walkable mix of uses. As at Columbia Pike, this transit-oriented retrofit of multiple properties has been led by the public sector—but this time working with, and on the properties surrounding, the large and long-standing Northgate Mall.[a] (See Figure A and Table A.)

Opened in 1950 as a large open-air center on a marshy site in what was then an undeveloped area north of the city limits, the mall is now owned by Simon Properties, the largest retail real estate investment trust (REIT) in the United States. The shopping center was expanded in the mid-1960s and enclosed in 1979. The Northgate area was annexed by the city in 1952 but remains suburban in form, consisting of residential subdivisions, garden apartment complexes, and stand-alone strip retail and office buildings, connected to downtown by Interstate 5,

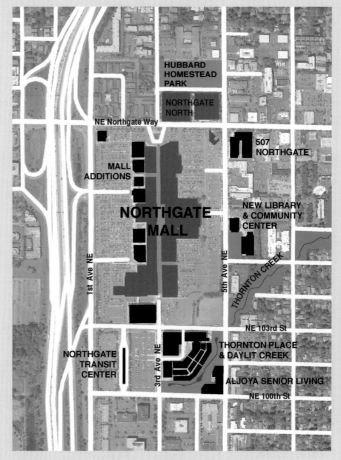

Figure A Retrofits around Northgate Mall, Seattle, Washington. Diagram by the authors.

which runs parallel to the west edge of the mall. Ten years after the 1979 renovation, in accordance with the relatively short financing cycles of suburban commercial real estate in the United States, the mall was due for an expansion. But the mall's owner ran into stiff legal opposition from local environmentalists who wanted to daylight a creek that, since the mall's construction, had been drained through a large storm pipe beneath the south parking lot.

In 2003, after many years of stalemate, an agreement was reached whereby Simon Properties would be permitted to demolish some vacant structures and add 230,000 square feet of retail space in exchange for a commitment to "use natural drainage methods, sustainable design and green building techniques and the city's new plans for Northgate area pedestrian circulation and open space."[b] These

"Before" use	"After" use	Developer and designer	Cost
Mall southeast parking lot (8.7 acres)	Thornton Place urban village (5 acres)	Lorig Associates LLC and Stellar Holdings Mithun Associates	$130 million Private funding with tax exemption
	Aljoya Thornton Place retirement housing (1 acre)	Era Living Weber Thompson architects	N/A Private funding
	Thornton Creek Water Quality Channel (2.7 acres)	Seattle Public Utilities SvR Design	$14.8 million Public funding
Goodyear tire store (3.5 acres)	Northgate community center, branch library, and park	City of Seattle Miller/Hull Partnership	$20.35 million Public funding
Corner-lot gas station (1.5 acres)	507 Northgate	Wallace Properties Baylis Architects	$54 million Private funding with tax exemption
Pedestrian-unfriendly arterial road	Fifth Avenue NE streetscape improvements	Seattle Department of Transportation	$2.1 million Public funding
Park-and-ride lot (3.73 acres)	Hubbard Homestead Park	City of Seattle Mithun Associates	$4 million Public funding

Table A Multiple retrofits surrounding Northgate Mall. Source: Courtesy of the authors.

priority items signaled a recognition that auto-oriented patterns were not serving all of the neighborhood's residents, especially the very young and the old. The mall's owner was also required to seek input from a newly formed Northgate stakeholders' group. Both the REIT and the mall's tenants would have representation in the twenty-two-seat group, as would the environmentalists. Also included was an advocate for senior housing.

The negotiated deal was critical to spurring reinvestment in the area, designated as one of six growth areas in Seattle's 1993 Comprehensive Plan. The surface parking lots of the shopping mall were prime opportunities to retrofit the neighborhood with the higher density and mixed uses that are critical to making mass transit viable.[c] (One quadrant of the mall's parking lot is already a bus transit center with almost eight hundred weekday bus trips, and plans for a light rail terminus are in the works.) Also critical are streetscape designs that support a pleasant and continuous walking experience, safe options to ride bicycles, and use of best practices to handle surface runoff, especially in Seattle's rainy climate.

A key provision in the 2003 agreement was an option for the city to purchase 2.7 acres on the southeast parking lot of the mall to provide for open space and a natural drainage solution for the piped portion of headwaters of the south branch of Thornton Creek. This provision was critical to jump starting the redevelopment of what has become Thornton Place. It represents a groundbreaking (literally!) retrofit of under-performing asphalt into a new mid-density pattern of mixed residential and commercial uses centered on the daylit creek.

Completed in 2009, Thornton Place was part of the pilot program of the LEED for Neighborhood Development (LEED-ND) rating system[d] for sustainable urban design and comprises nine buildings containing 530 dwelling units, 50,000 square feet of retail and restaurants, a fourteen-screen theater, and two stories of below-ground parking. The parking is shared, leading to a significant reduction in the number of spaces that would otherwise have been required. The site has two development parcels that bracket the 2.7-acre Thornton Creek Water Quality Channel. This publicly accessible park, also a sophisticated biofiltration swale

Before and after views of the Northgate Mall south parking lot, redeveloped as Thornton Place. In the foreground is the 8-story, 143-unit Aljoya senior living facility. Courtesy of Sky-Pix Aerial Photography.

that handles surface runoff for 680 acres, is flanked by age-integrated housing, with units designed for singles, couples, small families, and seniors: 109 condominiums, including 12 live/work spaces; 278 apartments of which 20 percent are income restricted; and 143 age-restricted units (age sixty-two plus).[e]

Aljoya Thornton Place, viewed from the Thornton Creek bioswale. Photograph by Mel Curtis, courtesy of Era Living.

The senior units are in an eight-story building (the Aljoya by Era Living) designed to rethink the conventional continuing care retirement community (CCRC) concept. The Aljoya does away with the traditional assisted living wing and instead treats patients in their own units, as necessary. "Score points for privacy and dignity," a review in *Seattle Met Magazine* raved.[f] The new continuing care protocol was developed jointly with the University of Washington School of Nursing. A restaurant is open to the public and animates the ground floor of the building. The location is proximate to Northwest Hospital and a bevy of health care providers. Also nearby is North Seattle Community College, a source for lifelong learning.

The Thornton Creek bioswale is an impressive element within this suburban retrofit project. It represents the highly successful integration of a regreening component into a redevelopment-type retrofit. The resulting amenity reintroduces environmentally cleansing vegetation and animal habitat into the landscape in a way that daylights a portion of the headwaters of the creek. When the mall expanded in 1965, the south branch of the creek was channeled into a sixty-inch-diameter underground pipe. In the final landscape design, realized by SvR Design Company under the auspices of Seattle Public Utilities, the pipe remains, but runoff is diverted to the unusually deep bioswale (up to twelve inches), where the water is partially cleansed by tall and attractive sedges, reeds, and rushes.[g]

One example of new more affordable housing, and the first multiunit housing built in Northgate in a generation, is 507 Northgate, which encompasses 163 units over retail. The site was formerly a gas station. The developers of both 507 Northgate and Thornton Place took advantage of programs for a property tax exemption of up to twelve years in exchange for providing a fixed percentage (up to 30 percent) of apartments with lower rents.[h]

Seattle is also heavily committed to legalizing the accessory dwelling units that are already common in many residential neighborhoods and to easing the path to building new units as backyard cottages. These offer a way for seniors to either downsize while living near family and staying in a familiar neighborhood or to remain in their homes with a separate unit for a live-in caretaker or rental income. A demonstration project was built in Licton Springs, a residential neighborhood in the Northgate area, as an example of a backyard cottage (a substitute term deemed less alienating than the more official "detached accessory dwelling unit," or DADU).

A backyard cottage in the Northgate neighborhood of Licton Springs. Courtesy of Chad Rollins and Christine Gregory.

In Northgate, the many changes—both small and large—intended to infill around the mall and evolve the area into a pedestrian-friendly, transit-supported, dynamic, and affordable place for new and existing residents are starting to pay off. Older adults can now experience a seamless, pleasant, and safe stroll from Thornton Place, around the reeds and rushes of Thornton Creek, to and through the shops and restaurants in the mall, and on to programs at the Northgate Community Center and Northgate Branch Library, built just a couple of blocks up Fifth Avenue on the site of a former tire store. This is no small achievement for a place built entirely and comprehensively around the primacy of the automobile.

[a]Meredith L. Clausen, "Northgate Regional Shopping Center: Paradigm from the Provinces," *Journal of the Society of Architectural Historians* 43 (1984): 144–61.

[b]From a City of Seattle press release, "Mayor, Council Announce Momentous Agreement on Northgate," announcing City of Seattle Resolution Number 30642, adopted December 8, 2003.

[c]Balancing parking, density, and transit while retrofitting is complex. Shopping centers built prior to 1965 tend to provide two to three times the number of parking spaces per square foot of gross leasable area as the Urban Land Institute and the International Council of Shopping Centers have since recommended. Transit access further reduces the number of needed parking spaces, freeing up more of the former parking lot for new uses. Research suggests that the minimum gross density to support transit is at or above seven dwelling units per acre, or fourteen jobs and residents per acre. See Robert Steuteville, Philip Langdon, and special contributors, *New Urbanism: Best Practices Guide*, 4th ed. (Ithaca, NY: New Urban Publications, 2009).

[d]LEED, which stands for Leadership in Energy and Environmental Design, is a third-party rating system developed by the US Green Building Council: http://www.usgbc.org.

[e]A biofiltration swale, or bioswale, is a gently sloped landscape element designed to use plantings to remove silt and pollution from storm water runoff.

[f]Kristin Cordova, "The New Old Age," *Seattle Met Magazine*, December 2009.

[g]"Former Seattle Parking Lot Now Treats Runoff, Provides Open Space," *Civil Engineering*, August 2009, 33–34.

[h]The rates are tied to the area median income (AMI). At 507 Northgate, 30 percent of the apartments are keyed to 70 percent AMI; at Thornton Place, 20 percent of the apartments are keyed to 80 percent AMI.

A Hopeful Future

But how welcome are these changes? Many suburban communities regard any proposal that increases density and connectivity between neighborhoods as a threat, principally due to fears of increased traffic. As a result, many redevelopment proposals are denied or watered down during the rezoning application process. Similarly, senior housing is often kept out of suburban communities as part of a blanket negation of multiunit housing. Senior housing has even been kept out of some suburban retrofits, despite the obvious benefits.[12] But the tide appears to be turning, and not only because of successful lawsuits challenging age discrimination. As but one example of many, the village of Park Forest, Illinois, helped invest in town houses oriented to seniors on a portion of the recently retrofitted shopping mall's parking lot as a way to boost the area's comparable property prices.

As the baby boomers in suburbia age, many will find that the same suburban physical design characteristics that at one time made the house a welcome retreat from the larger world may now lead to unwelcome isolation and costs, especially as driving becomes an issue. Retirees may first have to cope with the burden of rising fuel costs on a fixed income, only to then face surrendering independent mobility. Research shows that the average American male who reaches age sixty-five will outlive his ability to drive by six years, and the average American female by ten years.[13] Because of this, successful aging in place in suburbia will require more than remodeling of individual homes. There is a fundamental need to enhance alternative modes of travel, integrate more opportunities for social and physical activities, and provide compact, walkable, urban places with housing choices that appeal to older adults and seniors. Now is the time for communities to step up and begin the retrofitting process through grayfield redevelopment initiatives and changes to zoning laws, street design standards, and transit and park programs that address the needs of the aging population and tap into the strength of the boomer market to advance healthier communities for all.

Notes

1. Our focus here is on suburban *form*, wherever it is found, rather than on suburbs as defined by political boundaries. While urban form is characterized by walkable block sizes and buildings that face sidewalks and frame the space of the street as part of a mostly continuous street wall, suburban form is characterized by "object" buildings surrounded by parking lots or yards and a block and street system that is predominantly oriented to automobiles. There are many areas that are suburban in terms of form but are located within the boundaries of cities. Conversely, there are many walkable, connected, transit-served town centers that predate postwar suburbanization but are located within suburbs, though often surrounded by suburban form.

2. In 2008, 71 percent of "preseniors" (aged fifty-five to sixty-four) lived in the suburbs, according to the Brookings Institution Metropolitan Policy Program's report, *The State of Metropolitan America: On the Front Lines of Demographic Transformation*, p. 77, http://www.brookings.edu/metro/StateOfMetro America.aspx.

3. According to research sponsored by AARP, 84 percent of people aged fifty or older hoped to stay in their current residence as long as possible. Andrew Kochera, Audrey Straight, and Thomas Guterbock, *Beyond 50.05: A Report to the Nation on Livable Communities: Creating Environments for Successful Aging* (Washington, DC: AARP Public Policy Institute, 2005), 48. However, the 2005 Del Webb Baby Boomer Survey by Harris Interactive for Del Webb/Pulte Homes found that 59 percent of respondents aged forty-one to forty-nine planned to move to a new home upon retirement, and 45 percent expected to move out of state. http://library.corporate-ir.net /library/14/147/147717/items/191323/2005%20Baby %20Boomer%20Survey.pdf.

4. Del Webb, the largest provider of active adult communities in the United States, reports in its 2010 Baby Boomer Survey that 9 percent of today's fifty-year-olds and 20 percent of today's sixty-four-year-olds would prefer to move to an age-restricted community. This compares to 43 percent of fifty-year-olds and 35 percent of sixty-four-year-olds who would prefer a community with all ages. The remainder indicated no preference. http://dwboomersurvey .com/2010_Baby_Boomer_Survey.pdf. Sarah Kirsch, senior principal at RCLCO, a leading real estate consumer research company, in an e-mail message to Ellen Dunham-Jones on July 16, 2010, stated that RCLCO's past research indicated the percentage of boomers interested in age-restricted communities at 9 to 14 percent.

5. Study results on the preference for age-restricted communities vary, and many show that current residents of age-restricted communities have the highest satisfaction levels. In general, interest in age-restricted communities grows with age.

6. Good resources for research in this expanding area are linked at the US Centers for Disease Control and Prevention's Healthy Community Design Initiative website, http://www.cdc.gov/healthyplaces.

7. Development patterns that increase impervious surface and reduce tree cover and moisture, such as grayfield retrofit sites, have been linked with increases in the frequency of both extreme heat waves and cold fronts, both with particularly deadly consequences for older adults. The number of heat wave days in major US cities has doubled since the 1950s and has almost tripled in the country's most sprawling cities. Green roofs, tree-planting programs, and other regreening efforts can measurably dampen the severity of these events and save lives. Brian Stone, "Land Use as Climate Change Mitigation," *Environmental Science and Technology* 43, no. 24 (2009): 9052–56.

8. Ellen Dunham-Jones and June Williamson, *Retrofitting Suburbia: Urban Design Solutions for Re-*

designing Suburbs (Hoboken, NJ: John Wiley and Sons, 2009).

9. Douglas Storrs, telephone interview with Ellen Dunham-Jones, April 2009.

10. While there are many significant variations, high automobile use and high per capita heating and cooling energy use mean that people living at suburban densities have approximately two to four times the carbon footprint of those living at urban densities and hence a greater impact on climate change. There are numerous studies. See, for example, Jonathan Norman, Heather L. MacLean, and Christopher A. Kennedy, "Comparing High and Low Residential Density: Life Cycle Analysis of Energy Use and Greenhouse Gas Emissions," *Journal of Urban Planning and Development* 132, no. 1 (March 2006): 10–21.

11. In addition to the growing number of older adults in suburbia served by retrofits, the growth in suburban jobs has led to high numbers of young professionals, many of whom are also attracted to the more urban lifestyles suburban redevelopments offer within suburban locations. See Richard Florida, "The Case for Suburban Renewal," *Wall Street Journal*, October 9, 2010.

12. James Kraft, a developer and attorney specializing in senior housing law, has tried twice to introduce assisted living to Mizner Park, the oldest mall retrofit in the country and now routinely recognized as the "downtown" of Boca Raton, Florida. In a telephone interview with Ellen Dunham-Jones on July 20, 2010, he speculated that the reason the city's redevelopment agency would not meet with him regarding either proposal was its desire instead to maintain the area's successful focus on young professionals and nightlife. "It's age discrimination and it's illegal, but they may have felt that wheelchairs in the public park would take away from their brand."

13. Daniel J. Foley, Harley K. Heimovitz, Jack M. Gurainilk, and Dwight B. Brock, "Driving Life Expectancy of Persons Aged 70 and Older in the United States," *American Journal of Public Health* 92, no. 8 (2002): 1284–89.

Chapter 16

Longevity and Urbanism

Elizabeth Plater-Zyberk and Scott Ball

> Longevity was a great gift of the 20th century. Learning what to do with that gift is the challenge of the 21st.
>
> *Kathryn Lawler, Director of External Affairs, Atlanta Regional Commission*

Introduction

In a society with increased focus on sustainable building design and decreased resources, compactly built environments provide efficiencies and supports for aging communities. Compact "urban" environments offer the proximities necessary for a collective sense of identity and closeness through shared experience of place. Closeness in physical and social structures relates well to the needs of an aging society, offering informal interaction, "eyes on the street" for safety, and greater efficiencies in caregiving. The gift of longevity may be the catalyst that allows Americans once again to have a full appreciation of closeness in both physical and social relationships.

Urban environments can exist in a wide range of settings, from small towns in

ELIZABETH PLATER-ZYBERK is dean of the University of Miami's School of Architecture. She also is a principal of Duany Plater-Zyberk & Company, Architects and Town Planners (DPZ). She is a founder of the Congress for the New Urbanism and currently serves on the board of the Institute of Classical Architecture and Classical America. She has coauthored two books: *Suburban Nation: The Rise of Sprawl and the Decline of the American Dream* and *The New Civic Art*. She received her BA in architecture and urban planning from Princeton University and a master's in architecture from Yale University.

SCOTT BALL is a senior project manager with Duany Plater-Zyberk & Company, Architects and Town Planners (DPZ). He has managed several poststorm redevelopment efforts for DPZ along the Gulf Coast. Previous to his work with DPZ, he worked on numerous hurricane recovery housing efforts, including the creation of Louisiana's Road Home and Mississippi's Home Again programs. He served as the executive director of the Community Housing Resource Center in Atlanta. He authored the *Aging in Place Tool Kit and Lifelong Communities: A Regional Guide to Growth and Longevity for the Atlanta Regional Commission*. He has a BA from Bowdoin College and a master's in architecture from Yale University.

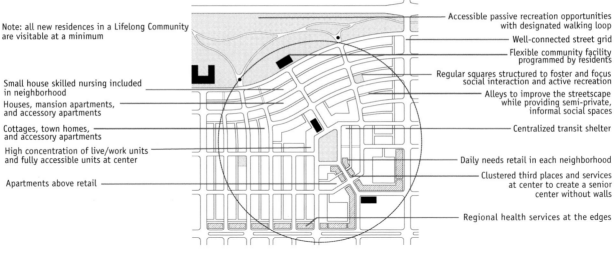

Note: all new residences in a Lifelong Community are visitable at a minimum

Small house skilled nursing included in neighborhood

Houses, mansion apartments, and accessory apartments

Cottages, town homes, and accessory apartments

High concentration of live/work units and fully accessible units at center

Apartments above retail

Accessible passive recreation opportunities with designated walking loop

Well-connected street grid

Flexible community facility programmed by residents

Regular squares structured to foster and focus social interaction and active recreation

Alleys to improve the streetscape while providing semi-private, informal social spaces

Centralized transit shelter

Daily needs retail in each neighborhood

Clustered third places and services at center to create a senior center without walls

Regional health services at the edges

Figure 16.1 Diagram of a lifelong community. Courtesy of the authors.

rural settings to neighborhood centers in suburban communities to city centers in metropolitan areas. Urbanism evolves in a range of environments, including building new communities and retrofitting existing suburbs; it does not imply mass migration to a single-city form.

A "Lifelong Neighborhood"

There are six design elements of urbanism that form what we call a "lifelong neighborhood." Other terms for these types of neighborhoods include age-friendly, healthy, walkable, or livable. These descriptors are used by those who share a growing understanding of good planning practices that serve all age groups well. Figure 16.1 diagrams a lifelong community.

The six primary design elements that shape quality urban places are as follows:

1. Connectivity
2. Pedestrian access and transit
3. Diverse dwelling types
4. Neighborhood retail and services
5. Public spaces that foster social interaction
6. Accommodation of existing residents

A NEIGHBORHOOD DEFINITION

The combination of a geographic focus and defined limits helps create a sense of neighborhood. A square, green, or important street intersection provides a public gathering space for the community with civic buildings, shops, and workplaces nearby. Private residences can be arranged around public spaces while still retaining private areas.

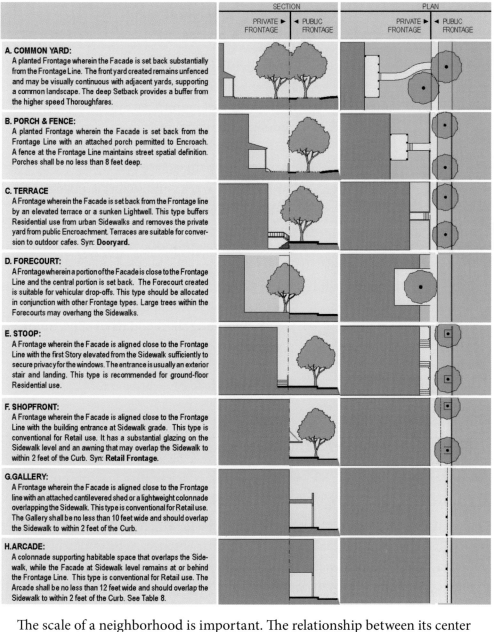

	SECTION		PLAN	
	PRIVATE ► FRONTAGE	◄ PUBLIC FRONTAGE	PRIVATE ► FRONTAGE	◄ PUBLIC FRONTAGE

A. COMMON YARD:
A planted Frontage wherein the Facade is set back substantially from the Frontage Line. The front yard created remains unfenced and may be visually continuous with adjacent yards, supporting a common landscape. The deep Setback provides a buffer from the higher speed Thoroughfares.

B. PORCH & FENCE:
A planted Frontage wherein the Facade is set back from the Frontage Line with an attached porch permitted to Encroach. A fence at the Frontage Line maintains street spatial definition. Porches shall be no less than 8 feet deep.

C. TERRACE
A Frontage wherein the Facade is set back from the Frontage line by an elevated terrace or a sunken Lightwell. This type buffers Residential use from urban Sidewalks and removes the private yard from public Encroachment. Terraces are suitable for conversion to outdoor cafes. Syn: **Dooryard.**

D. FORECOURT:
A Frontage wherein a portion of the Facade is close to the Frontage Line and the central portion is set back. The Forecourt created is suitable for vehicular drop-offs. This type should be allocated in conjunction with other Frontage types. Large trees within the Forecourts may overhang the Sidewalks.

E. STOOP:
A Frontage wherein the Facade is aligned close to the Frontage Line with the first Story elevated from the Sidewalk sufficiently to secure privacy for the windows. The entrance is usually an exterior stair and landing. This type is recommended for ground-floor Residential use.

F. SHOPFRONT:
A Frontage wherein the Facade is aligned close to the Frontage Line with the building entrance at Sidewalk grade. This type is conventional for Retail use. It has a substantial glazing on the Sidewalk level and an awning that may overlap the Sidewalk to within 2 feet of the Curb. Syn: **Retail Frontage.**

G. GALLERY:
A Frontage wherein the Facade is aligned close to the Frontage line with an attached cantilevered shed or a lightweight colonnade overlapping the Sidewalk. This type is conventional for Retail use. The Gallery shall be no less than 10 feet wide and should overlap the Sidewalk to within 2 feet of the Curb.

H. ARCADE:
A colonnade supporting habitable space that overlaps the Sidewalk, while the Facade at Sidewalk level remains at or behind the Frontage Line. This type is conventional for Retail use. The Arcade shall be no less than 12 feet wide and should overlap the Sidewalk to within 2 feet of the Curb. See Table 8.

Figure 16.2 Diagram of frontages, yards, and fences. Courtesy of the authors.

The scale of a neighborhood is important. The relationship between its center and edge is determined by an optimum walking range—a quarter mile (five-minute walk) from center to edge. A neighborhood gathers residents within walking distance of shopping, work, schooling, recreation, and dwellings of all types. A ten-minute walking distance (a half mile) may be required to access transit, optimally serving several neighborhoods at their edge. Perceptual boundaries define the neighborhood within a larger community without requiring fences and control gates. Figure 16.2 illustrates these perceptual boundaries, with a range of frontages for private and public places.

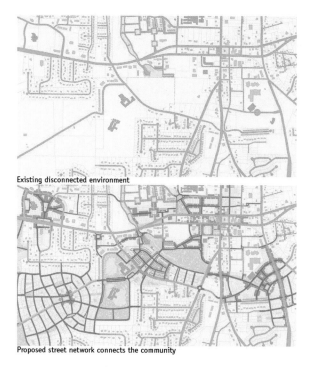

Existing disconnected environment

Proposed street network connects the community

Figure 16.3 Connectivity diagrams: the contrast between connected and disconnected street networks. Courtesy of the authors.

Planning Considerations

CONNECTIVITY

Connectivity is the single most important characteristic in community planning. It is the primary tool for maximizing access and minimizing traffic congestion.

The primary indicator of connectivity is the character of the street network. A well-connected network forms a grid with frequent intersections that provide multiple route choices. The grid can be composed of winding or straight streets. Connectivity determines a street system's ability to:

- Disperse traffic and modulate vehicle speeds.
- Support a vibrant pedestrian realm.
- Support neighborhood retail opportunities.
- Support easy movement between neighborhoods.
- Create a safe environment for people of all ages.

Figure 16.3 demonstrates the difference between connected and disconnected street environments.

Connectivity and Older Adults

Connectivity is an important urban characteristic for all ages, but older adults are more vulnerable than the general population to its absence. Accessibility of streets and sidewalks in the form of ramps, signal timing, seating, and other necessary accommodations for the disabled and the elderly is important. However, these elements are not substitutes for a well-connected street grid.

A poorly connected street network reduces the customer catchment area for local retail. It makes it difficult to establish a mixed-use neighborhood center where daily needs can be met without a car. It is difficult to serve with transit and can isolate those who do not drive. A poorly connected network collects and concentrates traffic on high-speed arterials that are dangerous to enter from the lower-speed local roads. For older drivers, abrupt intersections of local streets and arterials can be quite frightening and hazardous. Figure 16.4 demonstrates the difference between well-connected and poorly connected neighborhood plans.

Assessing Connectivity

There are a number of measures for optimum connectivity that balance pedestrian comfort and automobile mobility:

- The intersection spacing is frequent, typically 200 to 500 feet.
- The distance for walking the perimeter of the block is no more than a quarter mile, or 1,320 feet.
- The number of street intersections per square mile is generous, ranging from 120 to 240.
- The ratio of four-way intersections to three-way intersections is telling: obviously, four-way intersections provide more connection than three-way intersections.

Connectivity allows multiple modes of mobility besides the automobile, including walking, bicycling, electric carts, and transit.

The Cost of Connectivity

In new construction, a highly connected street grid is usually the most efficient subdivision pattern. A grid provides more buildable lots and a more efficient ratio of street and associated infrastructure to buildable lot. Streets that are not cul-de-sacs can be narrower. Figure 16.5 illustrates a grid of highly connected streets.

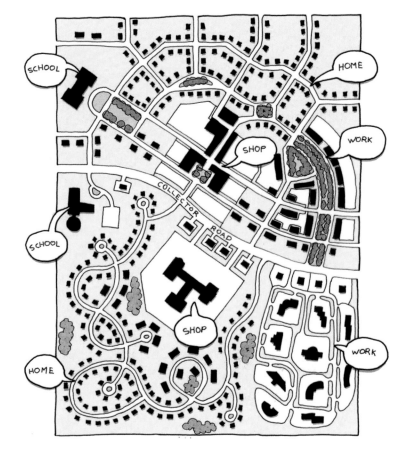

Figure 16.4 Example of well-connected neighborhood plan (top) and poorly connected plan (bottom). Courtesy of the authors.

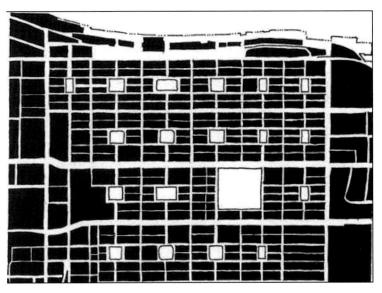

Figure 16.5 Example of connected street grid. Courtesy of the authors.

Improving connection in existing areas is a more challenging proposition. Reconnecting streets that are disconnected requires even more skillful and strategic design in order to minimize the need to purchase or condemn land from existing owners. Land acquisition is both time consuming and expensive. Careful design can mitigate displacement of current residents in an existing neighborhood.

Common Misconceptions about Connectivity

One common misconception is that residential density is the cause of traffic congestion. In fact, the opposite is true. Conventional development practices limit pedestrian access and separate uses and neighborhoods from each other. People are required to use cars, even for destinations that are close by, resulting in traffic congestion and isolating those who do not drive. When people have many routes to choose from to reach their destinations, they may do so using a variety of means, resulting in ease of access to the necessities of daily life, whatever an individual's level of mobility.

PEDESTRIAN ACCESS AND TRANSIT

Pedestrian access and transit are related; they are both parts of a continuous mobility network. While it may seem obvious that transit systems should mesh with walking routes and help people with their daily transportation routines, this pattern is not the goal of many transit systems. The primary focus of transit in most metropolitan regions is regional congestion mitigation rather than enhanced individual mobility. Such a system works well for commuters. It is less effective for those who are retired or work out of a home office and need transit for daily errands. Reorienting the focus of transit planning from congestion mitigation to individual mobility is particularly important for older adults who must rely on public transportation as they age. For these riders, an efficient alternative is the local circulator buses.

Assessing Pedestrian and Transit Mobility

Circles of a half-mile radius overlaying a plan of transit routes are an indication of the area around a transit stop that can comfortably be reached by foot, wheelchair, or scooter. Planners refer to this circular area prescribed by the half-mile radius as a "pedestrian shed." In an ideal pedestrian and transit plan, each half-mile pedestrian shed would be centered on a small daily-needs retail area at the transit stop.

DIVERSE DWELLING TYPES

For older adults who wish to remain in their current neighborhoods, downsizing to reduce maintenance and expense seems practical, but seeking a new dwelling often means moving a great distance, if there is not a mix of housing types and affordability levels within the neighborhood.

With a diverse housing stock in close proximity, moving allows one's social network to remain constant. It is possible that the stated preference of most older Americans to stay in their current home is misleading. The results may reflect limited options within their community rather than a desire to remain in the same house. Figure 16.6 shows a map of a neighborhood with a mix of housing types and affordability levels.

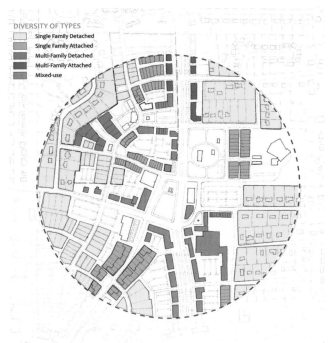

Figure 16.6 Diagram of diverse housing types. Courtesy of the authors.

Housing Diversity and Development Methods
In the case of newly built communities, a variety of housing types may require a more incremental approach to developing housing than is currently provided by high-volume development methods. Tract housing developments are often built like snapshots in time, tailored to a predevelopment market study based on prior success rather than future projection of need. That process can lead to highly repetitive uniform housing. The process has become increasingly pronounced over the past decades as mass finance and production methods have amplified the scale of these snapshots.

The result is subdivisions of homes, whether houses or apartments, built within a tight range of size and price point. The purchasers are likely to be at a similar stage in life. A typical subdivision may be developed for young families at about the same income level and with children or anticipating children. The development method itself tends to homogenize residents at the same life stage, precluding an intergenerational community.

Perhaps a lesson from the 2007–2009 recession is instructive and will encourage greater diversity in development patterns. A development that begins with larger, more expensive homes may also plan for smaller single-family and multifamily areas so that particular sections can be built as the economy fluctuates.

NEIGHBORHOOD RETAIL AND SERVICES
Having basic services within walking distance is a great convenience for all residents, but it is particularly important for an aging population.

In many places across the nation, zoning laws require the separation of commercial and residential areas. Development practices of the past half century have made it difficult to provide retail services for daily needs within residential areas. Zoning laws frequently require separation of uses to such a degree that they can only be accessed by car.

A first step to including neighborhood retail is to address the limitations of the local land use and building codes to allow mixing of uses in close proximity. To better serve older adult residents, existing neighborhoods often have to redesign and rezone areas for local commercial activity. Other useful zoning changes might include allowing home health offices in the neighborhood as well as community-appropriate skilled nursing facilities.

Zoning to Mix Uses and Housing in Close Proximity

Changes to land development regulations require a public hearing process. This process can be fraught with political anxiety, as homeowners close to the site of proposed changes voice concern about possible adverse effects such as increased traffic and loss of property values. Community opposition to change can grow to such extremes that identifying acronyms have been coined: NIMBY, "not in my backyard"; and BANANA, "build absolutely nothing anywhere near anything!" As a general rule, the more specific a community can make the zoning and entitlement process, the better the result for everyone. Homeowners need to know that the character of their community will be protected even as the uses within it diversify, and investors need to know what they can expect before purchasing a parcel for development.

Several approaches can accomplish the zoning changes that are needed: spot zoning, overlay zoning, and/or a new type of zoning called the form-based code. While all three approaches can apply to existing built forms, for new community design the form-based code is most effective.

Spot zoning is an exemption from existing zoning requirements for a single development proposal.

Overlay zoning is the term used to describe a voluntary provision added on top of an existing zoning area.

The *form-based code* is the most holistic zoning approach for retail and service integration. It provides the greatest degree of predictability and is correlated directly with a community master plan. Form-based codes primarily emphasize the shape, form, and character of the whole place rather than focusing on the individual use of each property. The form-based code was developed to advance pedestrian-friendly, traditional neighborhood planning principles. It regulates individual private developments so that they contribute to and shape the public space, producing a

AGING OVERLAY ZONES

Cities are not often viewed as ideal places to grow old. High traffic, a fast pace of life, expense, and safety are often cited as concerns. But cities also already have in place some of the most difficult to implement infrastructure features that support aging in place—public transportation, close proximity of medical care, and high-quality walkable destinations. Recognizing the realities of their aging populations, as well as the potential economic benefits of keeping seniors in their homes, some cities have begun to experiment with "age-friendly districts." These districts are intended to integrate some of the advantages of retirement communities into existing neighborhoods by doing things like extending red light times to allow more time to cross the street, providing additional benches for resting, convincing store owners to make public restrooms available, and providing buses to and from the grocery store.[a]

An even more aggressive version of this concept is the "senior overlay district." In this case, a formally defined boundary is drawn within a municipality in which special senior-friendly zoning laws are implemented. For example, a senior overlay district may allow multiple residents in what is traditionally a single-family home, enabling accessory dwelling units (ADUs) that would otherwise be impossible.

Additional requirements may also be implemented in the district, such as for concentrated services, health care facilities, ramps, and recreational planning.[b]

New York City is one of the leaders in taking this approach. The Age-Friendly New York City (Age-Friendly NYC) initiative was launched in 2008 as a partnership among the New York Academy of Medicine, the Office of the Mayor, and the New York City Council to implement the recommendations of the World Health Organization's Age-Friendly Cities program.[c] The partnership has launched two pilot age-friendly districts, one in East Harlem and one on the Upper East Side. The districts will initially be administered by the New York Academy of Medicine, but eventually will be transferred to local community groups. The final details remain to be defined, but the goal is "to create a public-private partnership that would encourage businesses to voluntarily adopt amenities for the elderly. Examples could include window stickers that identify businesses as age-friendly, extra benches, adequate lighting, menus with large type, and even happy hour for older residents."[d]

[a] Anemona Hartocollis, "Fast-Paced New York Promises Safety and Comfort to Older Residents," *New York Times*, July 19, 2010.
[b] Cori Menkin, "Senior Citizen Overlay Districts and Assisted Living Facilities: Different but the Same," *Pace Law Review* (January 1, 2001): 481–509.
[c] Age-Friendly New York City, http://www.nyam.org/agefriendlynyc.
[d] Hartocollis, "Fast-Paced New York Promises Safety and Comfort to Older Residents."

place of specifically intended character. The form-based code is focused on public spaces—streets, sidewalks, and parks—and how buildings on private parcels face them. The form-based code is typically more focused on the pedestrian experience than on that of the automobile, when regulating street and building details. While a conventional zoning code tends to separate buildings from the street and from each other, the form-based code focuses on orchestrating individual buildings so that, together, they produce a safe, comfortable, and interesting street space.

Retail Merchant Considerations

In suburban and rural settings, retail and service business models are often of a large scale; they depend on a regional market that, in turn, requires arterial road access. The smallest big-box operation may be unable to succeed below a minimum of thirty thousand square feet. A single neighborhood may not be able to accommodate more than a few thousand square feet or provide enough customer base for chain merchants.

On the other hand, older adults can provide an important market segment for smaller retail merchants, particularly when they are retired and do not need to function on the same 8:00 a.m., 12:00 p.m., and 5:00 p.m. peak retail demand hours of working adults. Under ideal circumstances, a neighborhood café is a morning coffee venue for parents dropping off children at school and heading on to work. After 3:00 p.m., it is an after-school hangout for teenagers, and again serves parents returning from work in the evening. Neighborhood retail requires these types of multiple market shifts throughout the day in order to survive. Older adults can play an important role in the daily retail cycle, as they provide a customer base for those otherwise slow midday hours when working adults are at their jobs and children are in school.

Integrating retail and service provision into the neighborhood requires both zoning reform and entrepreneurial innovation. Older adults can be advocates for this change as well as an important part of the market that will fuel the change. The corner store thrives in many older neighborhoods, and there are many new examples of mixed-use neighborhood development sprouting up across the country. As business models evolve, those communities that have adopted zoning ordinances to support neighborhood-based retail may be the first to receive new investment.

PUBLIC SPACES THAT FOSTER SOCIAL INTERACTION

Public spaces are an important feature in every community. To foster social interaction, public and semipublic spaces should be supervised, programmed, and differentiated. Public space is best supervised by surrounding buildings with facades and functions that enable a visual connection between indoors and out. "Eyes on the street" is the planner's phrase for informal monitoring or supervision of public open space from inside buildings or other activity spaces. These features are important for all age groups, but especially children and seniors.

Public space is programmed by structuring intentional uses within it, giving residents reasons to spend more time in public. A focused activity can lend a sense of purpose to being in public and prolong the time spent in a public setting. Sports such as shuffleboard, chess, and golf have long served as such a purposeful public recreation for seniors, and community gardening is becoming increasingly popular as a public activity.

Chess tables in Washington Square Park, New York City. Courtesy of http://en.wikipedia.org/wiki/File:Washington_Square_Park_Chess_Players_by_David_Shankbone.jpg.

Public space is differentiated in acknowledgment of the differing needs of various activities and age groups. Older adults may avoid areas that are teenage hangouts and perceived as unsafe, unfriendly, or too rambunctious. Teenagers may avoid areas where too many older adults gather that are perceived as uncool. Public space is not always neutral and open to all. Designing spaces for social interaction must anticipate and provide opportunities for differentiation, either by offering a wide array of smaller congregating areas distributed across the community or by subdividing larger public spaces so that they can be occupied differently by distinct groups in close proximity.

The goal is to provide opportunities for gathering, but gathering variously: to collect but individuate. Differentiating public space deters a single group's ability to monopolize a space, while encouraging a collective sense of neighborhood identity.

Washington Square Park in New York City provides an excellent example of differentiated space. It has broad paths that lend themselves to strolling in conversation, small formal flower gardens that invite sitting in contemplation, a long and winding perimeter trail for running and bicycling, safe playgrounds for small children, fountains that serve as meeting and people-watching places, and stone chess tables located adjacent to the playground. Benches for a pause and rest are evident. There is an intergenerational invitation to visit Washington Square Park.

ACCOMMODATION OF EXISTING RESIDENTS

The first five considerations of this chapter described community characteristics and implementation tools such as urban design and zoning laws. When we face the challenge of changing an existing residential area in which residents are already aging in place, two issues merit discussion: how to make an existing residential area more amenable for seniors with small changes and how to redevelop a residential area with major changes.

In the first case—that of making a residential area more amenable with only small changes—various improvements can be made. These include adding or improving sidewalks, street trees, and lighting; changing signal timing for longer pedestrian crossings; adding pedestrian shortcuts through long blocks; adding benches; allowing accessory dwelling units (ADUs) in single-family zones; inserting other types of housing appropriate for the elderly; and inserting a corner store. There are trade-offs with a piecemeal approach, but it enables people to stay in place in their existing community.

In the second case—major redevelopment—we must consider the effects on existing residents. Outdated and underutilized areas ripe for redevelopment often house a high percentage of older adults who are already aging in place. Any move is traumatic, and frail elderly individuals can experience confusion and diminished self-help capacity when relocated to unfamiliar settings. Careful relocation strategies must be employed when redeveloping existing communities. The right to return to the renewed or new development should be convincingly guaranteed to those who want it, and, at a minimum, US Department of Housing and Urban Development relocation requirements should be fulfilled.

Conclusion

It is critical to consider the principles of urbanism as we plan for an aging society. Connectivity and pedestrian access, diverse dwelling types, and a mix of neighborhood retail and services are key qualities. Public spaces and the accommodation of existing residents are essential. These urban design considerations will better allow residents to thrive in community. If longevity was the great gift of the twentieth century, it lays the groundwork for a return to great communities to be the gift of the twenty-first.

Chapter 17

Neighborhood Development

Christopher B. Leinberger and Michael Glynn

Introduction

The built environment is where America puts more of its wealth than any other asset class—more than stocks, bonds, or cash. It represents over 35 percent of the wealth of the country. The majority of this investment is in real estate, which includes housing, workplaces, retailing, public buildings, and medical facilities. The balance is in the infrastructure that supports this real estate. This huge investment affects most aspects of life.

Real estate is the catalyst for major changes in the economy, as demonstrated by the recession of 2007–2009, which was sparked by the collapse of the housing market. How we design the built environment fundamentally affects how people live their daily lives. In a society that is aging, the built environment can have a particularly significant impact on the ability of older people to remain safely and productively in housing of their choice.

America has a domestic public policy that implicitly favors one form of the built environment, known as "drivable suburban." Virtually every trip from home is by car, which means that this form of development consumes significant amounts of land. In fact, little investment has been made in other public transportation systems

CHRISTOPHER B. LEINBERGER is Visiting Fellow at the Brookings Institution and focuses on "walkable urban" places. He is a founding partner of Arcadia Land Company and a professor at the University of Michigan. His most recent book was *The Option of Urbanism: Investing in a New American Dream*. He received his BA from Swarthmore College and an MBA from the Harvard Business School. He also attended the Martin Luther King School of Social Change and the Institute of Social Research at the University of Michigan.

MICHAEL GLYNN is an independent consultant advising senior housing companies on strategic planning and business development. Previously, he was a health care services analyst in the US equity division at Credit Suisse in New York City. He is a CFA Charterholder and a LEED Accredited Professional. He holds a BA from Columbia University and a master's degree in urban/regional planning and graduate certificate in real estate development from the University of Michigan.

(such as rail and bus) or in alternative transportation (such as walking and biking). This form of the built environment is characterized by the following:

- Low density (0.05 to 0.40 floor area ratio, or FAR[1])
- Exclusively car/truck served
- Single uses separated from other uses (e.g., only owner-occupied housing in one district, only retail in another district)

The alternative development pattern is known as "walkable urban," which is how American metropolitan areas were predominantly built in the previous centuries.[2] Walkable urban places are characterized by the following:

- Higher density (FARs generally between 1.0 and 5.0, although some examples of even higher densities, such as Midtown Manhattan in New York City, exist)
- Served by a variety of transportation options, including transit, biking, autos/trucks, and walking
- Inclusive of multiple land uses, such as residential, office, medical, retail, and recreational, within walking distance (tends to be between 1,500 feet [a quarter mile] and 3,000 feet [a half mile])

Real estate project developments on the periphery of urban areas or in the suburbs can be more easily reduced to formulas than can infill urban development. Development within urban areas must accommodate the existing built environment. As a result, suburban real estate, which is most prevalent in the United States, can be commoditized. There are nineteen standard real estate product types that are easily understood by the real estate and financial services industries, as well as local planning and zoning agencies. These include such well-known products as mobile home parks, entry-level homes, and move-up homes.[3]

What about older Americans and where they live? The National Association of Home Builders 50+ Housing Council and the MetLife Mature Market Institute describe four types of communities of households for those aged fifty-five and older: age-qualified active adult, other fifty-five-plus communities, age-restricted rentals, and other fifty-five-plus households.[4]

There were 39.5 million fifty-five-plus households in the United States in 2009. Of these households, over 27 million (69 percent) were located in neighborhoods that are neither age qualified nor even occupied primarily by people over fifty-five (other fifty-five-plus households). Approximately 8.2 million fifty-five-plus households are found in neighborhoods where most of the residents are also over fifty-five (naturally occurring retirement communities). Just over 1 million households are in age-qualified active adult housing in the tradition of Del Webb's Sun City. Approximately 1.6 million households are age-restricted rentals.

Structural Shift in Market Demand toward Walkable Urban

Walkable urbanism has become more prevalent.[5] After sixty years of building drivable suburban development, the market appears to be saturated. There has been overbuilding of suburban housing[6] that has led to an unprecedented crash in home values. While a large segment of the senior housing market will still live in the suburbs, others will be drawn to urban settings.

Other evidence can be found in many metropolitan areas, where the highest housing values per square foot have shifted from drivable suburban neighborhoods in 2000 to walkable urban neighborhoods by 2010. Examples include high housing values in 2000 found in Great Falls, Virginia, in the suburbs of Washington, DC, and in Highland Ranch south of Denver, Colorado, shifting to walkable urban neighborhoods in 2010, such as Dupont Circle in Washington, DC, and the lower downtown historic district (LoDo) of Denver, Colorado. The lines crossed in the past decade. The last time the lines crossed was in the 1960s, and they were heading in the opposite direction.[7]

According to *Real Estate Issues*, "Boomers tend to seek maintenance-free living, easy lifestyles, more leisure time, new experiences, and prefer multiple options, customization and control."[8] Studies show that boomers favor dense, walkable environments with a concentration of easily accessible services.[9] The Congress for the New Urbanism reports that the older end of the baby boom wave is more likely

PARK PLACE AT CHATHAM, CHATHAM, MASSACHUSETTS

Park Place at Chatham in Chatham, Massachusetts, is an example of walkable urban senior living demand being met through the vision of a local suburban developer. Although the property's full apartment units are senior-friendly and high quality, this independent living facility keeps monthly costs at a minimum by tapping the synergies of the surrounding community and enabling residents to create a customized solution by purchasing only services they need. Home health services can be provided on more attractive terms because of economies of scale and group negotiation. Park Place's setting next to Chatham's historic town center brings walkable community access to its doorstep. This allows residents to easily take advantage of entertainment, social networks, and other services in the community at large without explicitly paying for them. The local library, retail and restaurants, Cape Cod baseball league games, parks, concerts, festivals, and public bus transportation to neighboring towns are also within walking distance.

ARLINGTON COUNTY, VIRGINIA

Walkable urban senior living demand was addressed indirectly through Arlington County's general land use plan. The success of the Rosslyn–Ballston Metro Corridor is a result of long-term planning to address the demand for walkable urban development in general. It is the foremost example in the country of the redevelopment of former strip commercial into walkable urban places. That it is an attractive place for senior housing is just one small part of the overarching strategy. In fact, only a limited number of new units specifically dedicated to senior housing have been developed in Arlington County. Yet the community is amenable to aging in place as a result of the top-notch public transportation and easy access to social networks and services.

Arlington, Virginia. Courtesy of Coalition for Smarter Growth, www.smartergrowth.net.

than any other age group to prefer living in "a townhouse in the city," perhaps more open to change as they become empty nesters.[10] From within the baby boomer category, those who are wealthier and more highly educated have demonstrated a higher likelihood of moving from isolated neighborhoods to walkable urban places, whether in the center city or the suburbs.[11]

The demand is not limited to center cities. There is much evidence that walkable urban development is as likely to transform the suburbs, such as in Valencia, California. Many smaller cities, like Santa Fe, New Mexico, Flagstaff, Arizona, Asheville, North Carolina, and Bend, Oregon, are attracting empty nesters and retirees, partially due to the walkable urban nature of their downtowns.

This type of development is attractive to older people for a number of reasons. As more restaurants, housing, office space, and hotels are built in a walkable urban place, home values and quality of life increase. For older individuals, there is increased access to entertainment, stimulation, care, education, and public services. This can preserve independence, especially when driving a car becomes a challenge. This type of community is also a positive for environmental sustainability reasons and meets the needs of all ages as well as varied multifamily housing types. It also means getting incidental exercise through the best possible means: walking. Financially, the ownership of a car is the second largest category of household expenditures after the cost of housing. By not requiring car ownership to participate in society, the cost of living can be reduced substantially.[12]

However, there are many challenges to walkable urban development. Over 90 percent of the jurisdictions in the country do not allow this form of urban development under their zoning codes. Changing the zoning laws or obtaining an exception requires significant time and financial resources without the assurance of success. There is considerable NIMBY (not in my backyard) opposition to allowing increased density even in urban places. There have been scattered examples of NIMBYs becoming "YIMBYs" (yes, in my backyard) with the recognition that high-density urban housing may increase the quality of life and housing values.

Other challenges revolve around the lack of experience and track record of financiers and developers. Standard senior housing product types are well understood, as are their risks. Given the size of the investment required and following the financial meltdown of 2007–2009, it is difficult for developers or their banks to feel comfortable with "new" concepts whose pitfalls are unknown.

There is yet another complication: walkable urban places need intensive management. Often, this responsibility is taken on by a not-for-profit management organization, such as a business improvement district (BID). There are over twelve hundred BIDs in North America, and using their existing management infrastructure would be extremely cost effective in better integrating various forms of senior housing into a broader community. BIDs have the incentive to do this as

Village of Park Forest Farmers' Market. Courtesy of the village of Park Forest, Illinois.

well; maintaining new or existing customers in the street life of a walkable urban place adds life and economic value.

Management is also important for senior housing in naturally occurring retirement communities (NORCs) and housing with services where seniors are staying in place. The Village to Village Network, which provides coordinated services in communities, is a new example of providing management to maintain the independence of seniors.

PARK FOREST, ILLINOIS

The village of Park Forest, Illinois, created walkable urban senior living by transforming a dying mall into its downtown. With dead and dying malls proliferating as a result of long-term structural changes in the way consumers shop, "grayfields,"

as dead malls are referred to, are in desperate need of new uses. The village of Park Forest used senior living as a key component for the adaptive reuse of a grayfield as a walkable, mixed-use town center. In place of an old Sears building, Victory Centre at Park Forest offers senior apartments and assisted living in a walkable community.

Senior Housing Standard Products

As with most real estate product types in America, the financial industry has forced senior housing into standardized categories—independent living facilities, assisted living facilities, memory care, and nursing care.

The distinguishing factor of senior housing is that it is "needs based" and that property managers offer services to address these needs. The real estate investment category "senior apartments" does not include needs-based services; therefore, it is more often categorized with basic multifamily real estate.

Senior housing categories are primarily defined by the intensity of on-site services related to health, hospitality, and social programming. These services may represent up to 75 percent or more of the operating cost structure[13] and may be collectively referred to as long-term care (LTC)—the assistance that individuals with disabilities receive to help them with everyday life. Below are descriptions of the four senior housing standards.

INDEPENDENT LIVING FACILITIES

Independent living facilities (ILFs) typically include only a small service component, as residents are healthier than those in other types of senior housing. Thus, ILFs are the least regulated and most loosely defined of the four standard senior housing categories. To enable aging in place, ILFs have an elder-friendly design and provide certain nonmedical services, such as food service, transportation, and social programming. Since health services are not included, residents often contract separately with providers, such as home health agencies. The National Investment Center for the Seniors Housing and Care Industry (NIC) estimates there are 693,000 ILF units in the United States[14] with an average monthly rate of $2,705.[15]

ASSISTED LIVING FACILITIES

In addition to the hospitality and social programming services akin to those offered at independent living facilities, assisted living facilities (ALFs) offer health services. Residents often receive assistance with medication management and activities of daily living, which are key determinants in the varying levels of care and associated monthly rents. NIC estimates there are 532,000 assisted living facility units in the United States[16] with an average monthly rent of $3,525.[17] The operating fee structure is roughly 65 percent for services and 35 percent for housing.[18] Like independent living facilities, ALFs are mostly private pay and therefore cater more to higher-income individuals. Regulation of ALFs varies by state.[19]

MEMORY CARE

Memory care, often considered a subcategory of assisted living, is dedicated to serving the needs of those with dementia. The fast growth of this category is associated with the increased number of Americans with diagnosed Alzheimer's disease, which accounts for 60 to 80 percent of dementia cases.[20] There are an estimated 114,000 memory care units according to NIC.[21]

SKILLED NURSING FACILITIES

Skilled nursing facilities (SNFs) are considered institutional settings since the average resident has limited independence and may warrant twenty-four-hour care and monitoring in a controlled setting. The service component accounts for about 75 percent of monthly fees compared to 25 percent for housing.[22] SNFs are the most regulated form of senior housing and, as a result, are the most standardized. There are approximately 1.5 million nursing care units in the United States,[23] and the average monthly cost is $7,943.[24] SNFs serve individuals of all income levels since Medicaid covers those with limited means.

These four standard types are often part of a continuum of care. One common type of such a continuum is the continuing care retirement community (CCRC). CCRCs usually include independent living and skilled nursing, but often have assisted living as well. CCRCs often have entry fees, which may be associated with a guarantee of increased services at a set price.

Commoditization of Senior Housing

Similar to the other standard real estate product types, the commoditization of senior housing helps lower the financial risk for investors, but has negative side effects. Many of these commoditized products are initially built by real estate developers, generally people who know how to build, but not manage, senior housing. Facilities are then sold or leased to operators, providing a possible disconnect between services required and the buildings delivered.

However, the major problem is that there is a disconnect between the senior housing units and the suburban communities in which they are built. There is often no connection between the immediate community and the senior housing facility. This arrangement ignores the role that the surrounding community and its transportation system play in residents' well-being. A resident's connection to a community can have a tremendous impact on health, quality of life, and cost of care. Assisted living and nursing facilities pay careful attention to standards of accessibility within a residence, but less attention to accessibility to the community.

It is important to realize that cost savings can accrue through the economies of scale available to walkable urban senior housing. By definition, long-term care strives to maintain optimal functioning through "a wide array of medical, social, personal, and supportive and specialized housing services."[25] If senior housing is isolated from walkable places, a rich set of community supports can be lost. The community has been developed at a cost that has been amortized over many years, and these supports must then be re-created at significant costs to the facility, which results in the higher rents and fees of traditional senior housing. A consequence of this is that a significant percentage of Americans are finding senior housing unaffordable and many institutional settings are struggling to survive.[26]

Financing Options in the Future

As financial markets recover and the real estate cycle begins anew, the senior housing market is in need of financial innovation to accelerate development in walkable urban environments to serve unmet demand.

The unique characteristic of senior housing, "that it is a combination of two sectors, housing and health care," may represent both the greatest barrier and the greatest opportunity to change. A US congressional commission reported, "The most striking characteristic of seniors' housing and healthcare . . . is the disconnection between the two fields. . . . The Nation can no longer afford the inefficiency of the current disconnect."[27]

Financial innovation can stem from the private sector through long-term care insurance (LTCI), which provides beneficiaries with additional income support at advanced ages. Incentives wrapped into LTCI contracts could encourage senior housing in walkable communities. For instance, LTCI policyholders could be given premium discounts if they reside in walkable communities. Or policyholders could realize greater reimbursement benefits if they reside in healthy communities.

Senior housing finance is in its early stages, and the financial services industry is reluctant to fund "nonconforming" investments. However, as successful senior housing models take hold, new financial products will result. Financial innovation is essential for the widespread development of walkable urban senior living in the decades to come.

Conclusion

Walkable urban senior housing options integrated into the surrounding community are crucial to providing the health care and social engagement that are most needed. This requires a focus on "place" within which seniors live, work, and play.

Finding and supporting models of walkable urban senior housing in all parts of the country is a crucial first step. Banks and developers are seeking new concepts, especially after the recession of 2007–2009, so showing how comparable projects work better and cost less is important. Likewise, funding new examples to demonstrate how projects can be developed or redeveloped will inspire confidence in the investment community. Finally, research is required to demonstrate the desirability of walkable urban senior housing for private investors, government, individuals, and their families.

Notes

1. FAR is a measure of density. It is the ratio of the square footage of heated living area to the land area on which it sits. For example, 20,000 square feet built on 100,000 square feet of land results in a FAR of 0.20. If 200,000 square feet were built on the same 100,000 square feet of land, the FAR would be 2.0.

2. Christopher B. Leinberger, *The Option of Urbanism: Investing in a New American Dream* (Washington, DC: Island Press, 2008).

3. Christopher Leinberger, "The Need for Alternatives to the Nineteen Standard Real Estate Product Types," *Places* 17, no. 2 (2005): 14.

4. *Housing Trends Update for the 55+ Market/New Insights from the American Housing Survey* (NAHB/MetLife, January 2011).

5. Leinberger, *Option of Urbanism*.

6. Christopher Leinberger, "Here Comes the Neighborhood," *Atlantic Monthly*, June 2010.

7. Leinberger, *Option of Urbanism*.

8. David Lynn and Tim Wang, "The US Senior Housing Opportunity: Investment Strategies," *Real Estate Issues* 33, no. 2 (2008): 33–51.

9. D. Myers and E. Gearin, "Current Preferences and Future Demand for Denser Residential Environments," Housing Policy Debate, 2001.

10. Congress for the New Urbanism, *The Coming Demand*, http://www.cnu.org/cnu_reports/Coming_Demand.pdf.

11. William H. Frey, *Mapping the Growth of Older America: Seniors and Baby Boomers in the Early 21st Century* (Washington, DC: Brookings Institution, 2007).

12. Leinberger, "Here Comes the Neighborhood." The cost of transportation for drivable suburban households is, on average, 24 percent of their budget; for walkable urban households, it is 12 percent.

13. Jeffrey Davis, *Senior Living and Long Term Care Properties: Institutional Investor Introductory Primer* (Chicago: Cambridge Realty Capital Companies, 2006).

14. National Investment Center for the Seniors Housing and Care Industry (NIC), "4Q 2010 Estimates," http://www.nic.org/research/faws1.aspx.

15. *Seniors Housing Market Insight: 2010 Mid-Year Review* (Del Mar, CA: Vant*Age Pointe Capital Management and Advisory, Inc.).

16. NIC, "4Q 2010 Estimates."

17. *Seniors Housing Market Insight*.

18. Davis, *Senior Living and Long Term Care Properties*.

19. "Oversight of assisted living communities is primarily in the hands of state governments rather than under federal regulation," *2009 MetLife Market Survey of Long-Term Care Costs*, http://www.metlife.com/assets/cao/mmi/publications/studies/2010/mmi-2010-market-survey-long-term-care-costs.pdf; *Brookdale Senior Living 2009 Annual Report*, http://www.annualreports.com/HostedData/AnnualReports/PDFArchive/bkd2009.pdf.

"Regulation of the senior living industry is evolving at least partly because of the growing interests of a variety of advocacy organizations and political movements attempting to standardize regulations for certain segments of the industry, particularly assisted livings"; and "state regulations governing assisted living communities require written resident agreements with each resident. Several of these regulations also require that each resident have the right to terminate the resident agreement for any reason on reasonable notice. Consistent with these regulations, many of our assisted living resident agreements allow residents to terminate their agreements upon 0 to 30 days' notice."

20. *Seniors Housing Market Insight*.

21. NIC, "4Q 2010 Estimates."

22. Davis, *Senior Living and Long Term Care Properties*.

23. NIC, "4Q 2010 Estimates."

24. *Seniors Housing Market Insight*.

25. Special Committee on Aging, *Developments in Aging: 1997 and 1998, Volume 1, Report 106-229* (Washington, DC: United States Senate, 2000); *Fact Sheet: Selected Long-Term Care Statistics* (San Francisco: Family Caregiving Alliance, 2005).

26. Phillip Moeller, "Senior Housing: The New Reality of Senior Communities," *US News and World Report*, March 3, 2010.

27. *A Quiet Crisis in America* (Report to Congress by the Commission on Affordable Housing and Health Facility Needs for Seniors in the 21st Century, Washington, DC, June 30, 2002).

STRATEGIES FOR CHANGE

Each of us must not only take personal responsibility for how we will age, but we must also think about our responsibility as citizens. Public policies that assist the most vulnerable in our society to age in place are challenging; it is important that aging in place not mean "stuck in place" for the very poor.

Because of the 2007–2009 recession, the financial security that many older people planned for may be significantly reduced. The alternatives for providing retirement income include personal savings, long-term care insurance, and, for homeowners, reverse mortgages and home equity lines of credit (HELOCs).

The recent recession has underscored the importance of Social Security and Medicare for all but the wealthiest Americans. Medicaid long-term care has been essential as a safety net for the very poor elderly. These entitlement programs are under tremendous budget pressure, just as the number of older people dramatically increases.

We must implement new financial strategies for aging in place, quickly, particularly for the oldest old. There are proven and promising initiatives, but accomplishing a cohesive system of private and public support based on home and community services requires research, advocacy, media attention, and legal and electoral action. Although enormously challenging, a new vision for very old age is simple: that old people might age in the homes of their choice with the support they need to thrive.

Chapter 18

Vulnerable Populations

Fernando Torres-Gil and Brian Hofland

My Experience: Fernando Torres-Gil

Having contracted polio at a young age and undergoing years of surgeries and rehabilitation, I have benefited from a lifetime of thinking about how I would adjust to longevity and how I would want to age in place with a disability. I have had the opportunity to see firsthand the environmental and infrastructure challenges that are involved with remaking neighborhoods to accommodate individuals like me. I served for many years as vice chair of the Los Angeles Planning Commission, later as a harbor commissioner for the Port of Los Angeles, and currently as a member of the Los Angeles Airport Commission. These experiences showed me firsthand the value that individuals attach to their homes and their understandable reluctance to accept changes in neighborhoods and communities.

I realized that, for me, I would need to think through a "personal longevity plan," which would accept the reality that someday I would not be able to walk and would have to rely on a wheelchair and power scooter. Some years ago, my wife and I, who live in a hillside single-family home, purchased a condominium in Downtown Los Angeles. At the time, Downtown LA was considered an

FERNANDO TORRES-GIL is associate dean of academic affairs at the UCLA School of Public Affairs. He is also professor of social welfare and public policy and the director of the Center for Policy Research on Aging. He was appointed as the first assistant secretary for aging in the US Department of Health and Human Services, and he serves on the board of AARP. He was coeditor of *The Art of Aging Well: Lessons from Three Nations* and *The Art of Caring for Older Adults*. He received his MSW and a PhD in social policy, planning, and research from the Heller Graduate School in Social Policy and Management at Brandeis University.

BRIAN F. HOFLAND is director for economic justice at the AARP Foundation. He was formerly director of the Atlantic Philanthropies Global Aging Program and was the first president of Grantmakers in Aging. He currently serves on the board of Lutheran Services in America. He received his BA in psychology from the University of Wisconsin and his MS and PhD in human development and family studies from Penn State University.

undesirable location, with drug addicts, the largest number of homeless of any US city, abandoned buildings, and minimal nightlife. In the years since, however, a consensus emerged that Downtown LA was vital to the future economic and social prosperity of the city and the region. Fast-forward to today: a growing population of middle- and upper-income professionals, a growing number of white and minority families with children, a return of retirees to the central city from surrounding suburban areas, dramatically reduced crime levels, reduction in the homeless population and expanding housing options, a vibrant nightlife, a major expansion of transit options, and improved property values.

My personal longevity plan will include moving to a fully accessible condo that has twenty-four-hour concierge service, an on-site deli, cleaners, restaurant, and retail and is close to educational and cultural attractions as well as medical facilities. I will use my personal power scooter with which I can access all the urban amenities of that area, such as the Walt Disney Concert Hall in the Los Angeles Music Center, without having to drive or walk. In fact, I intend to be fully engaged in civic activities, including volunteering to teach part-time at a new high school two blocks away, which will allow me to "scoot" over in my power chair. This school—the Edward R. Roybal Learning Center—is a magnet school for inner-city Central American and immigrant students. New public schools in Los Angeles are supported by a community concerned that a poor public school system would not only be a disservice to minority and immigrant children but would also lower property values in Los Angeles.

In time, if I need an assisted living facility, my wife and I will consider a Hispanic-oriented life care retirement community in Boyle Heights close to Downtown Los Angeles. Why a Hispanic-oriented facility? Because we choose to age in place with a racial/ethnic community in which we are comfortable. My personal journey is one example of how we can adjust to differences and respond to aging and diversity while working toward transforming our locales to account for old age. Through innovative practices, I believe that we can promote a quality of life with multiple preferences for housing, transportation, health, and long-term care. We can succeed if society becomes receptive to the changes that are needed.

But what happens when economic and social conditions prevent individuals and families from having choices? What if local communities and those with power and influence fail to pay attention to the demographic and social changes that will alter the landscape? What if cities resist innovative approaches to aging in place? When we write about the benefits of aging in place for older Americans, we need to consider those vulnerable individuals who may actually be "stuck in place" because of economic, social, physical, and racial conditions.

Setting the Stage: A Conceptual Framework

Current demographic and economic trends reveal a downsizing of the American dream and the possibility that older Americans may experience poverty or at least an insecure retirement. We have a responsibility to provide innovative solutions, new public policies, and private sector options to enable low-income senior citizens to enjoy a decent quality of life.

Private sector innovations and choices for housing, transportation, recreation, leisure, and social activities are focused on the affluent seniors in our society, which begs the question: What about those less affluent? Who represents their interests?

As the baby boomers age, society will encounter new challenges and opportunities; the needs of this population group will change as they age. The increasing diversity of our population will complicate how we respond to those who want to grow old in their homes and neighborhoods. What key population subgroups will require attention? Figure 18.1 provides a conceptual framework that identifies key subgroups to which many older people will belong, assuming a future of declining prosperity and resources.

This framework suggests that greater numbers of individuals may find themselves

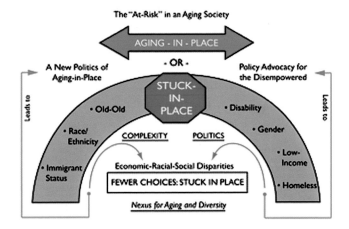

Figure 18.1 Aging in place: the nature of limited choice. Source: Fernando M. Torres-Gil and Diana N. Lam (2010).

"stuck in place" with fewer options for enhancing their quality of life as they try to age in place. Those "stuck in place" could include diverse segments of the population such as the oldest old, racial and ethnic groups, immigrants, people with disabilities, the poor, the homeless, and women. These vulnerable groups will require that policy and political advocates understand and represent their needs. Greater numbers of disabled, poor older minorities in gentrifying neighborhoods may bring new tension to the politics of aging in place.

There is a need to develop ways to address the needs of these vulnerable groups. In doing so, we need to consider the macro trends that will impact our ideas and recommendations for enhancing options for aging in place.

The Great Risk Shift: Shifting Macro Trends

How do today's economic changes alter how older people will fare in the future? An intriguing perspective is provided by Jacob Hacker in his seminal book, *The*

AT-RISK POPULATIONS: A CONVERSATION WITH ANDREW SCHARLACH AND BOB MCNULTY

In 2009, as the *Independent for Life* book project was in its initial phase, Fernando Torres-Gil posed a series of questions about aging and at-risk populations to his fellow contributors. The following are Torres-Gil's questions, and the responses from Andrew Scharlach (Chapter 6) and Bob McNulty (Chapter 14).

How do we ensure that at-risk populations are not overlooked?

Andy Scharlach: We need to be aware that housing by itself is not enough, and that services and supports are necessary to supplement the built environment. Particular attention must be given to those populations with the least political and economic capital, for whom additional infusions of social resources are needed.

Bob McNulty: Nationally, the model offered by AARP is a good example of channeling the power of a diverse population with a few uniform characteristics. Locally, many communities have "Senior Neighbors" or some such organization which serves the aging population in terms of services and voice.

How do we increase the political and policy influence of at-risk populations?

AS: We need to pay particular attention to program models that not only meet the needs of at-risk elderly populations, but enhance individual strengths, social capital, and community capacity. Policy advocacy is essential.

BM: Effective organization of any population (at risk or otherwise) is the only answer.

How do we ensure that minority groups and at-risk populations are not overlooked?

AS: Innovative responses to the needs and sensibilities of diverse population groups are needed, particularly for programs targeted to minority and at-risk populations.

BM: Organize.

How can we respond to the needs of persons with disabilities, those living in rural areas, older women in poverty, and those who are homeless or living at the margins economically?

AS: Community services and supports can help to bridge the gap between existing physical and social

Great Risk Shift.[1] Hacker argues that a massive transfer of economic risk from government to the individual has occurred over the last generation. This transfer has changed the economic circumstances of Americans, regardless of age and income level. These increased risks are evident in the transition from defined benefit pension plans to defined contribution savings plans, the demise of retiree health care coverage, and the erosion of employee benefits. An increasing proportion of employees are without health care coverage, face decreased health care benefits, and/or have a lack of long-term employment. The eroding employer-based social safety net has pressured governments to shoulder more of the burden of social services. Taken together, Hacker suggests that this transformation is structures and the needs of the most vulnerable groups and individuals. We need to respond to the needs and concerns of persons with disabilities, those living in rural areas, older women in poverty, and those who are homeless or living at the margins economically.

BM: There are local, state, and even federal agencies, but churches and nonprofit organizations are often better equipped to address such needs.

How do we promote coalition building, community organizing, media acceptance, and political empowerment of at-risk groups?

AS: We need to focus on integrative approaches to community support, which move beyond meeting individual needs to enhancing social capital and community capacity. Examples include community initiatives designed to build local coalitions, enhance community empowerment, and impact the policy environment.

BM: A local community cannot address these problems without a well-organized, professionally staffed, and adequately funded agency solely devoted to the creation, care, and feeding of a comprehensive network of neighborhood organizations. This should be "job one" for any city or other local government attempting to

have an impact on the needs related to aging in place.

How do we respond to NIMBYism [a derivative of "not in my backyard"] and LULUs [locally unwanted/ undesirable land uses]?

AS: We need to consider two types of discrimination: economic based (against people who are less affluent) and function based (against people who are disabled). Aging-in-place efforts, if successful, inevitably raise the specter of individuals continuing to reside in their existing communities as they become more impaired and less affluent. Community activities and services that facilitate the development of enduring interpersonal bonds and a sense of community may help to ameliorate some of the ageism and economic discrimination that otherwise might develop. The same principles, albeit more challenging in America's individualistic and class-driven society, may help to overcome obstacles to integrated neighborhoods and programs. Ultimately, enlightened self-interest may be the only potentially viable solution.

BM: The only way to overcome fear and resistance is familiarization—promoting and even forcing diverse groups to meet, talk, and seek a level of mutual respect and understanding.

not a one-time occurrence or linked to a specific recessionary period, but rather it is a long-term, permanent shifting of risk, insecurity, and responsibility to the individual.

This shift is most evident in a declining middle class, creating an intense level of insecurity among most Americans. Even those who followed the traditional steps toward securing a comfortable retirement (education, investing in a home, saving for retirement) are feeling deflated. Hacker's original analysis was made prior to the start of the 2007–2009 recession, and his prognosis has become even starker. In 2010, he noted that even the election of a progressive president did not alter the nature of this risk shift, given that "the bad economy has sidetracked many proposals" that might have benefited the middle class. What are the implications if Hacker's assessment is enduring for the long-term American economic experience?

Various scenarios emerge from Hacker's "great risk shift": pessimistic predictions of increased poverty among the elderly, an electorate that is less generous in supporting taxes and public programs, and intergenerational tension. Advocates may face a public that is skeptical about programs designed to serve seniors who are poor, disabled, homeless, minority, undocumented, black, single, and/or female. Such a public may be unaccustomed to diversity in their neighborhoods. Resistance to inclusionary policies may intensify.

The Bad News: Accepting the New Reality

A farsighted student of these trends is Elizabeth Warren, whose analysis of "the long road to retirement" summarizes the growing inability of the middle class to contemplate a retirement of economic security and leisure.[2] She illustrates the issues: escalating personal debt, increased foreclosures and bankruptcy, and declining pensions and savings. She portrays a future where the public sector will have limited tools because of unsustainable entitlements, federal deficits, and payments on the national debt. Figure 18.2 illustrates bankruptcy rates among various age groups.

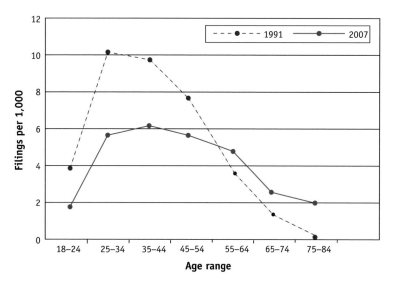

Figure 18.2 Bankruptcy filing rates per 1,000, by age. Source: Elizabeth Warren, "Middle Class in Crisis: The Long Road to Retirement" (presentation to AARP, Harvard Law School, Cambridge, MA, 2010).

In addition, the 2007–2009 recession dramatically affected the future economic security of baby boomers. Workers were impacted by unemployment, business downsizing, and other cutbacks; 401(k) plans and other defined contribution savings plans were hard hit by stock market losses; and over a third of workers have no pension or retirement savings.

The mortgage and foreclosure crisis is having a significant impact on older people. The loss of a home has inordinate repercussions, since older people have few resources for recovery. This crisis may often mean that old people are forced to move from where they had hoped to age in place to a child's home or to an apartment in an unfamiliar community. AARP's first assessment of this growing phenomenon found that, by the end of 2007, people over fifty years of age represented 28 percent of all delinquencies and foreclosures.[3] In addition, African Americans and Hispanics who were fifty and older had foreclosure rates of 0.51 percent compared to 0.19 percent for Caucasians in that age group.[4] By 2010, the more insidious aspect of the 2007–2009 recession was visible from the increase in homelessness among Americans who were sixty-two years of age and over.[5] The trend of homelessness among the elderly did not begin with this recession, but it is expected to increase as the baby boomers age.[6] M. William Sermons and Meghan Henry of the Homelessness Research Institute have projected there will be 95,577 elderly who are homeless by 2050, up from 33,754 in 1990. If these predictions hold, we will face a larger subset of the older population to which the concept of aging in place will have little or no relevance, as they will have no home.

Disability

We may also see a commensurate increase in the disabled. The Americans with Disability Act (ADA), which celebrated twenty years in 2010, covers approximately fifty-four million individuals with physical or mental impairments that substantially limit daily activities of working, walking, talking, and/or caring for personal needs. Growing numbers are people over fifty years of age. In 2007, 30 percent of people aged sixty-five to seventy-four and 53 percent of individuals aged seventy-five and older reported having one or more disabilities. These disabilities were the result of chronic illness, declining vision or hearing, decreased physical fitness, and other age-related impairments. With increased numbers of older people who are evidencing greater likelihood of difficulties with activities of daily living, including bathing, eating, toileting, and dressing, we can fully expect to see older Americans comprising the majority of the disabled.[7]

Poverty

During the Great Depression, older people and children were the most vulnerable to economic stress. Older people were more likely to lose their homes and savings and become dependent on their children, neighbors, or charitable organizations. Without those resources, they were forced into homelessness. It was the sight of elderly people seeking food in garbage containers in Long Beach, California, in the 1930s that sparked the first senior citizen movements: the Townsend movement of the 1930s and 1940s and the McLain Organization in California of the 1940s and 1950s.[8] These groups advocated for minimum incomes and pensions for older people and were the precursors to today's old-age advocacy groups, including the National Council on Aging, Families USA, the National Committee to Preserve Social Security and Medicare, the National Hispanic Council on Aging, and AARP. The resulting politics of aging gave older voters extraordinary electoral and political influence and helped lead to a host of categorical and entitlement programs predicated on age (Medicare, Social Security, the Older Americans Act). We might see a new politics of aging from the pending vulnerability facing baby boomers as a result of the recent recession.

Will the next generation of vulnerable baby boomers reach a level last seen among the elderly in the 1930s? Various analysts[9] are convinced that a large segment of baby boomers will be "at risk" as they age, with some speculating that the one-third of baby boomers today without a college degree, pension plan, or adequate savings may be ill-housed, ill-fed, and poor.

A measure of economic vulnerability is the federal poverty guidelines, which display numbers and percentages of older people falling below a poverty benchmark. One of the great success stories of the last century is the dramatic decline of elderly living in poverty, from roughly 70 percent of older people in the 1930s to a record low of 9.7 percent in 2007.[10] This decline in poverty among the elderly was in contrast to a dramatic increase in children living in low-income households. Much of the decline was due to the expansion of social policies and the entitlement programs of Medicare, Social Security, and Medicaid. But the official poverty measures may be understating the actual federal poverty rate today. In 2007, the federal poverty guidelines were $10,210 for a single person and $13,690 for an older couple.[11]

The problem with the federal poverty guidelines is that they are based on a 1960s consumption survey, which focused on what individuals spent for food. It mistakenly assumes that food accounts for one-third of a family's budget. In reality, the preponderance of an older person's budget is spent on housing and health care, which are not accounted for in the official poverty index. Efforts are under way to introduce legislation to create a new Elder Economic Security Standard Index that would more accurately account for the high cost of housing and medical care most relevant to a retiree.[12] Because the poverty index determines eligibility for means-tested programs (Medicaid, Supplemental Security Income [SSI], in-home supportive services, food stamps), this effort would increase the proportion of older people classified as poor and have a direct impact on spending and fiscal obligation. Figure 18.3 charts the difference between current and proposed poverty measures.

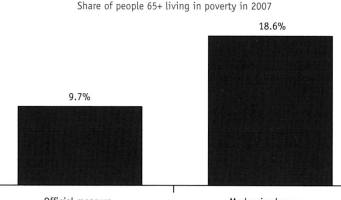

Share of people 65+ living in poverty in 2007

18.6%

9.7%

Official measure
(3.6 million elderly poor)

Modernized measure
(6.8 million elderly poor)

Figure 18.3 The official poverty measure underestimates the share of elderly Americans living in poverty. Source: AARP Public Policy Institute Economic Team, "Older Americans and the Recession" (2008).

Regardless of how poverty is measured among the elderly, current fiscal trends do not bode well for the future of more than eighty million baby boomers reaching retirement age. This scenario is further complicated by demographic forces that will alter the American landscape.

Nexus of Aging and Diversity: More Complexity and Seeds of Opportunity

By 2050, the United States will look, feel, and sound very different than it does today. Much attention is paid to the controversies over immigration and diversity, arguments over driver's licenses for undocumented immigrants, in-state tuition for native-born children of undocumented parents, and even revising the US Constitution to prohibit citizenship for children born of undocumented parents. What relevance does this have to aging in place?

The relevance is that the coming nexus of aging and diversity means that our neighborhoods, our political system, and the nation's racial-ethnic profile will be very different during the latter stages of the baby boomers' lifetime. This reality will have a profound effect on how we address aging in place. Figure 18.4 illustrates the concept of the nexus between aging and immigration.

The framework above illustrates the societal journey the United States will take between 2010 and 2030 as we witness lower fertility rates and increased life expectancy among Anglos and higher fertility rates among the immigrant population. Baby boomers will grow older, and the younger working-age population will be more diverse, made up of immigrants and minorities. Public policy, the culture, and the economy will be influenced by these twin developments.

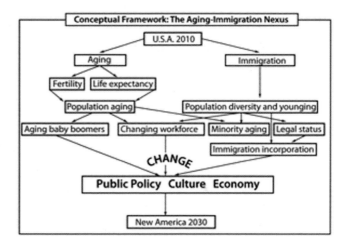

Figure 18.4 Conceptual framework: the aging-immigration nexus. Source: F. Torres-Gil and J. Treas, "Immigration and Aging: The Nexus of Complexity and Promise," *Generations: Journal of the American Society on Aging* 32, no. 4 (2009): 6–10.

Dowell Myers argues for "rediscovering the intergenerational social contract" by convincing aging baby boomers that they have a stake in how minority and immigrant groups progress and integrate into American society. He raises policy dilemmas about the future funding of entitlement programs and the burden on young minorities and immigrants to pay the taxes to sustain public benefits for older people. He highlights the need to educate and invest in the productivity of a diverse workforce. He also raises the critical question: Who will buy older people's houses?[13] The reality for many aging baby boomers is the expectation that someone will be willing and able to purchase their homes for a price that will enable them to have the liquidity they need for a health emergency or to move to housing with increased services.

As Myers illustrates, potential buyers will come from a younger generation and increasingly will be from Latino and other immigrant backgrounds. In 2009, for example, Spanish surnames among homebuyers accounted for six of the top ten names nationwide and two of the top five in California.[14] Aging baby boomers will be dependent on the purchasing power of future buyers to enable them to have choices as they sell their homes. Herein lie the seeds of a "new politics of aging in place," one in which Hispanics and other minority and immigrant groups will have a direct connection to how future elderly live.

The fact that Hispanics and other minorities will eventually account for the bulk of the working-age population, and that the nation will accrue economic productivity based on their employment, raises some important questions: What are the financial and economic futures of these groups? Are we investing in their future education, employment, health, and well-being? The trends are unsettling. Recent data show that the wealth gap between whites and African Americans has quadrupled since the mid-1980s.[15]

Financial assets among white families grew from a median value of $22,000 to $100,000 from 1984 to 2007, while those of African Americans showed a statistically insignificant increase. This wealth disparity can be seen in the severe financial problems facing today's African American and Latino elderly. Recent research by the Heller School at Brandeis University documents that three-fourths of African American and Hispanic seniors do not have sufficient financial resources to fund projected lifetime expenses.[16] In addition, high housing costs put six of every ten African American and Latino seniors at risk because 44 percent of African American and 38 percent of Latino seniors will not have the home equity required to sustain their later years.[17] These data indicate that minority seniors may not only be at risk of poverty in old age but are also less likely than whites to have the financial resources that allow choices for how and where they age. They are more likely to be "stuck in place."

While much attention has been focused on the over seventy-eight million baby boomers about to move into old age and the growing Hispanic population in the United States, the group that connects these two larger populations—Latino baby boomers—is only now coming into focus. Figure 18.5 illustrates the overlap between aging baby boomers and the emerging Latino majority.

Latino baby boomers account for a hidden population of eight million people and are a barometer of the future aging of Latino and other minority elderly. Studies conducted by the University of California at Los Angeles (UCLA) and

AARP reveal the risks this subgroup faces.[18] Latino boomers are less likely than whites or African Americans to have pension coverage and are more likely to rely on Social Security for their retirement income. Almost half of Hispanic boomers during the 2007–2009 recession had serious problems meeting basic subsistence bills. They were more likely to divest their 401(k) plans, and many felt that they were not financially prepared for retirement.

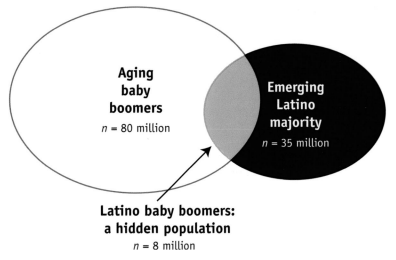

Figure 18.5 The confluence of two important demographic groups. Source: US Census Bureau; Z. D. Gassoumis, K. H. Wilber, L. A. Baker, and F. M. Torres-Gil, "Who Are the Latino Baby Boomers? Demographic and Economic Characteristics of a Hidden Population," *Journal of Aging and Social Policy* 22, no. 1 (2010): 53–68.

Preparing for the New America: Macro-Level Responses and Innovative Solutions

The social and political implications of aging and diversity are boldly stated by Ronald Brownstein in his article on the gray and the brown.[19] He reveals "a contrast in priorities" arising between a heavily nonwhite population of younger people and an overwhelmingly white cohort of older people.[20] He reinforces the "great risk shift" that will lead to an "age of diminished resources" and integrates the nexus of aging and diversity to paint a disturbing scenario of an "intensifying confrontation between the gray and the brown."

Brownstein foresees growing tensions and potential generational and racial conflicts as baby boomers age. The extent to which these tensions can be mitigated will depend heavily on the extent to which senior baby boomers take responsibility for ensuring that the next generation of Latino and African American youth have the education, health care, job training, and equal opportunities to succeed and become willing and productive taxpayers and homebuyers.

Conclusion

In time, most of us will experience a personal journey in our aging process that will bring unexpected circumstances and events. Some of us will have adequate resources to deal with our challenges. Some of us will face limited choices. But all of us will benefit from foresight and education, in order to maximize our opportunities for growing old in the places we choose with options that will

Personal Longevity Plan

Traditional retirement planning	Expanded longevity goals	Social/personal goals
• Savings • Pension • Investments • Social Security	• Transportation • Housing • Long-term care • Wellness and healthy living • Aging in place • Lifelong learning	• Reciprocity • Spirituality • Social support network • Emotional/psychological rebalancing • Accepting physical, mental, and chronic limitations and conditions

Figure 18.6 Personal longevity plan. Source: Fernando Torres-Gil and Diana Lam (2010).

enable us to enjoy our longevity. It is essential that we plan ahead to account for the demographic changes that will soon transform our country. Figure 18.6 shows the elements of a personal longevity plan that we might think about.

The critical message is that we need to account for differences among groups within our society and to recognize that all sectors of society—private, public, not-for-profit, for-profit, and religious—have a stake in the future of our communities.

Notes

1. Jacob Hacker, *The Great Risk Shift: The New Economic Insecurity and the Decline of the American Dream*, rev. ed. (New York: Oxford University Press, 2008).

2. Elizabeth Warren, "Middle Class in Crisis: The Long Road to Retirement" (presentation to AARP, Harvard Law School, Cambridge, MA, 2009).

3. Alison Shelton, "A First Look at Older Americans and the Mortgage Crisis," *Insight on the Issues*, September 9, 2008.

4. Ibid.

5. M. William Sermons and Meghan Henry, "Demographics of Homelessness Series: The Rising Elderly Population" (Homelessness Research Institute, April 2010).

6. Ibid.

7. Fernando Torres-Gil and Valentine Villa, "Social Policy and the Elderly," in *The Handbook of Social Policy*, ed. J. Midgley et al. (Thousand Oaks, CA: Sage, 2000), 209–20.

8. Ibid.

9. Alicia Munnell, "Risk in Motion: The National Retirement Risk Index," *Public Policy and Aging Report* 17, no. 2 (2007): 16–19.

10. S. Wallace and C. Molina, *Federal Poverty Guidelines Underestimate Costs of Living for Older Persons in California* (Los Angeles: UCLA Center for Health Policy Research, 2008).

11. Ibid.

12. Ibid.

13. Dowell Myers, "Aging Baby Boomers and the Effect of Immigration: Rediscovering the Intergenerational Social Contract," *Generations: Journal of the American Society on Aging* 32, no. 4 (2009): 20.

14. Ibid., 18–23.

15. Tatjana Meschede, Thomas M. Shapiro, Laura Sullivan, and Jennifer Wheary, *Severe Financial Insecurity among African American and Latino Seniors* (Waltham, MA: Institute on Assets and Social Policy, Brandeis University, 2010).

16. Ibid.

17. Ibid.

18. AARP Public Policy Institute Economic Team, "Older Americans and the Recession" (2008).

19. Ronald Brownstein, "The Gray and the Brown: The Generational Mismatch," *National Journal* (July 24, 2010): 14–22.

20. Ibid., 14.

Chapter 19

Housing Finance

Richard K. Green and Gary D. Painter

Introduction: More Old People/Fewer Resources

The aging of the baby boom generation will have wide-ranging consequences across many sectors of the economy. While much has been written about the implications of this demographic transition on federal budget obligations, there has been less attention paid to its impacts on housing markets and financial well-being.[1]

The aging of America is well documented, as is the fact that old people in the future may not be as affluent as those in recent generations. According to the 2007 Survey of Consumer Finances, the median income of people aged forty-five to fifty-four barely budged between 1989 and 2007, increasing from $62,100 to $64,200 (all numbers are in 2007 dollars).[2] Net-worth growth for this age group looks a little better, rising from $159,000 in 1989 to $184,900 in 2007, but much of this net worth came from housing equity, and house prices were at their peak in 2007. Today, national house prices are about 9 percent lower than they were in 2004. This means that the real net worth of people who will be approaching retirement over the next two decades may actually be lower than it was in 1989.[3]

At the same time, the retirement income of old people in the 2020s and 2030s may be less secure than it is for current seniors. The share of households with defined benefit pensions has been dropping. For those born between 1936 and

RICHARD K. GREEN is director and chair of the Lusk Center for Real Estate at the University of Southern California. Before joining the USC faculty, he was the Oliver T. Carr, Jr., Chair of Real Estate Finance at the George Washington University School of Business. He coauthored *The Housing Finance Revolution* for the Thirty-First Annual Federal Reserve Bank of Kansas City Economic Symposium. He received his MS and PhD in economics from the University of Wisconsin at Madison.

GARY D. PAINTER is professor in the School of Policy, Planning, and Development at the University of Southern California. He has been research director for the Lusk Center for Real Estate at the University of Southern California since 2002. He was a contributing author to *Redefining Urban and Suburban America*. He received his BA in quantitative economics and decision sciences from the University of California at San Diego and his PhD in economics from the University of California at Berkeley.

1940, nearly 60 percent of those with pensions have defined benefit pensions.[4,5] In contrast, 50 percent of those who are just retiring now—and who have pensions— have defined benefit pensions and only 44 percent of those who will be retiring in approximately twenty years will have defined benefit pensions.

These changes will have profound impacts on the housing market and will likely change how we think about where older people live. The stereotype of elderly housing is congregate care, which includes continuing care retirement communities (CCRCs), active living communities, and assisted living facilities. But most elderly people do not live in such communities, at least in part because they can be quite expensive. For most people, the cost-effective housing option is to remain at home, either in single- or multifamily settings, as long as they are physically able to do so.

What Do We Know about the Housing Choices of the Aging?

Most older homeowners remain in their homes until they die, as do those older people who rent their housing. Only a small fraction of homeowners downsize to own a smaller home,[6] and fewer sell their homes to become renters.

There are a number of theories why older homeowners sell their houses.[7–9] Many studies find that households may not view housing wealth as retirement wealth at all and therefore are unlikely to liquidate housing wealth[10] to pay for the living expenses of normal aging. Instead, households may view housing wealth as a source of precautionary savings or bequeathable wealth.[11–13] The primary motivation for such precautionary savings may be to protect against adverse health events. This fact is particularly true for generations that did not have access to a well-developed long-term care insurance market.

Studies highlight three noneconomic reasons to explain why homeowners choose to sell their homes.[14–19] First, the dissolution of a family union such as a divorce or the death of a spouse may change the demand for housing size and/ or quality and lead a household to transition from homeownership. Second, a household may wish to reduce the physical responsibility of maintenance and choose to be renters. This change is likely to be especially true for households that live in housing that does not have universal design components.[20] Finally, households may make decisions about where the parents will live in order to be near their children.

Age turns out not to be directly related to housing transitions for older households.[21] Life-changing events, such as significant health care expenses or the loss of a spouse, may cause homeowners to sell and downsize to smaller homes. Having wealthy children seems also to encourage parents to sell their current homes. Those with the lowest incomes are less likely to sell their homes and purchase smaller residences.

What Does This Mean for Aging in Place?

There is no single strategy that will help seniors make preferred housing choices. For those with sufficient resources, choices appear to be driven by changes in marital status, changes in health status, and proximity to children. People with fewer resources may be forced to move or rent because of adverse health events. As individuals age, they depend on personal savings, pensions, and government support. Home equity loans or reverse mortgages may provide support for households that lack sufficient cash flow or financial wealth to provide for their needs. In the absence of supplemental health or long-term care insurance, health-related financial pressures can force the elderly to sell their homes, even when they would prefer to age in place.

Aligning aging-in-place goals with the ability to finance them is a challenge. There is no single program available to help seniors modify existing homes, and there are no substantial programs to fund housing with universal design elements. In addition, few government programs exist to prevent the elderly from being forced out of their homes because of health-related financial stress. Programs such as Community Development Block Grants, the Section 202 Supportive Housing for the Elderly program, and housing trust funds are discretionary in design, and while they could be used for helping the aging to remain in their homes, they may be dedicated to other competing needs. They are also funded at very modest levels.

Funds to build new housing with universal design elements and to adapt existing communities are typically derived from resources that do not have aging in place as a primary focus. Beyond personal resources, government programs like the low-income housing tax credit and state housing trust funds could be directed to the needs of an aging population. Even the Section 202 program from the US Department of Housing and Urban Development (HUD) does not require that units include universal design features and could do so.

It may make the most financial sense for government agencies to prioritize their support to the naturally occurring retirement communities across the nation. Providing transportation infrastructure improvements and community health clinics may facilitate aging in place and help to prevent expensive subsidies for long-term care or other housing-related subsidies.

Methods of Self-Financing Aging in Place

Given that governments devote limited resources for helping the elderly age in place, seniors could use the equity in their homes in order to remain in place. The two options currently available are reverse mortgages and home equity lines of credit.[22]

REVERSE MORTGAGES

Reverse mortgages come in a variety of flavors, but the most straightforward allows the borrower to liquidate home equity into cash without making current interest payments on the amount borrowed. Principal accrues over the life of the borrower. At the borrower's death, if the house is worth more than the mortgage balance, heirs sell the house and pay off the principal and interest of the mortgage; if the house is worth less than the mortgage balance, the estate pays the lender the net sales price of the house and extinguishes its obligation. The arrangement essentially sets up the possibility of a no-fuss short sale.

The federal government's guaranteed reverse mortgage program is the Home Equity Conversion Mortgage (HECM), which is administered through the Federal Housing Administration (FHA). An HECM enables homeowners aged sixty-two and older to withdraw some of the equity in their homes. Reverse mortgage borrowers tend to average seventy-seven years of age, with more than 22 percent aged eighty-five and older, perhaps due to the fact that eligibility requirements decrease while HECM loan limits increase with the age of the borrower. The limit that can be borrowed is $625,000, but low-income homeowners are more likely to use reverse mortgages to supplement their income, and more than half of all seniors with reverse mortgages have homes that are valued between $100,000 and $250,000.[23]

Every borrower must have counseling about the use of this financing alternative, but *Consumer Reports* cautions that counseling can be "skimpy" and some consumers may not understand that interest and fees can "balloon."[24] Recently, the FHA introduced the Home Equity Conversion Mortgage Saver, which reduces the mortgage insurance premium for borrowing reduced sums.[25]

The reverse mortgage option may seem particularly attractive for the house-rich, cash-poor elderly. One could imagine that this arrangement might be the difference between living a comfortable life while remaining in one's home and feeling the need to move. The problem is that, from the standpoint of financial institutions, such loans are risky: they have substantial duration risk and a modicum of default risk. For investors in reverse mortgages to manage the uncertainty of duration risk, they need to hold a relatively large portfolio of such mortgages, which means their attractiveness might be limited to securities holders and large financial institutions.

To be compensated for their underlying risks, lenders charge fees for originating mortgages and may require borrowers to purchase mortgage insurance. At the same time, because the mortgage interest is accruing, the amount of money borrowers can receive at origination is limited to some fraction of the value of the house—a reverse mortgage does not allow households to monetize all of their equity. Reverse mortgage borrowers typically pay fees of 2 percent at origination along with a mortgage insurance premium over the life of the loan.[26] For those whose home values have dropped, a reverse mortgage may be undesirable because of the diminished value of the loan.

Recent changes in HUD rules have made some younger surviving spouses more vulnerable to foreclosure than under previous rules, which is the subject of litigation filed in 2011 by AARP. HUD allows only those who are over age sixty-two to borrow under its HECM program, so if there is a spouse who does not meet this age requirement, in order to qualify, title to the home would be transferred and held in the name of the older spouse only. If so, and the older spouse were to die, the younger spouse would not receive the loan proceeds and would be liable for repaying the full amount of the loan.

HOME EQUITY LINE OF CREDIT

The home equity line of credit (HELOC) is another alternative for households to use to access their home equity. Old people have often used HELOCs in order to remain in their homes in the presence of economic and health shocks.[27] Without the availability of relatively low-cost credit in the form of HELOCs, homeownership rates of those above the age of eighty would be five percentage points lower.

So long as capital markets are operating smoothly, HELOCs allow the elderly to tap the self-insurance they have obtained through home equity. However, we cannot count on capital markets to operate well under all circumstances. Because the elderly cannot predict when a health shock might happen, the lack of reliability of capital markets to provide HELOCs becomes a serious problem. Perhaps the government should take on a backstop role as a lender to allow the elderly to have access to their home equity when needed.

Challenges

FORECASTING FUTURE NEED

It is difficult to forecast how those currently at middle age will behave when they become elderly. Just because one age cohort has a particular trajectory of income, consumption, and housing preferences doesn't mean that the following age cohort will have the same (or even a similar) trajectory. In 1989, scholars forecast a 47 percent reduction in housing demand between 1987 and 2007, but even in the aftermath of the 2007–2009 housing crisis, housing demand is higher than it was in 1987.[28]

It is also difficult to infer housing assets held by one generation based on the amount held by the previous generation. The trajectory of housing assets across ages does not seem to be constant from one generation to the next. As we prepare for the financial needs of those trying to stay in place, we face a degree of uncertainty about what those needs might be.

JAPAN AND THE UNITED KINGDOM: AGING-IN-PLACE SOLUTIONS

Clearly, the United States is not alone in struggling to come up with solutions to help its aging population deal with their housing needs. The South Korean government recently commissioned a series of reports to learn how other governments are responding to these housing challenges.[a,b] These reports highlight how programs in Japan and the United Kingdom have worked to help address the demographic realities facing each country. As noted in the accompanying tables, both countries have focused their policy emphasis on aging in place. Citing a report from the Foundation for the Housing Problem of the Old in Japan, Shin-Young Park notes that the net present value of retrofitting existing properties to accommodate the increasing disability of the elderly would exceed 11.5 trillion yen (US$104 billion in 2006).[c] The report suggests that it would cost the government about 8.2 trillion yen (US$74 billion) but would reduce the cost of medical care and other services for the elderly by over 19.7 trillion yen (US$179 billion).[d]

In both countries, provisions are made for assessing the need for retrofitting existing properties of the aging. If it is determined that there is a need for repair and that people are unable to pay for it themselves, both countries try to connect the repair need to the disability programs of both governments. As noted in the accompanying tables, the countries differ in their approach as to how to help those who are not able to pay for the repairs and in their connections to the not-for-profit community.

The programs in Japan and the United Kingdom give some clues about what US policy could help facilitate aging in place. First, linking health care dollars to the housing needs of the aging has the potential to save the government money in the long run. However, if federal agencies do not view the program spending in a holistic manner, then it may be difficult politically to build support for programs that cross boundaries. Second, there is an important educational and support role for local governments and not-for-profits in providing help and information to aging households. If governments and not-for-profits could provide free advice as to the range

THE FINANCIAL CONDITION OF THE FUTURE ELDERLY

When asked what they thought about their financial condition for the future, the only age group where a plurality felt that they had saved enough was the group born before 1941.[29] These feelings have some foundation. As already noted, it is possible that adults currently in their fifties have less wealth than previous generations at a similar age.

People in their fifties today also have larger mortgage obligations relative to incomes than did previous cohorts. The older generation paid off their mortgages; 70 percent of households headed by someone over the age of sixty-five have no mortgage at all.[30] Loan amortization became a mechanism for forced saving and may help explain why older generations have a greater feeling of control over their finances than younger generations.

Japan	
Overall system	Each local government must develop a residential stabilization plan for the elderly in accordance with guidelines of the Ministry of Land, Infrastructure, Transport, and Tourism and the Ministry of Health, Labour, and Welfare.
Program structure	Local government provides technical assistance to aging households. This includes both counseling and case management. Some of the details are performed by not-for-profits.
Financing	If eligible, disability insurance pays 90 percent. Subsidies from local governments for the very low income. Loan programs from the Public Savings of Housing Finance or Public Pension programs (a type of reverse mortgage).

United Kingdom	
Overall system	Created a website (www.foundations.uk.com) to coordinate efforts of the 230 local home improvement agencies (covers 90 percent of the country).
Program structure (typical)	Provide free home inspection to determine the needs for repairs and retrofitting. Provide counseling and support services. Help determine whether financial assistance is available to pay for rehabilitation of the structure. Connect households to reliable contractors.
Financing	Agency will try to connect households with public benefits like disability to pay for repairs. The foundation has an Independent Living Trust Fund to help those who do not receive public assistance and have hardship (average grant size of £423 [approximately $630] during 2009/2010). Loans from commercial or credit associations, including reverse mortgages.

of options available to age in place, then aging households could make better decisions. Finally, the government could help provide loans for health retrofits to households based on equity in one's house. Perhaps the government could do this by providing insurance.

[a]Shin-Young Park et al., *A Study on the Residential Support and Management System of Rental Housing for the Elderly* (Sungnam, South Korea: Housing and Urban Research Institution, Korea National Housing Service, 2009).
[b]Shin-Young Park, "Housing Policy for the Elderly in Korea: Current Situation and Policy Issues," in *Facing the Future: Policy Changes in the Ageing Era* (Policy Forum on Low Fertility and an Ageing Society, Seoul, September 13–14, 2006).
[c]Ibid.
[d]Ibid.

Home equity is an important ingredient for allowing the elderly to remain in their homes. While, in principle, the elderly can have a mortgage as well as equity at the beginning of retirement, the absence of debt at retirement helps the elderly feel more secure financially.

The baby boom generation had much easier access to mortgage refinancing than previous generations. The combination of technological innovation and a race to the bottom to originate mortgages substantially reduced the cost of refinancing loans. The year 2003 was an extraordinary one, when a record $3.8 trillion in mortgages were originated, of which the Mortgage Bankers Association of America estimates that $2.5 trillion were refinances.

When the baby boom generation was on its best financial behavior, it engaged regularly in rate and term refinancing. While this was smart from the standpoint of managing interest rate costs, it also slowed amortization. Almost every time the mortgages were refinanced, amortization schedules were reset and mortgage payoff periods extended. In principle, borrowers could take the money and put it in other savings vehicles, but it is not clear that borrowers did that. Forced saving was slowed.

But this is not the worst of how people handled their mortgages. A substantial fraction of borrowers pulled equity out of their houses and spent those funds rather than reinvesting them, putting themselves on a lower savings path even in the absence of falling house prices.

Conclusion

The most likely method for allowing elderly homeowners to remain in their homes is to ensure that they have a path to using their home equity to do so. The problems with this approach are that older households in the future may not have as much home equity as their counterparts in previous generations. This conclusion is due to differences in savings behavior and substantial reduction in house prices between 2007 and 2009. Further, we cannot rely on capital markets to be available at all times. In addition, it is unlikely that governments at any level will be in a position to subsidize large numbers of the elderly who attempt to remain in their homes.

Notes

1. Dowell Myers and SungHo Ryu, "Aging Baby Boomers and the Generational Housing Bubble: Foresight and Mitigation of an Epic Transition," *Journal of the American Planning Association* 74, no. 1 (2008): 17–33.

2. Federal Reserve Board, *2007 Survey of Consumer Finances*, http://www.federalreserve.gov/pubs/oss/oss2/2007/scf2007home.html.

3. *S&P/Case-Shiller Home Price Index*, http://www.standardandpoors.com/indices/sp-case-shiller-home-price-indices/en/us/?indexId=spusa-cashpidff—p-us——.

4. Barbara Butrica, Howard Iams, Karen E. Smith, and Eric Toder, *The Disappearing Defined Benefit Pension and Its Potential Impact on the Retirement Incomes of Boomers* (Washington, DC: Urban Institute, 2009), http://www.urban.org/url.cfm?ID=411831.

5. The share of the population with any non–Social Security pension has remained relatively flat at around 63 percent for people born between 1946 and 1995.

6. Gary Painter and KwanOk Lee found that over one-third of the sample were homeowners who never left their dwelling. They also found that about 8 percent of the sample downsized their house, but re-mained homeowners. Gary Painter and KwanOk Lee, "Housing Tenure Transitions of Older Households: Life Cycle, Demographic, and Familial Factors," *Regional Science and Urban Economics* 39, no. 6 (2009): 749–60.

7. Lawrence D. Jones, "The Tenure Transition Decision for Elderly Homeowners," *Journal of Urban Economics* 29 (1997): S505–S509.

8. Menahem E. Yaari, "Uncertain Lifetime, Life Insurance and the Theory of the Consumer," *Review of Economic Studies* 32 (1965): 137–50.

9. Lawrence D. Jones, "Housing Tenure Transitions and Dissaving by the Elderly," *Canadian Journal of Economics* 41 (1996): 243–63.

10. Michael D. Hurd, "Research on the Elderly: Economic Status, Retirement, and Consumption and Saving," *Journal of Economic Literature* 28, no. 2 (1990): 565–637.

11. Louise Sheiner and David N. Weil, *The Housing Wealth of the Aged* (Providence, RI: Brown University, 1993), http://ideas.repec.org/p/nbr/nberwo/4115.html.

12. Thomas Davidoff, "Home Equity Commitment and Long-Term Care Insurance Demand," *Journal of Public Economics* 92, no. 1–2 (2010): 44–49.

13. Lina Walker, "Elderly Households and Housing Wealth: Do They Use It or Lose It?" (Research Paper WP2004-070, Retirement Research Center, University of Michigan, Ann Arbor, 2004).

14. Peter McCarthy and Bob Simpson, *Issues in Post-Divorce Housing* (Aldershot, UK: Avebury, 1991).

15. Friedel C. Filius, *Household Dissolution and Departure from the Housing Market in an Ageing Society* (Utrecht: Royal Netherlands Geographical Society, 1993).

16. Peter G. VanderHart, "An Empirical Analysis of the Housing Decisions of Older Homeowners," *Journal of the American Real Estate and Urban Economics Association* 22, no. 2 (1994): 205–33.

17. Frans M. Dieleman, William A. V. Clark, and Marinus C. Deurloo, "Falling Out of the Home Owner Market," *Housing Studies* 10, no. 1 (1995): 3–15.

18. Roland W. Goetgeluk, *Trading Off Housing Preferences: Housing Market Research with Decision Plan Nets* (Utrecht: Utrecht University, 1997).

19. Peteke Feijten, "Union Dissolution, Unemployment and Moving Out of Homeownership," *European Sociological Review* 21, no. 1 (2005): 59–72.

20. Molly F. Story, James L. Mueller, and Ronald L. Mace, *The Universal Design File: Designing for People of All Ages and Abilities* (Raleigh: Center for Universal Design, North Carolina State University, 1998).

21. Painter and Lee, "Housing Tenure Transitions of Older Households."

22. Another possibility is shared equity arrangements, where the elderly "cash out" potential future appreciation. Such arrangements have been floated in the market, and the take-up rate has been very small. See Andrew Caplin, Sewin Chan, Charles Freeman, and Joseph Tracy, *Housing Partnerships: A New Approach to a Market at a Crossroads* (Cambridge, MA: MIT Press, 1997), xiv, 265.

23. "Home Equity Conversion Mortgages for Seniors," http://portal.hud.gov/hudportal/HUD?src=/program_offices/housing/sfh/hecm/hecmhome.

24. "Reversals of Fortune/The Next Financial Fiasco? It Could Be Reverse Mortgages," *Consumer Reports*, September 2009.

25. "Home Equity Conversion Mortgages for Seniors."

26. National Reverse Mortgage Lenders Association, "Typical Costs in Getting a Reverse Mortgage," http://www.reversemortgage.org/AboutReverseMortgages/TypicalCostsinGettingaReverseMortgage/tabid/237/Default.aspx.

27. Makoto Nakajima and Irina Telukova, "Home Equity Withdrawal in Retirement" (working paper, 2010), http://dss.ucsd.edu/~itelyuko/nt_paper.pdf.

28. As well as real house prices. N. Gregory Mankiw and David N. Weil, "The Baby Boom, the Baby Bust, and the Housing Market," *Regional Science and Urban Economics* 19, no. 2 (1989): 235–58, http://ideas.repec.org/a/eee/regeco/v19y1989i2p235-258.html.

29. Paul Taylor, Cary Funk, and April Clark, "We Try Hard, We Fall Short: Americans Assess Their Savings Habits" (Washington, DC: Pew Research Center, 2007), http://pewresearch.org/assets/social/pdf/Saving.pdf.

30. US Census Bureau, *American Housing Survey*, http://www.census.gov/hhes/www/housing/ahs/ahs.html.

Chapter 20

A Political Strategy

Shirley Franklin and Jane Hickie

Introduction

> The old old are disproportionately women, living alone, often
> physically ill or mentally frail, unable to work, and in possession of
> only meager savings and modest pension benefits. When widowed,
> women's Social Security benefits decline by one-third. When
> incapacitated by long-term illness or disability, their needs extend
> beyond the protections offered by Social Security and Medicare,
> forcing them to rely on Medicaid's means-tested benefit.[1]

It is clear that the fear of inappropriate nursing home placement is strongly
linked to many older Americans' determination to age in place. The study on aging
in place commissioned by Clarity and the EAR Foundation (the Clarity/EAR study)
found that old people fear dependence and placement in a nursing home more
than they fear death itself.[2] It is possible that fear of inappropriate nursing home
placement drives the almost universal determination to age in place. Experts such
as Robert Hudson emphasize that "there is a growing awareness of the circular
relationship between income, housing, and health for older adults."[3]

Curtailing the costs of health care and maintaining Medicare solvency are far
beyond the scope of this chapter. However, the debate over how these costs and

SHIRLEY FRANKLIN was the first African American woman to be elected mayor of a major southern city.
She served two terms as mayor of Atlanta, Georgia, from January 2002 through January 2010. She received her
BA from Howard University and her MA from the University of Pennsylvania.

JANE HICKIE is senior research scholar and director of the Politics, Scholars, and the Public Program at the
Stanford Center on Longevity. She previously led the government relations practice at Public Strategies, Inc.;
was a partner in the law firm of Verner, Lipfert, Bernhard, McPherson and Hand based in Washington, DC; and
served as the director of the Texas Office of State and Federal Relations in Washington, DC. She received a BA
from Mount Holyoke College and a JD from the University of Texas.

solvency issues are resolved must not ignore the ability of the oldest old to afford the out-of-pocket costs and premiums required. The Employee Benefit Research Institute found that "a woman retiring at age sixty-five in 2009 will need anywhere from $98,000 to $242,000 in savings to cover health insurance premiums and out-of-pocket health costs for a 50–50 chance of having enough money, and $164,000 to $450,000 for a 90 percent chance."[4]

Innovative housing finance strategies are also well outside the parameters of this discussion, but housing costs are the largest expense in household budgets at all ages. On average, 34 percent of all household expenditures are devoted to housing; with a household head over age sixty-five, $36,844 (on average) was spent on housing.[5] Policies to manage and reduce those costs are essential. Strategies might include property tax relief or sales tax relief for home maintenance and remodeling products. Freezing seniors' water and sewer fees and subsidizing energy costs are other public measures that can be employed. Home maintenance, repair, and remodeling programs could offer senior discounts on property and casualty insurance for seniors' homes that are well maintained. Strict enforcement of landlord/tenant laws could benefit older renters. Funding research and development in manufactured housing for safety, aesthetic, and financial innovation would be another important action.

Successful aging in place encompasses housing, finances, health and care services, and community improvements. These are reforms that are normally considered separately, but for transformative progress to occur, they must be integrated. This chapter approaches aging-in-place policies through the lens of affordability and describes the efforts needed to bring public policies into national political debates. There is an urgent need for increased awareness and sustained debate about solutions for an aging America not only by program and academic experts but also among the larger public and its elected officials.

Public policies reflect both our society's priorities and the success of sustained advocacy campaigns. There are three interrelated strategies that would improve aging in place, each of which requires disciplined advocacy efforts:

1. Decreasing the cost of living for old people while improving the quality of community life
2. Increasing access to housing and supportive services
3. Increasing the purchasing capacity of disabled elderly

Although there are powerful forces and precipitating events driving change toward aging in place, there is no consensus on priorities or specific policies for advocacy. Advocacy coalitions exist, but there is a need to bring together aging and disability communities with other interest groups, including professionals whose expertise is in the built environment. An aging-in-place coalition must have prominent bipartisan leadership. With goals as ambitious as improving financial capacity, providing housing and supportive services, and developing livable neighborhoods, the president and Congress must recognize that these are important priorities for the United States.

Goal 1: Decreasing the Cost of Living While Improving the Quality of Community Life

"Warren Buffett is not the typical Medicare beneficiary. Instead, the prototype is an older woman with multiple chronic illnesses living on an income of less than $25,000 who spends more than 15 percent of her income on health care."[6]

Individual costs for housing and health care need to be made more manageable, and there are additional community-wide actions that could make a difference in affordability for older people. A variety of strategies are being developed locally to improve community life, including convenient public transportation, walkable neighborhoods, appropriate housing, nutritious food, safe streets, improved connectivity, and the shared use of public facilities. An important test of these initiatives might be: which of these important improvements will not only improve quality of life but also reduce the cost of living?

Will the public transportation system work well enough to allow an older woman to live without her own car, saving on maintenance, repairs, and insurance? Are neighborhoods planned in such a way that she can safely walk and have access to fresh produce markets, two factors that may help her stay healthier longer? Can weatherization programs be expanded to include home remodeling when she needs it, to create a safe environment that will also save on energy costs? Do zoning laws allow her to use her home for cohousing to share the costs of repair and maintenance and to help pay for home accessibility improvements? Are libraries and other public facilities welcoming to her and also used by young people in order to save capital and reduce operating costs? Are police, fire, and other community services being delivered in ways that maximize efficiencies, so that the local tax burden is appropriate?

Efficient coordination of existing programs will bolster community living initiatives while improving the affordability of living. For example, the United We Ride program addresses the fact that there are sixty-two different federal agencies providing transportation services plus numerous state and local systems. Given the multiplicity of transportation programs and the significant dollar amounts invested, more effective coordination is needed to ensure better service to more people, particularly when federal, state, and local budgets are under extreme pressure.[7]

"Affordability" varies from community to community. The Elder Economic Security Standard Index measures the minimum income older adults need to remain secure given the prevailing costs where they live. This measure finds that an older American in good health living alone would need about $16,300 annually to make ends meet if he or she owned a home free and clear; a higher amount would be required if he or she were still paying off a mortgage or renting. Incomes well above the poverty threshold are needed to make ends meet and age in place. "At the same time, updated measures of poverty show that many American elders have incomes below subsistence levels."[8]

Local governments have led community improvement efforts, with support from state and federal programs. A national campaign has not yet been developed to communicate effective local affordability initiatives. Efforts to promote local projects are scattered across foundations, professions, associations of public officials, and some environmental organizations. A cohesive national platform is needed to make affordability a goal of aging in place, so that excellent local models meeting that test are shared more systematically and efficiently.

Goal 2: Increasing Access to Housing and Supportive Services

As the renowned late gerontologist Dr. Robert Butler made clear, "Older people, unlike younger people, are not likely to ever escape poverty. This is particularly true for people over 85. Their working years behind them, they are left with no practical path, such as education or job-training programs, to improve their lives."[9]

In addition to those over age eighty-five, the most vulnerable older people are widowed spouses of low-income couples, retirees (usually women) with low benefits because of gaps in paid work, and low-paid service workers whose benefits fall short of meeting the poverty line.[10] "Among seniors, 28 percent of unmarried women, 33 percent of African Americans, and 28 percent of Latinos were poor or near poor. Seven out of ten elderly poor and near poor are female. Unmarried women of color have particularly high poverty rates."[11] For those most vulnerable, means-tested programs that are adequately funded and well administered need to be combined with a level of Social Security that is sufficient for a decent quality of life.

Publicly funded affordable housing and supportive services are under pressure in all government budgets. Government officials are cutting administrative and capital expenses, lowering overhead costs, stretching meal service supplies, leaving positions vacant, cutting planning and monitoring activities, increasing layoffs, adding furlough days, and providing less service to all.[12] A national advocacy campaign is needed just to maintain current funding for programs serving old people who are poor, such as the Older Americans Act, the Section 202 Supportive

Housing for the Elderly program, and Medicaid home- and community-based services.

Eligibility for Medicaid home- and community-based services requires extreme poverty. Old people who are eligible for both Medicare and Medicaid are called "dual eligibles." When a sample of these older, poor people were surveyed in 1999, more than half reported that they did not receive the assistance they needed. The lack of services meant that they were unable to bathe as often as they wanted, unable to dress themselves, fell out of bed or a chair, soiled themselves, and went hungry.[13]

Medicaid home- and community-based services is an option for states in the state-federal program that the states administer. Many states have innovative programs, but budget deficits threaten these optional approaches. Medicaid long-term care would have to be transformed to support the state innovations that will make successful aging in place the national standard.

The Older Americans Act funds programs intended for those at risk of losing their independence. Under the state and community programs, the Administration on Aging oversees a nationwide network of agencies and contributes to supportive services and home-delivered meals. Many states have now cut long-term services and supports funded through the Older Americans Act, even though demand for services has grown and will continue to grow.[14]

The US Department of Housing and Urban Development (HUD) Section 202 program is the only federal housing program specifically for older people. Section 202 housing is severely limited, and this housing stock is being lost at the same time that the population of old people needing affordable housing is increasing.[15]

With little expectation of increasing local, state, or federal funding, new approaches must be tried for financing housing and supportive services as America ages and more Americans join the ranks of the old, frail, and poor. There are policy debates about how long-term care services should be financed so that old people who are poor can remain in their homes and communities. Some proposals would create a federal Medicaid block grant, with states trading increased future federal funding for greater state control. Canada employs a block grant system, with federal support and provincial administration of programs.[16] Unlike the Canadian system, other advanced industrial nations have changed their long-term care welfare systems to federal social insurance financing.

Goal 3: Increasing the Purchasing Capacity of Disabled Elderly

Social Security is a social insurance system that has proven value in the United States. "Poverty among older adults declined dramatically from 35 percent in 1959

BACKGROUND: BRIEF OVERVIEW OF FEDERAL HOUSING AND SUPPORTIVE SERVICES PROGRAMS

In the past decade (2001–2011), there have been significant additions to available federal housing and supportive services programs. The following is a brief overview of recent developments in this policy area that could benefit aging in place.

The dominant feature of public policy for aging is Medicaid, a joint federal and state program for individuals with low incomes and few assets. Medicaid is the single largest source of financing for nursing homes. "While institutional care consumes 70 percent of Medicaid LTC [long-term care] spending, public demand and the 1999 *Olmstead* Supreme Court decision require that states expand alternative home- and community-based service programs."[a] Congress began funding the Real Choice Systems Change Grants for Community Living program to increase home- and community-based services in the Medicaid program.[b] Congress also enacted the Money Follows the Person (MFP) demonstration program to support former nursing home residents as they transition back to their home community.[c] Federal regulations now require that nursing home residents be asked directly if they would like to remain in an institution or if they would prefer to transfer back into the community.[d]

In addition to the Medicaid programs for home- and community-based care, Medicare-covered home health care and Title III of the Older Americans Act (OAA) are particularly important for older Americans. Medicare pays for limited days of skilled nursing and related services by certified home health agencies. Title III of the OAA oversees a nationwide network of aging agencies, supportive services, and congregate and home-delivered meal programs. The OAA also funds counseling and some caregiver respite programs.

An important partnership between the US Department of Health and Human Services (HHS) and the US Department of Veterans Affairs (VA) began in 2008. The Veterans Directed Home and Community Based Service Program is a package of services that enables veterans to live independently.[e]

In 2010, the administration announced the Community Living Initiative, in which HHS is partnering with the US Department of Justice, the US Department of Housing and Urban Development (HUD), and the Administration on Aging to signal enforcement of the *Olmstead* decision as well as provide technical assistance, grants, and ongoing guidance to governments to support aging in place.[f]

"The housing and service needs of seniors traditionally have been addressed in different 'worlds' that often fail to recognize or communicate with each other."[g] In April 2011, Shaun Donovan, the secretary of HUD, announced that HHS and HUD "are working together to compare data related to seniors living in HUD housing with data of seniors receiving Medicaid benefits—so that we can better understand who receives services and how we can improve access to them. [The] two agencies are also exploring the cost savings of connecting affordable housing and home and community-based services."[h]

The Congressional Research Service (CRS) reviewed HUD programs, including five assisted housing developments for low-income elderly: Section 202 Supportive Housing for the Elderly, the Section 221(d)(3) Below Market Rate program, the Section 236 program, and some public housing and Section 8 housing projects. All totaled, the CRS reported that these programs provided fewer than 625,000 units; of that number, 263,000 were in the Section 202 program.[i] In addition, HUD operates four supportive services programs to integrate service delivery: the

Congregate Housing Service program, the Service Coordinator, the Resident Opportunity and Self-Sufficiency (ROSS) Service Coordinator program, and the Assisted Living Conversion program.[j]

Other programs that provide assistance to low-income elderly households include HUD's Section 8 voucher program, HUD's mortgage insurance and reverse mortgage programs, and the US Department of Agriculture's rural housing programs. Housing choice vouchers assist with rental affordability. Mortgage insurance programs offer assistance with construction and rehabilitation of housing. The Section 515 Rural Rental Housing program and the Section 504 rural program also serve low-income families.

Additionally, there are the HOME Investment Partnership program, the Community Development Block Grant (CDBG) program, and Low Income Housing Tax Credits and Section 232 financing. The HOME program could help with gap funding to combine services with housing. CDBG funds are flexible and can be used to match other federal funds to offer reconstruction or rehabilitation of senior housing, construction of senior centers, and provision of public services. Low Income Housing Tax Credits are also designed to encourage investment in affordable housing. The Section 232 program offers financing for assisted living and nursing homes.

Secretary Donovan noted that, as of 2011, the Section 202 program served 130,000 older Americans; the Section 8 program, 430,000; and public housing, another 325,000, for a total of 885,000 older Americans.[k] With a current population of older Americans of approximately forty million, if even 10 percent are living under current poverty standards, there is a great and growing need for affordable assisted housing with supportive services for elderly people.

[a]Martin Kitchener, Terence Ng, Nancy Miller, and Charlene Harrington, "Medicaid Home and Community Based Services: National Program Trends," *Health Affairs* 24, no. 1 (2005).

[b]US Department of Health and Human Services, "New Freedom Initiative: Self Evaluation—Timeline of HHS Activities," http://www.hhs.gov/newfreedom/final/hhstimeline.html.

[c]Centers for Medicare and Medicaid Services, "Money Follows the Person Grants Deficit Reduction Act," https://www.cms.gov/DeficitReductionAct/20_MFP.asp.

[d]US Department of Health and Human Services, "Implementing the Affordable Care Act: Making It Easier for Individuals to Navigate Their Health and Long-Term Care through Person-Centered Systems of Information, Counseling and Access, Program Announcement and Grant Application Instructions," http://www.nasuad.org/documentation/aca/grants/CFDA%2093.071.pdf.

[e]US Department of Veteran Affairs, "Veteran-Directed Home and Community Based Services Program—Geriatrics and Extended Care," http://www.va.gov/GERIATRICS/Veteran_Directed_Home_and_Community_Based_Services_Program.asp.

[f]Centers for Medicare and Medicaid Services, "Community Living Initiative Community Services and Long Term Supports," http://www.cms.gov/CommunityServices/10_CommunityLivingInitiative.asp.

[g]*A Quiet Crisis in America* (Report to Congress by the Commission on Affordable Housing and Health Facility Needs for Seniors in the 21st Century, Washington, DC, June 2002), http://govinfo.library.unt.edu/seniorscommission/pages/final_report/finalreport.pdf.

[h]Shaun Donovan (speech, LeadingAge Annual Conference, Washington, DC, April 13, 2011), http://portal.hud.gov/hudportal/HUD?src=/press/speeches_remarks_statements/2011/Speech_04132011.

[i]Libby Perl, "Section 202 and Other HUD Rental Housing Programs for Low Income Elderly Residents" (Congressional Research Service, September 2010), http://aging.senate.gov/crs/aging13.pdf.

[j]*A Quiet Crisis in America*.

[k]Donovan, speech.

to around 10 percent today largely due to increases in Social Security benefits. The average monthly Social Security benefit for a retired worker is $1,153, or $13,836 per year."[17] Social Security is an important source of income for middle- and upper-middle-income elders as well as low-income retirees.[18]

The importance of Social Security and Medicare "cannot be overstated. Nevertheless, the costs of housing, out of pocket health care, transportation and food require more than three-quarters of spending for this age group, leaving few financial resources remaining for other expenses."[19] Further, the increasing age eligibility required for full Social Security benefits and the direct deduction of increasing Medicare premiums from Social Security payments means that, unless Social Security rates are raised, retiring sixty-five-year-olds will not receive the net wage replacement rates that have been in place for the last twenty-five years.[20] And these calculations do not include the cost of long-term care, which can overwhelm the budgets of all but the wealthiest families.

"If you are lucky enough to live a long life, then you are likely to end up needing some form of long-term care," although that is not inevitable.[21] An estimated ten million Americans needed long-term care in 2000.[22] The need for long-term care is unpredictable, and although it increases with age, 30 percent of sixty-five-year-olds will not need any long-term care by the time they die, but 20 percent will need care for more than five years.[23] Because the need for long-term care is a risk, not a certainty, it is logical to treat it like other unpredictable and potentially catastrophic events, that is, to rely on insurance rather than on welfare.

Briefly, a long-term care social insurance system allows younger workers to purchase a minimum amount of long-term care insurance. If later they have challenges with activities of daily living, they can receive services and/or a cash benefit to help them to purchase the housing and supportive services that they need and want without regard to their income level. Germany, Japan, Austria, and France, countries with older populations than in the United States, use social insurance systems to provide a greater range in service options. Programs in these countries provide supports that are more individualized and more autonomous and offer greater freedom of choice for the older individual.[24]

Driven by an aging population and proposed by a conservative government, Germany enacted a universal coverage social insurance program to replace its means-tested system. The program was implemented quickly with surprisingly few difficulties and continues to enjoy broad popular and political support.[25] The program is based on disability levels, not on poverty levels. Participants determine which services they want and can access those services from wherever they live. The program is funded by contributions from employees and employers.

Long-term care costs—whether in an institution or at home—are beyond the means of most Americans. In 2010, the cost of a private room in a skilled nursing facility was $75,190 annually, compared with $37,572 in an assisted living facility. Home care costs at $19 per hour for a home health aide averaged $43,472 annually.[26] Reverse mortgages and private long-term care insurance can supplement personal savings and Social Security benefits for those who have home equity and can afford private insurance. Unpaid caregiving from family and friends is a critical support.

But personal resources can quickly be exhausted, and if so, recourse today is to the Medicaid program. A long-term care social insurance program could dramatically alter this picture.

With a cash benefit, old people with disabilities would more likely be able to live where they choose. With improved financial resources, they could purchase the services they want and need. If increased deference results in part from a person's ability to purchase products and services, new social insurance benefits could help change attitudes toward the very old.

Federal legislation, known as the Community Living Assistance Services and Supports (CLASS) Act, was passed in 2010 that would introduce long-term care social insurance in the United States.

> The CLASS Act is the most significant change in financing
> of long-term care since the creation of Medicaid in the 1960s.
> CLASS is the first national non-means-tested financing program
> focused solely on long-term care. The CLASS program also
> provides a platform from which to launch future policy initiatives.
> CLASS opens the door to universal long-term care coverage in
> America.[27]

The CLASS Act offered a voluntary, privately funded, publicly administered social insurance program that would provide at least $50 per day in benefits to people who have difficulties with two or more activities of daily living. CLASS Act funds could be used to pay for whatever services are needed and wanted. "This program is about giving people more control over their own care."[28] Criticized as an unaffordable new entitlement program, legislation to repeal the CLASS Act was introduced in 2011.

Advocacy Campaigns: Aging in Place

Two models may be useful in considering an advocacy campaign for the three interrelated policy goals for aging in place. The first model is found in "The History of Social Security" by Peter A. Corning, in which he describes the process of successful federal advocacy that led to significant national change.[29] The second model focuses on systems change on a state level and is found in Steve Eiken's work for the Centers for Medicare and Medicaid Services (CMS), titled "Promising Practices in Long-Term Care Systems Reform: Common Factors of Systems Change."[30]

Older activists in Washington State. Courtesy of the Alliance for Retired Americans.

These models have been combined into the following framework with five key elements:

1. Recognition of precipitating events and powerful forces that drive change
2. A vision that describes the result that is sought, with effective messages to mobilize important segments of the public
3. A plan that sets out priorities for action-based expert analysis and consensus for action
4. An advocacy coalition of public and private interests for disciplined and sustained incremental reform and comprehensive change
5. Executive leadership from the president

RECOGNITION OF PRECIPITATING EVENTS AND POWERFUL FORCES THAT DRIVE CHANGE

"By 2040, the number of persons aged 85 years and older—the age range where the elderly are most likely to need long-term care—is projected to more than triple . . . to about 14 million. By then, the number of disabled elderly is projected to increase up to twice as much as today, reaching a high of 12 million." [31]

In the future, costs related to US demographic changes will explode. As experts with the Georgetown University Long-Term Care Financing Project stated, "The demographic bulge, represented by the baby boom cohort, [calls] into question a historic assumption that successive generations of workers would be willing to support earlier generations in their old age." If taxes were as "high as 60 percent of each paycheck, the next generation [would] have little incentive to work."[32]

These demographic and economic trends are important, but the precipitating cause for focusing on affordable aging in place is the 2007–2009 recession and the shocks that reverberated throughout the American economy. Alicia Munnell et al. found that 401(k) balances lost about 30 percent of their value in the twelve months following the market collapse in October 2007. "The collapse of the housing market triggered a broad decline in asset prices that greatly reduced the wealth of all categories of households. . . . Overall . . . older households lost much of their presumed gains relative to earlier cohorts and they will have less time to recover."[33] Fifty-one percent of households are at risk of falling more than 10 percent short of maintaining their living standards in retirement.[34] The result is that baby boomers will be far more dependent on Social Security and Medicare than prior generations.[35]

The financial crisis shines light on the critical role of Social Security in maintaining economic security for elders.[36] There are few, if any, replacements for the Social Security system to provide retirement income to the majority of Americans.[37] Demographic and economic trends mean that aging in place is coming into focus for baby boomers and policy makers. The recent recession and ongoing economic concerns make value awareness and cost-of-living issues even more important.

A VISION THAT DESCRIBES THE RESULT THAT IS SOUGHT, WITH EFFECTIVE MESSAGES TO MOBILIZE IMPORTANT SEGMENTS OF THE PUBLIC

In 1999, the US Supreme Court decided Olmstead v. L. C. and E. W., 527 U.S. 581 (1999), in which the Court held that the unjustified institutional isolation of people with disabilities is a form of unlawful discrimination. The Court ruled that institutional placement "perpetuates unwarranted assumptions that persons so isolated are incapable or unworthy of participating in community life and institutional confinement severely limits individuals' everyday life activities."[38] The *Olmstead* decision offers a platform for the development of an aging-in-place vision.

Donna Shalala, as secretary of the US Department of Health and Human Services, spoke about the *Olmstead* Supreme Court decision and articulated a compelling message for the rights of disabled people to live in community:

We can agree that no American should have to live in a nursing home or state institution if that individual can live in a community with the right mix of affordable support;

We can agree that we all have the right to interact with family and friends in our communities . . . to make a life.[39]

A vision statement for aging in place would include the following:

- American homes will be accessible.
- American communities will connect residents to needed services and community life.
- Older families will have the financial resources needed to manage the challenges of normal aging.

A PLAN THAT SETS OUT PRIORITIES FOR ACTION-BASED EXPERT ANALYSIS AND CONSENSUS FOR ACTION

Identifying the particular segments of the population with a financial interest in aging-in-place public policies and providing persuasive expert analysis is a critical first step in the advocacy process. Innovative packages in financial products, home remodeling, new homes, neighborhood retrofitting, and new neighborhoods must be developed. The first step is a communication effort by experts to other influential leaders who have a particular interest in this issue. As advocacy moves beyond informed elites to the larger public, baby boomers must be assured that, with aging in place, adequate supportive services will be available for their parents and themselves.

An advocacy plan for the larger public should be based on the fact that old people rarely move. They are clearly determined to age in place, whether or not care services are available. Their baby boomer children are concerned that supports are not in place to make aging in place a safe choice for their parents. However, baby boomers are determined that aging in place is the right choice for themselves.

In the Clarity/EAR study mentioned earlier, 94 percent of boomers say that it is important that their senior parents be able to age in place. However, 79 percent are concerned about their parents' ability to do so. And 75 percent say they are worried about the potential for falls/injuries, and 58 percent are concerned with their parents' ability to drive (if their parents do not move into a nursing facility).[40] Given these factors, a plan to support aging in place must persuade baby boomers that there are practical alternatives to institutional care. Such a plan must also convince boomers that the necessary housing and supportive services will be available and affordable.

AN ADVOCACY COALITION OF PUBLIC AND PRIVATE INTERESTS FOR DISCIPLINED AND SUSTAINED INCREMENTAL REFORM AND COMPREHENSIVE CHANGE

A successful plan calls for building a coalition of those who are already leading efforts to support aging in place, then reaching out in targeted directions to opinion leaders in the private and public sectors, other segments of the public, and elected officials and their staff. As a leading advocate for aging in place has said, "These issues must move from the social services office to the mayor's office."[41] In fact, they must move into the corner offices on Wall Street and to the Oval Office itself.

Active, older voters are important to almost any successful coalition of interests for needed government action. Older Americans are highly engaged in political participation. They vote, contribute to and work in political campaigns, contact public officials, and serve on local public advisory boards and councils on aging. In addition, millions of them belong to mass-membership organizations (particularly AARP) that engage in political activity. Older people "are indeed senior citizens, fully incorporated into social and political citizenship."[42]

Older voters participate in elections at a higher rate than voters of other ages. However, older voters are not a homogeneous group; their opinions diverge along a variety of "fault lines," including race, sex, and socioeconomic status.[43] Research completed in 2010 by the Stanford Center on Longevity demonstrated wide variations in opinions among older voters. In the center's study, differences among older voters in education, age, gender, race, and ethnicity are reflected in differing opinions about Medicare cost and management reform proposals.[44] Despite evidence of such diversity, "politicians . . . share the widespread perception that there is a huge, monolithic, senior citizen army of voters."[45]

Long-standing advocates for aging in place with supportive services must coalesce around a policy, vision, messages, and a plan in which aging in place is made a priority, not just another worthy program. A coalition of aging advocates and disability organizations is effective, but it must have strong bipartisan leadership and connect with a diverse range of organizations that are also powerful participants in public advocacy. In addition to private sector leaders, there are state officials who understand the urgency and scale of needed change. Experts from academic institutions and policy centers who have studied and written on these topics must participate. An advocacy coalition must reach well beyond the organizations whose participation would be expected. This coalition must be able to sustain and grow its membership, enjoying incremental successes as it builds toward comprehensive change.

There is no single political faction, organization, or leader who can cause a national transformation. What is required is a diverse coalition of organizations that are willing to participate in a shared agenda. That coalition must cross states, political parties, and economic, racial, ethnic, disability, and social chasms.

EXECUTIVE LEADERSHIP FROM THE PRESIDENT

Aging in place is a concept that involves a number of changes in a variety of systems that traditionally are disconnected. For example, "[if] disabled adults could draw down benefits under the CLASS Act, enriched with purchase power[,] they would still have the same broken system to navigate. . . . Advocacy must also improve care coordination, grow the needed direct care workforce, and expand home and community-based services under Medicaid to create a new system that is truly greater than the sum of its parts."[46] Unless homes and communities change so that they are healthy, more accessible, and more livable, they will add to the challenges and costs of aging in place. Livable communities should be affordable communities. Success ultimately depends on leadership from the executive levels of government that will make aging in place a priority for our society.

It remains to be seen if the president will seize every opportunity to take seriously how older Americans want to live. It also remains to be seen what the president himself will say about the role the federal and state governments should have and can afford as America ages. In order for scalable national change to occur, the president must take the lead, even at significant political risk. It is the president who commands the attention of the American public and who therefore could lead the nation to provide a "secure, positive, and meaningful later-life experience for all of our very oldest citizens."[47]

Conclusion

It is apparent that aging in place is not well understood. A clear vision must be developed and presented. Messages to and from experts and directed at the larger public are needed. There must be a plan with priorities for communication from an advocacy coalition that is broadly inclusive. The president must be engaged.

Old people want to remain independent, purchasing the housing, products, and services they need to age in place. If old and disabled people in our society have adequate financial resources, the private sector will respond. State governments could be freed from the responsibility of long-term care in the Medicaid program. If relieved of those costs, more state revenues could be available to meet other demands, including public education. Old people could be assured that they would not have to become publicly dependent, placed in a nursing home and subject to the uncertainties of government funding.

It is not enough to tinker with modest innovations on a local level or even to successfully increase funding for current state and federal programs. These programs are uncoordinated and fragmented, with divided authority, eligibility, purpose, scope, and measurement of results.

There are only twenty years before the baby boomers begin to reach advanced ages. A systematic social advocacy effort requires a clear vision of what should be done, described in ways that the public can imagine. It requires picturing the cost of failure to act. It requires a strategic plan and an effective coalition of supporters who can sustain disciplined advocacy. Bipartisan and nonpartisan experts must agree on new policies. The Congress must see the importance of constructive action. Most important, comprehensive national change must have leadership from the president. These actions would be promising signs of progress as demographic and economic realities become ever more apparent and a consensus comes into focus that much must be done very soon.

Notes

1. Robert B. Hudson, *The New Politics of Old Age Policy*, 2nd ed. (Baltimore: Johns Hopkins University Press, 2010), 14–15.

2. Prince Market Research, "Aging in Place for America Studies"; Clarity/EAR, "Seniors Fear Loss of Independence, Nursing Homes More Than Death" (November 2007).

3. Hudson, *New Politics of Old Age Policy*, 191.

4. Virginia P. Reno and Benjamin Veghte, *Economic Status of the Elderly in the United States* (Washington, DC: National Academy of Social Insurance, 2010), 24.

5. Adele Hayutin, Miranda Dietz, and Lillian Mitchell, *New Realities of an Older America: Challenges, Changes and Questions* (Stanford, CA: Stanford Center on Longevity, 2010), 68.

6. Drew Altman, quoted in Saul Friedman, "Alan Simpson and Teats: He Knows Whereof He Speaks," *Huffington Post*, December 6, 2010, http://www.huffingtonpost.com/saul-friedman/alan-simpson-and-teatshe-_b_792310.html.

7. National Council on Disability, "Creating Livable Communities," http://www.ncd.gov.

8. Reno and Veghte, *Economic Status of the Elderly in the United States*, 6–7.

9. Robert N. Butler, "Old and Poor in America" (Issue Brief, International Longevity Center–USA, New York, October 2001).

10. Kay E. Brown, "Older Americans Act: Preliminary Observations on Services Requested by Seniors and Challenges in Providing Assistance" (testimony before the Special Committee on Aging, US Senate, September 2010).

11. Reno and Veghte, *Economic Status of the Elderly in the United States*, 4.

12. Brown, "Older Americans Act."

13. Sheila P. Burke, Judith Feder, and Paul N. Van de Water, eds., *Developing a Better Long-Term Care Policy: A Vision and Strategy for America's Future* (Washington, DC: National Academy of Social Insurance, 2005), 8.

14. AARP, "Weathering the Storm: The Impact of the Great Recession on Long-Term Services and Supports," http://www.aarp.org/health/health-care-reform/info-10-2010/health-panel-10201.html.

15. Jon Pyonoos, Candace Baldwin, Kenneth Barbeau, and Kathy Rosenthal, "Linking Housing and Supportive Services for the Frail Elderly, Challenges and Opportunities" (National Health Policy Forum, George Washington University, Washington, DC, October 2009).

16. Pamela Doty, "Dispelling Some Myths: A Comparison of Long-Term Care Financing in the US and Other Nations," US Department of Health and Human Services, http://aspe.hhs.gov.

17. Hayutin et al., *New Realities of an Older America*, 14.

18. Reno and Veghte, *Economic Status of the Elderly in the United States*, 8.

19. Judith G. Gonyea, "The Oldest Old and a Long-Lived Society: Challenges for US Public Policy," in *The New Politics of Old Age Policy*, 2nd ed., ed. Robert B. Hudson (Baltimore: Johns Hopkins University Press, 2010), 196.

20. Reno and Veghte, *Economic Status of the Elderly in the United States*, 14.

21. S. Rogers and H. L. Komisar, *Who Needs Long-Term Care?* (Washington, DC: Georgetown University Long-Term Care Financing Project, May 2003).

22. Ibid.

23. P. Kemper, H. L. Komisar, and L. Alecxih, "Long-Term Care over an Uncertain Future: What Can Current Retirees Expect?" (Excellus Health Plan Inc., Winter 2005).

24. Doty, "Dispelling Some Myths."

25. A. E. Cuellar and J. M. Wiener, "Can Social Insurance for Long-Term Care Work? The Experience of Germany," *Health Affairs* 19, no. 3 (2000): 19.

26. Walter D. Dawson, "The CLASS Act and Long-Term Care Policy Reform: A Perspective," *Public Policy and Aging Report* 20, no. 2 (2010): 16–20.

27. Ibid.

28. Sebelius: CLASS Act "Totally Unsustainable" as Written, US Senate Republican Policy Committee, February 15, 2011.

29. Peter Corning, "The First Round—1912 to 1920," Social Security Online History Pages, Social Security Online, http://www.ssa.gov/history/corning chap1.html.

30. S. Eiken, *Promising Practices in Long-Term Care Systems Reform: Common Factors of Systems Change* (Washington, DC: Centers for Medicare and Medicaid Services, 2004), http://www.cms.hhs.gov/Promising Practices/Downloads/commonfactors.pdf.

31. James H. Schulz and Robert H. Binstock, *Aging Nation: The Economics and Politics of Growing Old in America* (Baltimore: Johns Hopkins University Press, 2008).

32. Hudson, *New Politics of Old Age Policy*, 15.

33. A. H. Munnell, F. Golub-Sass, and D. Muldoon, "An Update on 401(k) Plans: Insights from the 2007 Survey of Consumer Finance," Center for Retirement Research at Boston College, 9–5.

34. Reno and Veghte, *Economic Status of the Elderly in the United States*, 20.

35. Ibid., 19.

36. Ibid., 21–22.

37. Ibid., 23.

38. Olmstead v. L. C. and E. W. 527 U.S. 581, 600 (1999).

39. Donna Shalala (speech to the National Conference of State Legislators, July 28, 1999), http://www.accessiblesociety.org/topics/persasst /Olmstead_shalala.htm.

40. Prince Market Research, "Aging in Place for America Studies"; Clarity/EAR, "Seniors Fear Loss of Independence, Nursing Homes More Than Death."

41. Robert McNulty, private conversation, March 2010.

42. Robert H. Binstock, "Older People and Political Engagement: From Avid Voters to 'Cooled-Out Marks,'" *Generations: Journal of the American Society on Aging* 30, no. 4 (2006): 26.

43. Schulz and Binstock, *Aging Nation*, 178.

44. Hart Research, V. J. Breglio Inc., Health Survey Project: Reforming Medicare, September 2010, 32–34.

45. Binstock, "Older People and Political Engagement," 26.

46. Lisa R. Shugarman, "Health Care Reform and Long-Term Care: The Whole Is Greater Than the Sum of Its Parts," *Public Policy and Aging Report* 20, no. 2 (2010): 3–7.

47. Hudson, *New Politics of Old Age Policy*, 184.

Conclusion

Aging in Place

Henry Cisneros

It is our hope that, within ten to fifteen years, many American institutions will have recognized the challenges of an aging nation and will have enacted measures to maximize the "longevity dividend" generated by aging in place. Americans will need to be increasingly aware of the growing proportion of the population that is aging. This reality will become apparent in the fiscal pressures, workplace challenges, market adjustments, and demographic-related conflicts that emerge in our society. The economic and personal dividends derived from enabling elderly Americans to live in their own homes for as long as they can are so great that they require intentional aging-in-place strategies.

Aging-in-place strategies include adapting existing homes and neighborhoods and building new housing and communities that are age-appropriate and affordable. These ideas are important as a source of jobs, as a driver of community revitalization, and as a response to the determination of older Americans to live independently and with dignity.

The following lists outline the priorities that we see as a part of the solution. These priorities have been drawn from "to do" lists submitted by the chapter authors of this book.

Detailed "To Do" Lists from the Authors

AGING-IN-PLACE PRIORITIES
Housing and Community Priorities
Research
1. Conduct research to assess the cost benefits of aging in place versus institutional care across the wide variety of settings.
2. Evaluate the savings that could accrue in the Medicaid program with universal application of home- and community-based services and home health care.

3. Assess the application of the *Olmstead* decision on housing options for disabled elderly.

4. Review the adequacy of federal programs for frail elderly, especially "dual eligibles."

5. Identify the barriers and opportunities for expansion of the Program of All-Inclusive Care for the Elderly (PACE).

6. Identify and evaluate strategies for older Americans' financial security, such as long-term care insurance (LTCI), the Community Living Assistance Services and Supports (CLASS) Act insurance program, reverse mortgages, home equity lines of credit (HELOCs), annuities, etc.

7. Evaluate the US Department of Energy Weatherization Assistance Program and its possible service as a model for a national remodeling initiative.

Culture Change

1. Provide incentives to building professionals to develop remodeling packages such as age-appropriate homes in core product lines and mixed-use/aging-in-place neighborhood developments.

2. Develop a national contest to inspire innovations in housing options such as new models for cohousing and shared housing.

3. Link the wide array of resources, organizations, and individuals working in this field through a national coalition, establishing priorities for action, sharing information, and virtual connections.

Government Action

1. Tailor connectivity in transportation planning to the needs of older Americans, requiring systems to incorporate appropriate equipment and routes linking residences with amenities.

2. Make transportation policies appropriate, with senior discounts, liability protection for organizations that have volunteer drivers, and car donation programs.

3. Reduce the effects of vehicle emissions within concentrated pedestrian areas by separating housing from major transportation corridors.

4. Establish minimum levels of affordability and accessibility in all new developments.

5. Make zoning changes that assist livability such as form-based zoning, overlay districts based on statistical analysis of neighborhood concentrations of aging residents to allow for greater density, smaller lot sizes, accessory dwelling units, and other planning innovations.

6. Encourage city governments to create special units to assemble surplus public land for construction of mixed-use infill neighborhoods.

7. Encourage suburban jurisdictions to participate in repurposing obsolete commercial properties.
8. Modify zoning regulations to allow for mixed-use development in suburban neighborhoods.
9. Require community master plans to consider accurate demographic information, including the rapidly aging population.
10. Provide adequate affordable housing with services, appropriate for old and poor people in urban, suburban, and rural areas.
11. Enact incentives such as reduced water, energy, and property tax rates for older residents who are maintaining and remodeling their homes for accessibility.
12. Create means-tested programs to assist aging residents who are poor to afford home assessments, maintenance, and retrofitting for adaptability.
13. Provide incentives to builders and remodelers to construct smaller, age-appropriate, lifelong homes.
14. Provide federal loan support, regulations, and counseling for reverse mortgages.
15. Direct Base Realignment and Closure (BRAC) efforts to address the needs of an aging population.

Services Priorities

Research
1. Develop economically sustainable business models for villages and other neighborhood support models.
2. Measure the health costs and other quantifiable benefits of walkable communities.
3. Develop indicator systems widely adopted throughout the nation that accurately reflect measures that are beneficial to older people in housing, mobility, health, and social connectivity.
4. Develop affordable, replicable technologies and systems to more effectively deliver services to old people.

Culture Change
1. Urge school districts and other public entities to integrate older and younger people into physical facilities and programs, such as joint use of libraries and mentoring programs.
2. Make universal design a national standard in the building industry.

Government Action
1. Establish Neighborhood Watch programs through collaborations between older residents and police.
2. Enact new "volunteer" incentives for older volunteers, including stipends, tax credits, housing allowances, skills exchanges, and tuition rebates.

3. Launch a two-year national public service that could be fulfilled any time up to age seventy, including military service. Such a program could be completed in six-month segments. Retirement support could be linked to completion of the requirement.
4. Direct state-funded land grant universities to expand their traditional extension service missions to address aging-in-place challenges.

Education Priorities
Research
1. Investigate which aspects of education are most beneficial to long life, and why.
2. Determine and define the characteristics of naturally occurring retirement communities (NORCs) and identify their locations throughout the United States.

Culture Change
1. Expand the nation's focus on childhood obesity to include obesity in older people.
2. Address negative stereotypes about older people in the media, in employment, and in strategies for economic development.
3. Encourage personal longevity plans to help Americans of all ages with financial planning, health care, support services, mobility, and housing choices. Such plans could be included in a public education curriculum.
4. Create options to encourage older Americans to work longer, including part-time options and developing new skills.
5. Encourage older people's activism—from controlling their health care to leading villages to assuming leadership roles at the state, national, and international levels.

Government
1. Train older people to conduct asset-based community development (ABCD) assessments nationwide.
2. Establish local skills exchanges, especially intergenerational skills exchange.
3. Train local building departments to organize and regulate local remodelers to offer certified packages of home remodeling for accessibility.
4. Develop local and state training programs for aging-in-place specialists to provide outreach and support targeted to people living in villages and naturally occurring retirement communities (NORCs).
5. Train more gerontologists.
6. Invest in public education for young people, especially in long-neglected schools and neighborhoods.

Resources

2008 National Population Projections
> http://www.census.gov/population/www/projections/2008projections.html
> Estimates of the future US resident population from the US Census Bureau.

AARP
> http://www.aarp.org
> Not-for-profit group addressing the needs of people over age fifty.

AARP Bulletin
> http://www.aarp.org/bulletin
> Monthly magazine for AARP members.

AARP Foundation
> http://www.aarpfoundation.org
> Foundation "dedicated to serving vulnerable people over 50 by creating solutions that help them secure the essentials and achieve their best life."

AARP Public Policy Institute
> http://www.aarp.org/research/ppi
> Research and policy arm of AARP.

AbleData
> http://www.abledata.com/abledata.cfm
> A source of links to assistive technology.

Affordable Housing
> http://www.hud.gov/offices/cpd/affordablehousing
> Resource on affordable housing from the US Department of Housing and Urban Development (HUD).

Aging in Place: A Toolkit for Local Governments
> M. Scott Ball
> http://www.co.vernon.wi.gov/VCCP/documents/agingInPlace.pdf
> Recommendations and resources for communities to incorporate aging in place.

Aging in Place: Coordinating Housing and Health Care Provision for America's Growing Elderly Population
> Kathryn Lawler
> http://www.nw.org/network/pubs/studies/documents/agingInPlace2001.pdf

Outlines federal, state, and local connections between health care and housing for the elderly.

Aging in Place Innovative Service Model Summaries

Carey Wiant Nyberg

http://www.gcimpact.com/documents/AginginPlaceAlternativeModelsReport.pdf

Review of nine aging-in-place models of senior housing.

Aging Research Centre (ARC)

http://www.arclab.org

Links to recent aging-related articles, which are updated monthly; real audio features; and research projects of interest.

Alliance for Retired Americans

http://www.retiredamericans.org

A national organization that serves to protect the health and economic security of seniors and voice the opinions of retirees and older Americans.

A Long Bright Future: Happiness, Health, and Finaical Security in an Age of Increased Longevity

Laura L. Carstensen,

Pulbic Affairs, 2011

American Association of People with Disabilities (AAPD)

http://www.aapd.com/site/c.pvI1IkNWJqE/b.5406299/k.FBCC/Spotlight.htm

Information and support to those with disabilities.

American FactFinder

http://factfinder2.census.gov/faces/nav/jsf/pages/index.xhtml

Online data resource for US Census Bureau statistics.

American Housing Survey (AHS)

http://www.census.gov/hhes/www/housing/ahs/ahs.html

Historical results from US Census Bureau biannual surveys of the nation's housing supply.

American Institute of Architects (AIA)

http://www.aia.org

National professional association of architects; includes a Design for Aging forum.

American Seniors Housing Association (ASHA)

https://www.seniorshousing.org

An independent not-for-profit organization providing leadership for the seniors housing industry.

American Society of Interior Designers (ASID)

http://www.asid.org

Links to the organization's continuing education, government affairs, and information.

American Society on Aging (ASA)

http://www.asaging.org

An interdisciplinary organization in the field of aging.

Americans with Disabilities Act (ADA)

> http://www.ada.gov

> Provides information and technical support for implementing the Americans with Disabilities Act of 1990.

America's Families and Living Arrangements: 2007

> Rose M. Kreider and Diana B. Elliott

> http://www.census.gov/population/www/socdemo/hh-fam/p20-561.pdf

> A report on trends in household and family living arrangements from the US Census Bureau.

Archstone Foundation

> http://www.archstone.org

> A foundation focusing on issues related to older Americans.

Asset-Based Community Development Institute (ABCD)

> http://www.abcdinstitute.org

> Conducts research and provides support for "building community capacity."

Assisted Living Federation of America (ALFA)

> http://www.alfa.org

> Association of assisted living executives.

Beneficial Designs

> http://www.beneficialdesigns.com

> Engineering and design firm website that offers research, design, and education programs.

Beyond 50.03: A Report to the Nation on Independent Living and Disability

> http://www.aarp.org/health/doctors-hospitals/info-11-2003/aresearch-import-753.html

> The third in AARP's Beyond 50 series, an in-depth look at the roles of supportive services, family, and community.

Boomer Project

> http://www.boomerproject.com

> A market research group specializing in the baby boom generation.

Broadband and Health Care

> http://www.broadband.gov/issues/healthcare.html

> Outlines the health care effects of a plan to provide broadband infrastructure across the nation.

Building Environmentally Sustainable Communities: A Framework for Inclusivity

> Vicki Been, Mary K. Cunningham, Ingrid G. Ellen, Joe Parilla, Margery A. Turner, Sheryl V. Whitney, Ken Zimmerman, Adam Gordon, and Aaron Yowell

> A 2010 literature review with policy recommendations.

Building for Boomers: Guide to Design and Construction

> Judy Schriener and Mike Kephart

> McGraw Hill Construction Series, 2010

> Trade book for professionals building homes, apartments, and developments for baby boomers.

Caregiver.com

http://www.caregiver.com

Dedicated to caregivers and includes local, regional, and state sources as well as a regularly updated clearinghouse of links to caregiver resources.

CaregiverMN.org

http://www.caregivermn.org/HomePage.asp

Offers resources for caregivers, including confidential online advisory.

Caregiver Network

http://www.caregiver.ca/content_main.html

Information on the network's services, including seminars and care management, caregiver information, links to products, and other services.

Cash and Counseling

http://www.bc.edu/schools/gssw/nrcpds/cash_and_counseling.html

A grant program allowing frail older adults to manage goods and services based on their personal needs.

Center for Housing Policy

http://www.housingpolicy.org/toolbox/older_adults.html

Explores the challenges facing older adults and describes a range of promising policies.

Center for Inclusive Design and Environmental Access (IDEA)

http://www.ap.buffalo.edu/idea

A research and design group with the mission of "making environments and products more usable, safer and healthier."

Center for Retirement Research

http://crr.bc.edu/index.php

Research group studying retirement issues and informing policy decisions.

Center for Urban Transportation Research

http://www.cutr.usf.edu

An interdisciplinary transportation research group.

Centers for Medicare and Medicaid Services (CMS)

http://www.cms.hhs.gov/home/rsds.asp

Research results and data from the Centers for Medicare and Medicaid Services.

Changes in US Family Finances from 2004 to 2007: Evidence from the Survey of Consumer Finances

Brian K. Bucks, Arthur B. Kennickell, Traci L. Mach, and Kevin B. Moore

http://www.federalreserve.gov/pubs/oss/oss2/2007/scf2007home.html

Analysis of results from the Federal Reserve's Survey of Consumer Finances, showing income, saving, and spending trends.

Cohousing Association of the United States (Coho/US)

http://www.cohousing.org

Organization whose purpose is to promote and encourage the cohousing concept.

Columbia Pike Form-Based Code

http://www.columbia-pike.org/?page_id=298

An example of form-based code from the Columbia Pike Revitalization Organization, Arlington County, Virginia.

Communities for a Lifetime

http://www.communitiesforalifetime.org

A planning resource for communities and businesses developed by AARP and the Florida Department of Elder Affairs.

Community Connections

http://www.comcon.org

Links to HUD programs and initiatives, publications, and other resources such as federal programs and private funding resources.

Community Innovations for Aging in Place Initiative (CIAIP)

http://www.ciaip.org

Grant program for communities to implement aging-in-place strategies.

Community Partnerships for Older Adults

http://www.partnershipsforolderadults.org

A national program administered by the Robert Wood Johnson Foundation to provide resources to communities to support aging residents.

Concrete Change

http://www.concretechange.org

Construction guidelines and cost information; suggestions for a nationwide and international movement for basic access in all new homes.

Congress for the New Urbanism (CNU)

http://www.cnu.org

An organization of architects and planners working to promote walkable, mixed-use neighborhoods.

Connecting and Giving: A Report on How Mid-Life and Older Americans Spend Their Time, Make Connections and Build Communities

Alicia Williams, John Fries, Jean Koppen, and Robert Prisuta

http://assets.aarp.org/rgcenter/general/connecting_giving.pdf

An AARP report on the volunteering habits of older Americans.

Consumer Expenditure Survey

http://www.bls.gov/cex

Data tables and analysis of Bureau of Labor Statistics survey results on the buying habits of Americans.

Continua Health Alliance

http://www.continuaalliance.org

International industry group for health care and technology companies.

Cost of Falls among Older Adults

http://www.cdc.gov/HomeandRecreationalSafety/Falls/fallcost.html

Fact sheet about the costs of falls.

Creating Aging-Friendly Communities

> http://www.agingfriendly.org
>
> An online information clearinghouse for aging in place.

Current Population Survey (CPS)

> http://www.census.gov/cps
>
> Monthly survey of fifty thousand households by the US Census Bureau.

DataQuest

> http://dq.cde.ca.gov/dataquest
>
> Searchable statistics from the California Department of Education.

Demographics of Homelessness Series: The Rising Elderly Population

> http://www.endhomelessness.org/content/article/detail/2698
>
> A 2010 report by the National Alliance to End Homelessness on the risks and prevalence of homelessness among elderly people.

Demographic Trends in the 20th Century

> Frank Hobbs and Nicole Stoops
>
> http://www.census.gov/prod/2002pubs/censr-4.pdf
>
> An extensive review of historical US Census Bureau data.

Designing Walkable Urban Thoroughfares: A Context Sensitive Approach

> http://www.ite.org/emodules/scriptcontent/Orders/ProductDetail.cfm?pc=RP-036A-E
>
> Guidelines from the Institute of Transportation Engineers for including stakeholders in community planning and design.

Eden Alternative

> http://www.edenalt.org
>
> An alternative philosophy to traditional long-term care institutional settings.

Elder Care

> http://www.eldercare.com
>
> A not-for-profit, charitable organization with a national mission to assist the caregivers of the elderly with reliable information, referrals, and support.

Eldercare Locator

> http://www.eldercare.gov
>
> Local resources and contact information for state and local agencies, from the Administration on Aging and the US Department of Health and Human Services.

Fact Sheet on Older Adults

> http://www.completestreets.org/complete-streets-fundamentals/factsheets/older-adults
>
> Older adults benefit greatly from complete streets with safe pedestrian walkways and sidewalks.

Federal National Mortgage Association (Fannie Mae)

> http://www.fanniemae.com/portal/index.html
>
> Website of Fannie Mae; provides information on mortgage loans for single- and multifamily housing and community development.

FedStats

> http://www.fedstats.gov
>
> Clearinghouse for federal data and statistics.

Freddie Mac

> http://www.freddiemac.com
>
> Their mission is to provide liquidity, stability, and affordability to the U.S. housing market.

Frequently Asked Questions about HUD's Reverse Mortgages

> http://portal.hud.gov/hudportal/HUD?src=/program_offices/housing/sfh/hecm/rmtopten
>
> Information about the Home Equity Conversion Mortgage offered to approved lenders by the Federal Housing Administration (FHA).

Generations United

> http://www.gu.org
>
> Information on intergenerational policy, programs, and issues, with links to public policy, legislative alerts, training, special initiatives, services learning, and intergenerational programs.

Gerontological Society of America

> http://www.geron.org
>
> Multidisciplinary organization dedicated to the scientific study of aging and to the translation/dissemination of research for practice and policy.

Global Age-Friendly Cities: A Guide

> http://www.who.int/ageing/publications/Global_age_friendly_cities_Guide_English.pdf
>
> World Health Organization (WHO) guide to supporting older people in cities.

Green House Project

> http://thegreenhouseproject.org
>
> An alternative to nursing homes that provides professional long-term care services in a homelike setting.

Health and Retirement Study

> http://hrsonline.isr.umich.edu
>
> Results of a large-scale survey administered by the University of Michigan to over twenty-two thousand Americans over age fifty every two years.

HealthCare.gov

> http://www.healthcare.gov
>
> Resources on health care from the US Department of Health and Human Services.

Health Impact Project: Advancing Smarter Policies for Healthier Communities

> http://www.rwjf.org/files/applications/cfp/overview_HIAcfp2009.pdf
>
> A grant-awarding program for state, local, and tribal agencies making policy changes to improve health.

Hearings under the Home Ownership and Equity Protection Act (HOEPA)

> http://www.federalreserve.gov/communitydev/hoepahearingtranscripts.htm
>
> Records of hearings at the US Federal Reserve.

The Home Depot Foundation

> http://www.homedepotfoundation.org
>
> The foundation's mission is to improve homes and improve lives.

The Housing Bubble and Retirement Security

Alicia H. Munnell and Mauricio Soto

http://crr.bc.edu/working_papers/the_housing_bubble_and_retirement_security.html

A 2008 report from the Boston College Center for Retirement Research on the effects of the housing bubble's collapse.

Housing Research.org

http://housingresearch.wordpress.com

Information for housing professionals and consumers on major housing issues, the Hope VI program, and the continuum of supportive housing options.

HUD (U.S. Department of Housing and Urban Development)

http://hud.gov

HUD's mission is to create strong, sustainable, inclusive communities and quality affordable homes for all.

HUD's HOPE VI Program

http://www.huduser.org/portal

Program transforms public housing projects into mixed-income, diverse, and stable neighborhoods in order to attract middle-income people to developments that include a wide range of incomes and housing types.

Increasing Home Access: Designing for Visitability

Jordana L. Maisel, Eleanor Smith, and Edward Steinfeld

http://assets.aarp.org/rgcenter/il/2008_14_access.pdf

A 2008 report from the AARP Public Policy Institute about residential visitability design.

Institute on Assets and Social Policy

http://iasp.brandeis.edu

Research and policy analysis about financial stability for vulnerable populations.

Intel in Healthcare

http://www.intel.com/about/companyinfo/healthcare

Intel's health care research includes at-home technology.

International Interior Design Association (IIDA)

http://www.iida.org

Professional association of interior designers.

International Longevity Center

http://www.mailman.columbia.edu/academic-departments/centers/international -longevity-center

Formed to educate individuals on how to live longer and better, and advise society on how to maximize the benefits of today's longer lifespans.

Issues in Creating Livable Communities for People with Disabilities: Proceedings of the Panel

http://www.ncd.gov/publications/2007/Oct12007

Results from a 2007 panel conducted by the National Council on Disability.

Joint Center for Housing Studies

    http://www.jchs.harvard.edu

    Harvard University's center for information and research on housing in the United States.

LeadingAge (formerly the American Association of Homes and Services for the Aging)

    http://www.leadingage.org

    Consumer resources on savings, health care, and design for older adults.

Lifelong Communities: A Regional Guide to Growth and Longevity

    http://www.atlantaregional.com/File%20Library/Aging/ag_llc_regional_guide.pdf

    A report by the Atlanta Regional Commission on the results of a 2009 design charrette about livability design in five communities around Atlanta.

Livable Communities: An Evaluation Guide

    Mary Kihl, Dean Brennan, Neha Gabhawala, Jacqueline List, and Parul Mittal

    http://assets.aarp.org/rgcenter/il/d18311_communities.pdf

    A set of surveys published by AARP to assist community efforts toward livability.

John D. and Catherine T. MacArthur Foundation

    http://www.macfound.org

    The foundation is committed to building a more just, verdant, and peaceful world.

MacArthur Foundation Research Network on an Aging Society

    http://www.agingsocietynetwork.org

    An interdisciplinary research group exploring productivity and work for older people, intergenerational issues, and questions of inequality and age.

Meals on Wheels

    http://www.mowaa.org

    National organization whose aim is to end senior hunger.

MetLife Foundation

    http://www.metlife.com

    Empowering people to lead healthy, productive lives and strengthen communities.

MetLife Mature Market Institute

    http://www.metlife.com/mmi/index.html

    Papers and reports related to senior issues.

Metropolitan Policy Program

    http://www.brookings.edu/metro.aspx

    Research and articles from the Brookings Institution on metropolitan issues.

MIT Age Lab

    http://agelab.mit.edu

    Created to invent new ideas and technologies to improve health and enable people to "do things" throughout life.

The Mobility Needs of Older Americans: Implications for Transportation Reauthorization

    Sandra Rosenbloom

    http://www.brookings.edu/reports/2003/07transportation_rosenbloom.aspx

    Policy brief on the transportation requirements of older adults.

Monitoring Success in Choice Neighborhoods: A Proposed Approach to Performance Measurement

> Robin E. Smith, G. Thomas Kingsley, Mary K. Cunningham, Susan J. Popkin, Kassie Dumlao, Ingrid G. Ellen, Mark Joseph, and Deborah McKoy

> http://www.urban.org/publications/412092.html

> A 2010 proposal for measuring the outcomes of the HUD Choice Neighborhoods Initiative.

Monthly Labor Review

> http://www.bls.gov/opub/mlr

> Journal of the Bureau of Labor Statistics.

National Association of Area Agencies on Aging (n4a)

> http://www.n4a.org

> Advocacy group for the interests of older people and people with disabilities who want to live in their own homes and communities.

National Association of Home Builders (NAHB)

> http://www.nahb.org

> Trade association for the housing industry; coordinates the Certified Aging-in-Place Specialist (CAPS) certification program.

National Center for Health Statistics

> http://www.cdc.gov/nchs/index.htm

> Collection of data from the Centers for Disease Control and Prevention.

National Center for Home Equity Conversion

> http://reverse.org

> Information on reverse mortgages, as well as alternatives to reverse mortgage.

National Council on Independent Living (NCIL)

> http://www.ncil.org

> Advocacy organization that furthers the concerns of people with disabilities.

National Institute on Aging (NIA)

> http://www.nia.nih.gov

> As part of the US National Institutes of Health, the NIA supports research about aging and the lives of older adults.

National Investment Center for the Seniors Housing and Care Industry (NIC)

> http://www.nic.org

> Not-for-profit organization conducting research and offering information about investment decisions.

National Multi Housing Council (NMHC)

> http://www.nmhc.org

> Website with a legislative action center where people can send messages to Congress, respond to legislative alerts, and obtain information on renting versus owning.

National Reverse Mortgage Lenders Association (NRMLA)

> http://www.reversemortgage.org

> Information for consumers about reverse mortgages, including a reverse mortgage calculator.

New Realities of an Older America: Challenges, Changes and Questions
Adele M. Hayutin, Miranda Dietz, and Lillian Mitchell
http://longevity.stanford.edu/files2/New%20Realities%20of%20an%20Older
%20America_0.pdf
An overview of population aging in the United States and its effects on housing, work,
diversity, health, and finances.

NIA Demography Centers
http://www.agingcenters.org
Policy and university centers pursuing research on demographics and aging.

NORCs: An Aging in Place Initiative
http://www.norcs.org
Information and history of naturally occurring retirement communities (NORCs) in
the United States.

Northgate Revitalization, Department of Planning and Development, Seattle, Washington
http://www.seattle.gov/DPD/Planning/Northgate_Revitalization/Overview
Overview and progress updates from the Northgate Revitalizaion project.

Nursing Home Compare
http://www.medicare.gov/nhcompare
Comparison guide for Medicare beneficiaries researching nursing homes.

Older Americans 2010: Key Indicators of Well-Being
http://www.agingstats.gov
Recent data from the Federal Interagency Forum on Aging-Related Statistics on older
Americans in five subject areas: population, economics, health status, health risks,
and health care.

Oregon Center for Aging and Technology (ORCATECH)
http://www.orcatech.org
Oregon Health and Science University research group working to support successful
aging.

OurParents
http://www.ourparents.com
Consumer resource for finding local long-term care options.

Parentgiving.com
http://www.parentgiving.com
Resource for seniors, their adult children, and caregivers.

Partners for Livable Communities
http://www.livable.org
Not-for-profit organization focused on quality of life, economic development, and social
equity in communities.

Pew Research Center's Social and Demographic Trends Project
http://pewsocialtrends.org/about
Conducts public opinion surveys and uses published data to investigate "the behaviors
and attitudes of Americans."

Population Reference Bureau

http://www.prb.org

An international research and reference group focusing on population, health, and the environment.

Program of All-Inclusive Care for the Elderly (PACE)

http://www.cms.gov/pace

Coordinated service delivery program paid for by Medicaid and Medicare.

Project for Public Spaces (PPS)

http://www.pps.org

A not-for-profit organization working with community leaders to advance local placemaking.

Race, Ethnicity and the Economy Program at the Economic Policy Institute

http://www.epi.org/research/race-and-ethnicity

Studies racial inequality in the United States.

Rebuilding Together

http://www.rebuildingtogether.org

A national not-for-profit organization that rehabilitates the homes of low-income homeowners free of charge through volunteer efforts.

Research, Statistics, and Policy Analysis

http://www.ssa.gov/policy

Research reports and policy analysis from the Social Security Administration.

Resource List: Sustainable Planning for Aging in Place

http://www.michigan.gov/documents/miseniors/ICMA-ResourceList_222217_7.pdf

Planning resources for aging in place from the International City/County Management Association (ICMA).

Retirement Living Information Center

http://retirementliving.com/index.html

Resources for individuals planning and making decisions about their retirement.

"Retrofitting Suburbia"

Ellen Dunham-Jones

http://www.ted.com/talks/ellen_dunham_jones_retrofitting_suburbia.html

Short lecture about retrofitting suburban designs.

Retrofitting Suburbia: Urban Design Solutions for Redesigning Suburbs

Ellen Dunham-Jones and June Williamson

Includes many examples of redesign projects throughout the United States.

Reverse Mortgage Information

http://reverse.org

Consumer information on reverse mortgages.

Reverse Mortgages: Get the Facts before Cashing In on Your Home's Equity

http://www.ftc.gov/bcp/edu/pubs/consumer/homes/rea13.shtm

Fact sheet from the Federal Trade Commission on the different types of reverse mortgages.

The Secret Life of the Grown-Up Brain: The Surprising Talents of the Middle-Aged Mind
   Barbara Strauch
   Penguin Group, 2010
   Examines the latest scientific research on brain function to determine how the brain
      improves with age.
Section 202 Supportive Housing for the Elderly Program
   http://portal.hud.gov/hudportal/HUD?src=/program_offices/housing/mfh/progdesc
      /eld202
   Information about Section 202 housing, which is designated for very low income elderly.
SeniorNet
   http://www.seniornet.org
   Provides adults aged fifty and older with access to and education about computer
      technology and the Internet to enhance their lives.
SeniorResource.com
   http://www.seniorresource.com/house.htm
   Online encyclopedia of aging issues, including housing.
Senior Sites
   http://www.seniorsites.com
   A list of not-for-profit providers of senior housing, health care, and services throughout
      the nation.
SmartCode Central
   http://smartcodecentral.com
   A free form-based code manual for planning professionals.
Social Security Statistical Tables
   http://www.ssa.gov/OACT/STATS/index.html
   Data and statistics from the Social Security Administration.
Stanford Center on Longevity
   http://longevity.stanford.edu
   The center studies the nature and development of the entire human life span, looking
      for innovative ways to use science and technology.
The State of Society: Measuring Economic Success and Human Well-Being
   Erwin de Leon and Elizabeth T. Boris
   http://www.urban.org/publications/412101.html
   A 2010 report on alternatives to gross domestic product (GDP) as a measure of societal
      success.
The State of the Nation's Housing 2008
   http://www.jchs.harvard.edu/publications/markets/son2008/index.htm
   A report from the Joint Center for Housing and Studies of Harvard University that
      details the impact of the 2007–2008 fall in the housing market.
Strategies to Meet the Housing Needs of Older Adults
   http://www.aarp.org/home-garden/housing/info-03-2010/i38-strategies.html
   A 2010 report on housing older adults and associated fact sheets from the AARP Public
      Policy Institute.

Successful Aging

John W. Rowe and Robert L. Kahn

Dell Publishing, 1998

The authors present the work of the MacArthur Foundation Research Network on an Aging Society to address the realities of aging.

Sustainable Communities for All Ages: A Viable Future Toolkit

http://www.viablefuturescenter.org/VFC_Site/AgeProducts.html

A guide to sustainable planning practices.

Technology Research for Independent Living (TRIL) Centre

http://www.trilcentre.org

Research group based in Dublin, Ireland, that studies technology and aging, especially the ways in which technology can enable healthy lives.

UniversalDesign.com

http://www.universaldesign.com

Website hosted by Universal Designers and Consultants, Inc., an architectural design group specializing in universal design.

Urban Land Institute (ULI)

http://www.uli.org

International real estate organization.

US Department of Veteran Affairs (VA)

http://www.va.gov

Federal agency for military veterans; provides health care, financial benefits, and business services.

US Green Building Council (USGBC)

http://www.usgbc.org

Not-for-profit organization working to make green building technology accessible to all people; administers Leadership in Energy and Environmental Design (LEED) certification.

Village to Village Network

http://vtvnetwork.clubexpress.com

Resources for senior village communities.

Glossary

accessory dwelling unit (ADU)   Independent apartment, either attached or separate from the main structure, with own entrance, sleeping area, bathroom, and kitchen; also known as granny flat, ECHO (elder cottage housing opportunity) housing, in-law apartment, or mother-daughter apartment.[1]

active adult community   Community limited to residents of a particular age (often fifty-five and older) and emphasizing an active lifestyle, often with golf courses and other recreational facilities included; rarely provides care services to residents.

active life expectancy (ALE)   Variation on life expectancy; measures the number of years of life individuals in a given population will live without significant disability or impairment.

activity of daily living (ADL)   Bathing, eating, toileting, dressing, or other activity normally performed by an individual in daily life; often used as a measure of disability.

adapted housing   Home or apartment in which alterations have been made to accommodate residents in wheelchairs, walkers, or with other supportive needs.

adult day care   Program to provide daily activities and supervision—but not medical care—to older adults, many of whom are driven to the facility by caregivers who may have jobs during the day.

adult foster care   Private residence in which several older adults live and receive assistance with activities of daily living, meal preparation, and transportation from a care provider; regulation and definition vary from state to state.

age-restricted community   Community limited to residents above a particular age (often fifty-five and older); rarely provides services to residents.

age-targeted community   Community that appeals to older residents, often by advertising amenities aimed at older people, but does not exclude younger residents who may want to live in the community.

aging-friendly environment   Environment that supports the personal interests, activities, health care, social needs, and new sources of fulfillment and engagement for people of all ages.

aging in community   General term for efforts to support older people aging in their current neighborhood even if they move from their current home.

alternative transportation   General term for noncar transportation, including bicycles, buses, trains, and walking.

ASID   American Society of Interior Designers.

asset-based community development (ABCD)   Planning technique that maps and analyzes the assets and liabilities of a community.

assisted living, assisted living facility (ALF)   There are a variety of definitions of assisted living per the AARP. Most definitions include private rooms or apartments in a residential setting with twenty-four-hour supervision and a range of care, including housekeeping, meal preparation, and assistance with activities of daily living.

bedroom community   A community in which nearly all residents commute to work somewhere else; almost entirely residential and may not have any businesses.

CAPS   Certified Aging-in-Place Specialist; certification program administered by the National Association of Home Builders (NAHB).

cocooning   Describes an individual's withdrawal from society into the home.

cohousing   Form of independent living; residential development that locates multiple housing units around a central shared common area and emphasizes community interaction through design and management; can be limited to older adults or open to all.

comfort-height commode   A toilet with a seat height similar to a chair; often sixteen and a half inches high, to allow for easier sitting and standing.

community-based care   General term for health care and social services provided to people outside of institutional settings.

compression of morbidity   Trend in human aging in which an individual's functional ability remains high very late into life and then falls steeply during a short and final illness, in contrast to a long, slow decline into disability before death.[2]

congregate care   Model of housing for older adults with shared common spaces and some light services, but not skilled medical care.

connectivity   Characteristic of a community that describes the directness and number of different routes from place to place; can be measured in terms of intersections or distance traveled.

continuing care retirement community (CCRC)   Single-campus community that provides a continuum of care, meals, social events, and housing; housing ranges from self-contained apartments to skilled nursing facilities and is paid for by an entrance fee and monthly fees based on the services used.

drivable suburban or rural form   Neighborhood form characterized by the need to drive to nearly all destinations, as opposed to a walkable urban form.

drive to qualify (for a mortgage)   Because workers cannot afford housing located near their jobs, they must drive long distances between work and affordable communities.

floor area ratio (FAR)   Measure of the density of built structures on a piece of land; used in zoning and development.

form-based code   Planning technique that regulates the structure and form of buildings rather than their uses.

GIS mapping   Geographic information system (GIS); a technology for mapping various kinds of geographic information in a single, often searchable, map.

grayfield   Real estate that is obsolete or underutilized, often characterized by large parking lots, but does not require environmental remediation before redevelopment (as opposed to brownfield).

graying of suburbia   Demographic shift toward older age groups in suburbs.

Green House movement   Form of skilled nursing facility; model of supportive housing in which a small group of older adults live together in a house, receive support from staff, share common spaces, and eat meals together.

home health care   The provision of a wide range of health care services to individuals in their own homes.

hospice   Model for providing comprehensive end-of-life care at home or in any other setting.

independent living   Any noninstitutional living situation; can include some supportive care that is provided in the home.

independent living facility (ILF)   A form of elderly housing in an apartment or condo, with some light services, like transportation or meals, provided; home health care may or may not be included.

instrumental activity of daily living (IADL)   An activity that, while not essential to daily life, contributes to an individual's independence; includes paying bills, shopping, and preparing meals.

life expectancy   The age to which 50 percent of a given population is expected to live.

livable (home, neighborhood, community)   Concept used to describe a house, neighborhood, or community that is designed for people of all ages.

live/work home   A house or apartment that includes both living and working spaces for the residents.

longevity dividend   Economic, social, or health benefit to society that is anticipated to come with increasing life expectancy.[3]

long-term care (LTC)   Medical and nonmedical services for people who have chronic conditions or disabilities that prevent them from successfully accomplishing ADLs; can be provided in the home or in an institutional setting.

LULU   Locally unwanted/undesirable land use; term for development projects that local residents don't want nearby, even if the project is recognized as necessary (examples include prisons and landfills).

medical home/medical team shop   Health care provider or group responsible for coordinating all aspects of a person or family's health care.

NAHB, NAHBR   National Association of Home Builders, a construction industry trade group; the National Association of Home Builder Professional Remodelers is a smaller group of remodelers within the NAHB.

naturally occurring retirement community (NORC)   Community that was not planned as a retirement community but in which the bulk of residents are older (there is no strict age definition); some degree of services may be organized for residents; can be vertical or horizontal.

NIMBY   Not in my backyard. A land use term for development that local residents do not want nearby.

overlay zoning   Planning technique that designates a special area as an exception with its own zoning rules.

poverty line   Federal calculation of annual income, below which individuals and families are eligible for various forms of public assistance.

remodel   To make over in structure or style; recontruct.

remote patient monitoring   Technologies that allow medical professionals to track from a different location various health indicators with measurements taken at a patient's home by either the patient or a caregiver.

retirement community   General term for a community intended for older adults (usually fifty-five and older); the first was Sun City, built by Del Webb in Arizona in 1960.

retrofit   Improvements or reconstruction of a building to bring it up to modern standards.

rural area   Usually defined by exclusion as any place that is not a city or suburb; according to the US Census Bureau, a rural area has fewer than twenty-five hundred residents and is not adjacent to a metropolitan area.[4]

Section 202 housing   Federally funded housing program designed specifically for older adults and administered by the US Department of Housing and Urban Development; limited to people over age sixty-two who have incomes below 50 percent of the area's median income.

senior cooperative housing   Form of independent living; resident-owned housing in which people live in private apartments or townhomes but may share some services, including housekeeping or meal preparation.

shared housing   Arrangement in which a tenant pays rent and/or provides some services in exchange for reduced or eliminated rent; not strictly for older adults.

skilled nursing facility (SNF)   Institutional living arrangement in which residents have private or semiprivate rooms in a facility that provides skilled nursing care and a range of other services; also known as a nursing home.

socioemotional selectivity (aka positivity effect)   A theory that an individual's perception of time influences his or her life goals; generally speaking, when time is unlimited, people seek new experiences and knowledge; when time is short, people focus on emotional goals.

spot zoning   Exception to a zoning ordinance, in the form of a variance, special-use permit, amendment, or other special arrangement.

suburb   A city, town, or area with low population density, primarily residential buildings, and economic ties to larger cities nearby.

successful aging   "Avoidance of disease and disability, the maintenance of high physical and cognitive function, and sustained engagement in social and productive activities."[5]

supportive housing   Housing options that have a noninstitutional style—either houses or apartments—but are designed to provide some level of assistance to older adults.

telehealth, telemedicine Health care services that use communication technologies to allow patients and medical staff to interact remotely.

third place Urban planning term to describe spaces that are neither home nor work; third places provide opportunities for social and civic interaction.

universal design Design philosophy emphasizing products and buildings that are usable by all people without additional accessories or adaptations, coined by Ronald L. Mace.

urbanism, urban form Broad policy and development strategy that aims to restore the vitality of urban centers and towns within metropolitan regions to achieve environmental and social goals.

village model, senior village movement Not-for-profit organizations that coordinate the delivery of services to members, who live within the village's service area; services and membership fees vary.

visitability Home design that includes one zero-step entrance, thirty-six-inch-wide doors, and a wheelchair-accessible bathroom on the ground floor.[6]

walkable urban form Development and planning form that emphasizes multiuse spaces, with work, shopping, and housing all within walking distance (a pedestrian catchment is usually one-quarter to one-half mile).

YIMBY Yes, in my backyard. A land use term for development that local residents do want nearby.

zero-step entrance, low threshold An exterior door that has a ramp or is flush with the ground to allow wheelchair access; one of the three components of visitability.

Notes

1. This, and many of the definitions in this glossary, owe a debt to the American Planning Association's *Planners Dictionary*, which collects definitions from municipal laws around the country. See Michael Davidson and Fay Dolnick, eds., *A Planners Dictionary* (Chicago: American Planning Association/Planning Advisory Service, 2004).

2. Sherwin B. Nuland, *The Art of Aging: A Doctor's Prescription for Well-Being* (New York: Random House, 2007).

3. S. Jay Olshansky, Daniel Perry, Richard A. Miller, and Robert N. Butler, "In Pursuit of the Longevity Dividend: What Should We Be Doing to Prepare for the Unprecedented Aging of Humanity?" *The Scientist* 20, no. 3 (2006): 28.

4. Louise Reynnells, "What Is Rural?" (National Agricultural Library, 2008), http://www.nal.usda.gov/ric/ricpubs/what_is_rural.shtml.

5. John W. Rowe and Robert L. Kahn, "Successful Aging," *The Gerontologist* 37, no. 4 (1996): 433–40.

6. Concretechange.org.

Index

Italic page numbers indicate material in tables or figures.

defined benefit pension plans, 224, 233–234

defined contribution savings plans, 224

Del Webb, 55–56, 211

dementia, 23, 39, 65, 216

demographic trends in aging, 8, 35–37, 252–253

density, residential, 202

Denver, Colorado, 211

Design for Aging, 95

design for independent living, NAHB, 125

Designing Walkable Urban Thoroughfares (ITE), *186*

developers: caution following recession, 213; incentives for, *18*, 156, 187; inexperience of, 213, 216; openness to new concepts, 145, 186, 211, 217

development methods and housing diversity, 203

dialysis centers, travel to, 169

diet and nutrition: elderly neglect of, 58; farmers' markets and community gardens, 167–168, 206, *214*; fast food, 153; home-delivered meals, 53, 247; local government support, 167; and longevity, 25; neighborhood restaurants, 25–26; obesity rates, 36, 148, 152–155; Senior Farmers' Market Nutrition Program, 168

dimmers, 128

disability: and activity limitations, 38; among the elderly, 27, 227, 244; CLASS Act and, 75, 256; disabled veterans, 140–141; insurance for, 239; *Olmstead* decision and, 253–254; prevalence of, 139; rights advocacy for, 92; services for, 224–225

dishwashers, 118, 125

diversity: aging and, 35, 223, 229–231, 255; need for in housing, 113, 181, 203, 222

divorce, 234

Donovan, Shaun, 248, 249

doors: bathroom, 118–119; front entrance, 142; identical keying of, 129; pocket, 117, 125; width of, 92, 116, 125, 130; zero-step entrances, 11, *89*, 92, 115, 142

dooryard frontage, *199*

downsizing to smaller homes, 115, 186, 193, 202–203, 234

Downtown Los Angeles, 221–222

drawers/cabinets, 125, 131

driving: boomer concern about parents, 254; connectivity and, 150–152, 200–201; cost of ownership, 213; to dialysis centers, 169; independent transportation networks, *163–164*; losing access to, 49, 101, 149–150, 154, 163, 194–195; necessity of, 209; ridesharing boards, 102–103; traffic intersections, *151*, 200–201; volunteer driver programs, 103, 164. *See also* public transportation/mass transit

dropout rate, school, *47–48*

dryers, 118, 131

dual eligibles, 247

Dupont Circle (Washington, DC), 211

Dutcher, Wally, *143*

dwellings. *See* housing types

East Harlem, NYC, 205

e-care technologies, 107–110

economic-based bias, 82, 225

economic downturn. *See* recession of 2007–2009

economic drivers of housing decisions, 42–43

education: of citizens by civic leaders, 162–163; by government, 238–239; intergenerational school programs, 172–*173*; level attained and old-age outcomes, 27, 33, 75; lifelong learning, 170–171, 192; of minorities, 47–48; reduced-cost college courses for seniors, 177; senior academies, 173

Edward R. Roybal Learning Center (Los Angeles), 222

Eiken, Steve, 251–252

Eldercare Locator service, 76

elder cottage housing opportunity (ECHO), 11, 61–62, 182, *186*, 205

showers: blocking in, 114; controls for, 92, 125; curbless/roll-in, 4, 11, *119*, 125; difficulties for elderly, *89*; handheld, 125, 130; seats in, 92; tub-to-shower conversion, 119–121, *119*, 127

Shrenk, Michael, 139, 143

shuttle buses, 165

sidewalks, 149, 151, 154, 166, 176

SilverRide service, 78

single-person households, 40–41

sinks: adjustable-height, 125; roll-under, 11, 118–119

size and space (universal design), 92

skilled nursing facilities (SNFs)/nursing homes, 41, 65–66, 74, 216

Smart Growth America, 156

smart growth principles, 14

smart tags, 104

Smith, Eleanor, 92

social aging, 23–25

social contract, intergenerational, 39–40, 229–230

social health support system (SHSS), 101–102

social insurance systems, 250

social networking technologies, 103–104

Social Security: deductions from, 250; disincentives to work, 30; importance of, 219, 247–251; insufficiency of for many, 28; percentage of income, 42; and poverty decline, 43; ratio of workers to retirees, 8; widow's benefits, 243

social solar system display, 102

socioemotional selectivity theory, 24

Sound Steps program (Seattle), *165*, 169

South Korea, 238

spiritual support, end of life, 67

Sports for Life (San Antonio), 169

sports in public spaces, 169, 206

spot zoning, 204

SSPs (supportive services programs), 57, 60, 82, 180

stairs: carpeting on, 121; chairlifts, 125; contrasting colors on, 10; difficulties with, 88, *89*, 141; glide, cost of, *17*; handrails, 120; lighting of, 120; reducing number/ height of, 121; replacing with ramps, 4; zero-step entrances, 11, *89*, 92, 115, 142

standardization of affordable designs, 140

starter homes, modifying, 115

state and local initiatives, 76; funds for, *18*; integrating housing and community services, 79; laws and regulations, 64; need for coordination, 82

steps. *See* stairs

St. Louis, Missouri, 184

stoop frontage, *199*

Storrs, Douglas, 183

stoves/ovens, 91, 125, 131

St. Paul, Minnesota, 182–183

streetcars, 187

street connectivity, *151*, 200, 202

strength, 88

"stuck in place," 222, 223, 230

subdivisions, uniformity of, 203

subsidies for seniors: discounts on home maintenance/repair, 244; discounts on property and casualty insurance, 244; farmers' market vouchers, 168; freezing water/sewer fees, 244; for housing, 60–61, 136, 162; reduced-cost college courses, 177

suburbs: barriers to senior living in, 74, 216; boomers' desire to stay in, 13–14, 180; demographics of, 185; resistance to new housing types, 49; retrofitting of, 179–195

Sun City, Arizona, 55–56, 211

supportive care homes, 64

supportive housing, 55, 64–66

supportive services programs (SSPs), 57, 60, 82, 180

Supportive Technology and Design for Healthy Aging course, AIA, 95

surfaces, softer, *89*

sustainability, 130, 133, 177, 213

Sustainable Cities Institute (SCI), 130

Swampscott, Massachusetts, 28